MONSIGNOR

JAMES HORAN

A note on the editor

A native of Westport, Co. Mayo, Micheál MacGréil SJ is a lecturer in sociology at St Patrick's College, Maynooth. He has published numerous social surveys, including *Prejudice and Tolerance in Ireland*, which received the Ewart-Biggs Memorial Peace Prize in 1977. He directed the revival of the Máméan Patrician Shrine in the Maamturk Mountains of Connemara with some valuable advice from the late Monsignor Horan. Currently chairperson of the Pioneer Total Abstinence Association, he is also actively involved in the Irish language revival movement.

MONSIGNOR

JAMES HORAN

MEMOIRS
1911-1986

edited by
Fr. Micheál MacGréil sj

BRANDON

First published in 1992 by
Brandon Book Publishers Ltd,
Dingle, Co. Kerry, Ireland.

Text © Miss Nancy Horan 1992
Foreword and Epilogue © Micheál MacGréil 1992

British Library Cataloguing in Publication Data
Horan, James
  Memoirs, 1911-86
  I. Title II. MacGreil, Micheal
  280.92

ISBN 0 86322 146 7

Photo credits
Front cover photograph, Martin Nolan; back cover photograph by Eric Luke is reproduced by kind permission of the *Irish Press*. The photographs on pages 120, 122, 123 and 125 are reproduced by permission of *The Irish Times*. The photograph on page 121 is courtesy of *L'Osservatore Romana* and on page 125 courtesy of Frank Dolan, Westport.

Cover design: Stephen Hope
Typesetting: Brandon
Printed by Colourbooks, Dublin

Contents

Foreword	*vii*
Early Years	11
Schooldays	18
St Jarlath's College, Tuam	28
St Patrick's College, Maynooth	39
A Curate in Scotland	49
Curate in Tiernea	64
Illness and Recovery	74
A Curate in Tooreen	82
Raising Funds for Tooreen Hall	90
Curate in Cloonfad	108
The Observant Traveller	128
Parish Priest of Knock	133
The Pope's Visit to Knock	165
A Helping Hand	173
An Airport for Connaught	186
Airport Project Meets Hostility	202
Reprieve for Connaught Airport	214
Trouble on the Horizon	226
The Problem with the Media	234
Back on the Agenda	244
Epilogue	249

Editor's Foreword

THE MEMOIRS OF Monsignor James Horan provide a unique insight into the life and times of one of the most colourful and dynamic Irish priests of this century. The story of his life and ministry is a record of the events and activities of an Irish diocesan priest who came from a rural and relatively poor farming background in south-west Mayo, although his family and the neighbours he grew up with were richly endowed with a solid faith and a sense of communal solidarity. These were the background and circumstances of many priests of the time, and most of James Horan's pastoral experiences would have been shared by his colleagues and contemporaries in the Archdiocese of Tuam.

Beyond this, however, Monsignor Horan took on a number of projects which won for him fame and notoriety. Four of these get special mention in his memoirs. The building of the community dance hall in Tooreen, Ballyhaunis, which he worked for in order to improve the social life of the young people of his parish, was his first major achievement. It was followed later by the development of the Shrine of Our Lady in Knock and the building of the pilgrims' basilica, which Monsignor Horan regarded as the most important achievement of his life and which is now a monument to his memory. The leading role he played in Pope John Paul II's visit to Ireland, to mark the centenary of the apparition of Our Lady, was the third outstanding event of his life.

But it was his superhuman efforts to have a regional and international airport built on the hilltop plateau at Barnacúige near Charlestown, Co. Mayo, which brought him national and international recognition. He worked unstintingly for the airport project so as to contribute to the development of the West of Ireland which he felt had long been neglected, a situation which he knew could only be remedied by self-help and co-operation in the region.

While these achievements were important it would be wrong to focus on them to the exclusion of the more common and more pastorally representative aspects of the monsignor's career. His memoirs also give a very perceptive account of conditions on the land in the West of Ireland: his views on unemployment and mass emigration from the West and his admiration for the Irish in Britain, the USA, Canada, Australia and New Zealand; his opinions on Irish independence and the value of Irish language and culture. As a pastor he records decided views on the Church and the role of the priest in the community. He felt that the social and spiritual roles of the priest were complementary, and for him community development carried out in a spirit of unity and co-operation was a passionate objective.

There were three aspects of modern life which clearly annoyed Monsignor Horan: the negative effect which political rivalry had on the development of the West; the negative role played by the media as a result of its misrepresenting social and religious life; and the obstructive stance adopted by some state bureaucracy and vested interests in relation to community development.

In general the monsignor's memoirs concentrate more on issues and activities than on personal introspection, yet they are revealing of the character of the man who recorded them. At times the reader is given an insight into the deeper spiritual soul of the author; at times, too, his singlemindedness in the pursuit of what he believed in gives an impression of a very tough and astute leader. However, his conflict with politicians and with some people in the media was rarely personal, but was due to their evident opposition to his cherished projects and views. Monsignor Horan was a very human person, quite witty at times, and generous of spirit, a generosity which was fully expressed in his widely acknowledged hospitality. He was also a person of deep faith and a "man of the soil" who was very deeply attached to his family, his community and his country. In his priestly and pastoral roles his sympathies were with the people of his parishes, and he wished always to be close to them. On theological matters he was quite orthodox and very much a Church person: on many of these matter he was a man of his time.

The original manuscript was recorded by the monsignor over three years from 1982-85. His sudden death on 1 August 1986 prevented him from preparing the final text for publication. It fell to me to undertake the task of editing the final draft which is published here. I wish to acknowledge the valuable help I received from everyone who assisted me in the work. The late Monsignor Horan's sister, Nancy, and his brother, Bartley, have been most helpful. Special thanks is due to Peter Malone of

Foreword

Brandon for his expertise and valuable advice. The staff at Knock Shrine and at Horan International Airport were most co-operative while the Most Rev. Dr Joseph Cassidy, Archbishop of Tuam, and Rev. Professor Michael Casey OP were a tremendous help to me in the preliminary stages of the work.

The main work involved was in ordering events and commentaries in a chronological and logical sequence, but the content and style of the original manuscript have been maintained throughout. The first chapter and the epilogue are written by me. Chapter One gives a summary of Monsignor Horan's account of his family background and early childhood in Tooreen, Partry, Co. Mayo, while the epilogue records the major events in James Horan's life from the end of his recorded memoirs in 1985 until his death in 1986.

But may I end this foreword by inviting the reader to follow this story in much the manner in which it was told – as if he or she were listening to the monsignor telling it in his own words over a cup of tea. It is a story he wanted to tell in his own way, and it is a story worth listening to now and in the future. *Ní bheidh a leithéid arís ann, bail ó Dhia air.*

Micheál Mac Gréil SJ
Loughloon
Westport
Co. Mayo

EARLY YEARS

James Horan was born in the village of Tooreen in the parish of Partry, Co. Mayo, on 5 May 1911, the fair day in Dún a' Móna. He was the first-born in a family of seven children – four girls and three boys; there were two other children who had died in infancy. His father, Bartley, was a small farmer and tradesman; his mother, Catherine, formerly Catherine Casey, came from the nearby village of Kilkieran. Partry was a *breac-Gaeltacht* – where both Irish and English were spoken daily – while nearby Tourmakeady, a half-parish of Partry, was a *fíor-Gaeltacht* where Irish was the everyday language of the people.

James did not consider it to be a happy privilege to be the eldest member of the family. "Being the eldest," he later recalled, "meant having to rock the cradle and mind the children when other lads were out playing on the village green. Very often I was responsible for what others did. I was travelling new ground every time; I had nobody to look up to for guidance. Had there been somebody older who had done all of these things, I would have had more courage and confidence in facing them."

Large families were "a very natural thing at the time", as was a strong sense of kinship. James's grandparents, James and Margaret Horan, lived in the Horan household in Tooreen, while James had twelve cousins in the Casey family in Kilkieran. James had a deep attachment to his grandparents. Grandmother Horan, a native Irish speaker, died just as James began school. "The death of Grandmother Horan made a strong impression on me," he recalled. "I have a very distinct memory of the evening she died. I got up out of bed and saw my grandmother 'overboard', that is, laid out. I do not believe that I understood what had happened." He was particularly close to his grandfather, James Horan, who was a very widely read man. Because his parents were busily occupied providing for the family, and his father had to travel long distances to build houses, the grandparents had more time than they to spend with James and the other children. His relationship with the Casey grandparents was not as close, though Grandfather Casey would regularly visit the Horan home on Sundays after Mass. He gave James a gift of a ewe lamb once, and her progeny joined the family flock. Grandmother Casey died when James was a student in St Jarlath's College, Tuam.

James was baptised in Partry parish church by Fr James Corbett; his godparents were his father's sister, Mary, and his mother's brother, Patrick. His godmother was married to Pat Hennelly and lived in the nearby village of Carraneeragh on the shores of Lough Mask. Patrick Casey, his godfather, emigrated to the USA where he joined the navy during World War I, serving afterwards in the New York police force until his retirement.

The parish priest, Fr Corbett, was a prominent priest in the Archdiocese of Tuam, having served as secretary to the commission set up by Archbishop John MacHale to examine the witnesses to the apparition at Knock in 1879. Father Corbett's nephew was the world champion boxer "Gentleman Jim" Corbett, who donated money for the building of a wall and pillars outside the parish church; the wall was built by James's father. Cardinal Gibbons of Baltimore in the USA was a second cousin of Grandfather Horan, and this relationship with the eminent churchman would prove significant in young James Horan's decision to join the priesthood. His account of the family connection is noteworthy:

"Cardinal Gibbons's grandmother was Horan and was born in a thatched cottage on our farm. She married a local hedge-school master named Walsh – I was told he taught school in our barn. The couple had a daughter who went to America where she met and married a man named Gibbons from the village of Gort na Cuilcann in Tourmakeady. Their son was to become James, Cardinal Gibbons.

"I have seen copies of the letters written by Cardinal Gibbons to my grandfather in the 1890s. In the letters he was advising my grandfather against becoming involved in politics. At that time there were many movements in Ireland, for example the Land League, the Irish Republican Brotherhood and other groups. The cardinal advised that the Irish people should get their freedom by means of political activity rather than by any violent movement.

"Cardinal Gibbons visited Ireland as a priest, as a bishop and as a cardinal. His brother, John Gibbons, a merchant in New Orleans, used to send copies of journals like the *New York Times* to my grandfather during the First World War; they came regularly until John died. The cardinal, who had a great love of Ireland, was born in America but had lived in Ballinrobe as a young boy. His parents settled there for a time and had a shop in Bridge St, where J.B. Staunton's shop is now, and they also bought land in the district though they found it hard to collect any rent for it. But while they were in Ballinrobe a daughter of theirs died from the fever; the parents got scared and the family returned to the United States.

"James, Cardinal Gibbons, became a very famous prelate in America. He had great influence in relation to the development of American labour laws and of the American system of trade unions. He was a friend of a number of American presidents. It was always a great consolation to me when I thought of going to the priesthood to have had a relative, no matter how distant, who had gone the same way before me."

James's father, Bartley, was a carpenter and builder. He worked for the Congested Districts Board at first and later for the Land Commission. "My father was a builder and spent a lot of time on the road cycling to and from work over distances of up to fifteen and twenty miles. It was only when he was very far away from home that he would stay in lodgings. He built houses everywhere, though generally speaking he worked in the Ballinrobe, Castlebar and Westport areas. Even when he was working as far away as Finney he would always cycle there and back. Around the country I have met a lot of people who knew him and saw him cycling the roads. Houses at the time were built with mass concrete: my father would put up the shutters and the men with him would fill in the cement. They would build from fifteen to twenty houses at a time for the Land Commission."

Bartley played the accordion and was a keen Irish dancer. James was eager to learn to play music, but his attempts to have his father teach him did not work out well. "I asked my father to teach me. Although my father could play the accordion, he did not know anything about music and could not give me the technical knowledge about it. 'You haven't an ear for it,' he said. He always said I belonged to my mother's side of the family, as none of her family could sing or dance. Nevertheless, he did spend a week trying to teach me 'Pop Goes the Weasel'. At the end of the week he told me to give it up as I was only wasting his time. Afterwards I found out that it was not true that I had no ear for music. When I became a priest I always felt that my musical talent was badly neglected when I was young, and in every parish where I worked I always tried to get music teachers for the young children as I felt it was very important for them."

In all, however, James had very happy memories of his early childhood in Tooreen, situated between Lough Mask and Lough Carra. "I loved the village, the people and the scenic beauty of the whole surroundings. There was great neighbourliness in the village. Wandering from house to house was the only entertainment available. In every house there was a 'forum' – a long stool – for children like us to sit on listening to stories being told. However, the days of the *seanchaí*, the old storyteller, had vanished by then."

As a young lad James had the freedom of the countryside. "I would go out, barefooted, and traverse the bog looking for birds' nests, especially the *pilibín's* or green plover's. The *pilibín* always nested on the ground and I often got into trouble with the s*craith bhogáin* and places where one might be swallowed up in the bog. A *scraith bhogáin* was a place where there was a spring of water underneath and when you walked on it it moved up and down under your feet. The days you could go out into the sunshine and explore for yourself were marvellous days, and the sun seemed to be shining all the time."

The month of May was special, a month dedicated to Our Lady, Mary, the mother of God, and altars were put up in every home. "As a little boy I had a May altar in my bedroom in a place where nobody would disturb it. I had a statue of Our Lady and I would put vases of flowers in front of it. This was kept up during the month of May every year. I enjoyed going out to pull the flowers in an old fort called Lisheen. Because the fort would never be disturbed all kinds of flowers were growing there. I remember standing in wonder at the beauty of all these flowers – cowslips, bluebells and many others. May altars at that time were very popular with children and the local teacher encouraged them."

Bonfire's night on the eve of the feast of St John, 24 June, was a big event. "We prepared for it for days beforehand and collected turf from various houses. Old and young came out and sat around the bonfire. It was a very exciting time watching the fire burning, and we would stay there until eleven o'clock at night – when somebody came and lugged us home and put us to bed."

As autumn came, from late September until the first of November the young people picked hazel nuts and blackberries, and then at the turn of the year Christmas was celebrated. Christmas was especially memorable. On the Monday before

Christmas they went to the big market in Ballinrobe, where all the neighbours from the farms around gathered to buy and sell their produce – geese, ducks, chickens, potatoes, oats – or simply enjoy the fair. "Christmas night was a great night. A special ceremony was made of sitting down to eat the Christmas meal on Christmas Eve. Potato cake was a speciality for the night, accompanied by all kinds of sweet cakes and raisin cakes. Turkeys were rare at the time – geese and chickens were the popular dishes. The meal was a very happy one and was begun and ended with special prayers. We all looked forward to early Mass on Christmas morning. We had to walk three miles to Partry church for first Mass at seven o'clock." Before going to sleep on Christmas Eve James would hang up his stocking in the hope of receiving gifts. "At that time one would not get very much, but we always lived in hope and put the stockings on the bed." Sometimes he might get gifts of money from relations or neighbours. His mother used say that "the money was following him," but James would spend it all which, he recalled, caused his mother to remark that "even though I got all this money I would die a pauper".

Meitheal days, when neighbours came together to help one another bring in the harvest of hay and oats and draw home the turf from the bog, were notable events in the annual calender. "*Meitheal* days were marvellous days for bringing all the neighbours together. They were akin to feast-days when food and refreshments were provided. Everyone worked hard. Special *meitheal* days were organised to help widows and older people to do the work they were unable to do for themselves. The neighbours were very charitable in those days and they certainly looked after those in need in the village."

Farming smallholdings of less than ten acres, families ploughed the land, cultivated crops and raised animals. As a young lad James worked on his father's farm, learning the tasks and skills of farmwork: "I mowed hay, cut corn, bound the sheaves, made stacks of corn and did ploughing as well." He watched his grandmother as she churned cream in an old-fashioned dash churn. If a neighbour happened to call during the churning, it was customary for her or him to "take a turn at the churn. Before putting salt in the butter, my grandmother would take some unsalted butter and put it on a board which hung on the side of the wall. This was called *caoineach liath* or green mould. The *caoineach liath* would be applied, say, to an injured toe and helped to heal it. Unknowingly, my grandmother was anticipating Alexander Fleming's discovery of penicillin."

Old Moore's Almanac served as a calendar for fairs and other events. "The day on which the cow was due to calf was written on the back of the *Almanac*," and the day of the calving was a great event. The first milk from the cow on the day after calving – the beastings – was shared with all the neighbours. The annual killing of the pig was another big day in the life of the farm, and some of the fresh meat and the black pudding which the family made would, again, be shared.

The "land question", as the political and legislative attempts to solve competing claims of ownership to the land was called, was a major topic of concern for the Horan family during the early decades of the century. The division of the smallholdings and the complicated and complex subdivisions of fields and pastures were to become the first major social and economic issue which occupied James Horan's thinking. He knew at first hand the hardship which people endured as a result of the social and economic conditions prevailing at the time. Growing up in a community where each small field was given its own individual name, he developed firm views on the land issue.

"Michael Davitt had done a lot of good work for Ireland through the Land League. He gave farmers the authority to own their own land and, instead of them paying exorbitant rents for their land they paid a fixed rent, originally to the landlord and later to the state. The landlords eventually sold their estates to the Congested Districts Board and, later, to the Land Commission. With security of tenure the farmers could improve their lands and they could also sell it. I think, reading the history of Ireland from the beginning of the nineteenth century up to the present time, no political leader, with the possible exception of Daniel O'Connell himself, did as much for the Irish people as Michael Davitt. Unfortunately, I am afraid, he did not get full credit for it. Of course, Davitt was helped by Parnell, who was also a great politician, in getting the Land Acts through the British parliament. The two important Land Acts were those of 1893 and of 1903.

"There were four landlords with land in my village – Lynch, Byrne, Burke and Spellissy. Burke and Spellissy lost their claims for some reason, so Colonel Blas Lynch and Mr Byrne were the two landlords left. I remember my parents paying rent to Mr

Byrne, and they also paid rent to Blas Lynch. Eventually the Land Commission bought the lands of Lynch and Byrne, which made up two parts of the village. The other two parts belonged to the people of the village through prescriptive rights. This meant that the Land Commission could not take control of the whole village.

"There were twenty-one families in the village, each with a holding of between six and eight acres. A further two families from outside had holdings within the village, resulting in a total of twenty-three. These holdings were further divided, with smaller portions of land in different parts of the village. One day you would be working on the shores of Lough Mask and another day within sight of Lough Carra. In my village we had what was known as the rundale system of grazing. When I was young I realised this, so I would keep encouraging my father to swop land in the same part of the village – it would be more convenient and productive. The farmer could then manure the land, put a wall around it and do lots of other things with it which would be impossible otherwise. My father was anxious to build a new house for his family and he hoped to get an exchange of holdings from the Land Commission in East Mayo, in Co. Westmeath, or elsewhere. Unfortunately, the Land Commission could not exchange his holdings at the time due to the confusion of ownership over the village land. Part of his holding belonged to my father himself and part to the Land Commission, but nobody could say which part."

Later, when James Horan was a student, he helped to persuade farmers to give the Land Commission ownership of that part of the land in their possession, thus enabling the Commission to exchange land between farmers in the county, and indeed the country. "In the end the Land Commission exchanged half of the families and transferred them to farms around Kilmaine and Ballinrobe. The land in the village was then 'striped', or divided, and given to the remaining ten or twelve families. The farm of each family was then compact, and a house was built on it. So, they are very comfortable now and it is a different village and the old-time village has vanished. There is not, however, the same freedom of movement now as there was before."

In 1952 James's family were one of those given a different holding, in Kilmaine, in exchange for their old land in Tooreen.

Schooldays

At the age of six James was sent to the local, all-boys Partry National School. "I often wonder now if it would have been better to have been sent to a mixed school? Maybe we would have been more refined if we had to go to school with girls. Perhaps the master would not have been as cross as he was if there were girls there."

James remembered his schoolmaster in fond, if critical, terms. "When calling out the roll, the schoolmaster always commented on the different characters. He often referred to my card-playing, as he felt I was playing cards at night instead of doing my homework. If Dave Hennelly, one of my card-playing partners, had a sum wrong the schoolmaster would say, 'Well, if you were threepence up on Jimmy Horan's sixpence at card-playing, you would know all about that and you wouldn't make any mistake!' Whenever he wanted to be hard on me he would give me 'a lot of tongue'. He would tell me to go and buy a spade for myself because that was what I was destined for. Still, my schoolmaster was a very nice man and a marvellous teacher. I was very fond of him and had the honour of going to see him after my ordination, but I never knew exactly what ideas he had in his head about me. I often wonder about that.

"When I was going to the national school I had to walk the three miles there and back. We had no meals at school. Having taken a breakfast in the morning, and sometimes it was rushed, you went to school and you did not get anything to eat until you came home again. It was not customary for the big boys to take a lunch because eating a lunch at school was seen as something unmanly. It was rather a peculiar feature but that is the way it was.

"It was very hard to get books. I envy young people nowadays because they have libraries coming to the schools; we had no such advantages. I used go around cadging books from the neighbours. I got the names of all the families whose children had grown up and I borrowed books from them. At one stage I needed a dictionary. One day in the bog I met John Corcoran from Cushlough, who seemed to think I was scholarly. We started to talk about school and I told him about the dictionary. He told me he had one and would give it to me if I cycled down to his house on the following Sunday, which I did, and when he gave me the dictionary I would not call the Queen my aunt! I got readers [textbooks] from other families and these books served me well until I went to St Jarlath's.

"In order to study one had to get a candle and go into one's room. Of course, in the kitchen we had a paraffin-oil lamp; not the fancy kind that came later, but it gave sufficient light for reading. And we did not have the distractions of television and radio, so it was easier to study then. I was anxious to study and to get on. I do not know why: maybe my mother used to put a little ambition into me. In those days there were hardships in a country village and, I suppose, unconsciously one realised these hardships and felt there may have been a better life. I do not know.

"Partry was a *breac-Gaeltacht*. My grandfather spoke Irish and English and could also read both, which was unusual for people in those days, and my uncle Michael was very well versed in Irish and English at the levels of reading and writing. He helped me quite a lot in learning Irish and so did Lizzie, his wife. I did not learn Irish at school until I was in fourth class. My English was poor, like most of the people of my village. Our English was more or less Irish translated into English, and literal translations of Irish idioms did not make for good English, but as I read more and more English my difficulty with the language declined. At school English was taught very well. We read a number of Shakespeare's plays – *Macbeth* and *Julius Caesar*. We were also well advanced in arithmetic. I knew as much arithmetic when I left the national school as would enable me to pass the Intermediate Examination.

"After Fr James Corbett died, Canon Thomas O'Malley was appointed parish priest of Partry. He had been a curate in Robeen before being transferred to our parish. I loved Canon O'Malley; he was a very kind and fine priest who took his duties seriously. He was a man of prayer and I often saw him in the church praying when I went there myself. He was a sensitive man. When coming to the door, which was always open in the country at that time, he would call out 'Hello there!' as a warning that he was coming. Then he came in and talked to the family, and sat down for a while asking my mother how she was. His sacristan drove him round in a horse and trap, as there was no motor-cars in those days. Despite the transport difficulties he came around quite often; he was strong on sodalities and always spoke about them when visiting our house. Canon O'Malley told my parents that I was very good at school and he encouraged them to educate me as I showed great promise. That was when I got the notion of going to college and becoming a priest.

"I was a Mass-server along with other lads from our school and some from the school down in Derrow. There was great competition among us to wear the soutane and white surplice. My mother brought me to Ballinrobe to a dressmaker, not to a tailor, to have my soutane and surplice made. We bought the material in McCormack's drapery because they had a priest in the family and thus Mrs McCormack would know what was required. She was always very helpful and would give us credit for a little while if we were short of money.

"I think it was Napoleon who said that his Communion day was the greatest day of his life. I could say the same. Although we had not the means to dress up as they do now, we were nevertheless well dressed and my father and mother made a very big occasion of my first Holy Communion. Confirmation was another big day for me. I can remember the question the bishop, Dr Thomas Gilmartin, asked me: 'What is perjury?' It was a tricky question, but I answered it correctly and was very proud of myself."

The mission was a notable occasion in the life of the parish during James Horan's childhood.

"The Redemptorist Fathers always gave the mission in Partry when I was a boy. There was one mission in particular that I remember; it was given by Fr Conneely, a native of the Aran Islands. Those were the days when missioners were missioners! They gave much tougher sermons than missioners or priests give nowadays. That was the style of things in those days and the people liked it that way. They came out to the mission, while the missioners also went around to the houses to meet the people. I think they did a marvellous job. I always associate stalls outside the church with the mission; the stall-holders followed the missioners around from parish to parish. The display of religious goods fascinated me. You would always get something new at the stalls – a rosary beads, a prayer book, or something like that."

James's schooldays took place against the backdrop of a country fighting for its independence.

"I was at school when the Partry ambush took place in March

1921. I saw the cart carrying the dead soldiers to the church while we were in the play-yard for a break. The sad things about the Partry ambush was that the poor soldiers who were shot were actually on their way to Castlebar to be court-martialled.

"Going to school during 1920-21 we would see the Black and Tans passing along the road in lorries. They sat back-to-back with rifles in their hands, ready for action, the lorries raising dust on the road. I must say, however, they did not interfere with us at all. They said nothing and just drove by.

"The Rising in 1916 had not affected the people much: it was almost over before they knew it had started, and little news came out of Dublin about it. Rather it was the aftermath, the executions of the leaders, that really angered the people of Ireland. I remember my grandfather getting the newspaper, the *Freeman's Journal*, in 1916 and reading about the execution of the leaders. I was just five years old. It was as a result of those executions that we had the Rebellion of 1920-21.

"In the famous election of 1918 De Valera was elected not only for his constituency of Co. Clare but also for the constituency of East Mayo, so we had the privilege of having De Valera as our representative in the First Dáil. The election gave the Republicans a big majority but, when Ireland again failed to get Home Rule in 1919, something was bound to happen. The people laboured under this terrible disappointment and the memory of the 1916 executions was still very much alive, so the period 1920-21 saw terrible fighting. During the War of Independence Keel Bridge on the road between Castlebar and Ballinrobe was blown up to cut communications between the two towns, which were both military centres. There was great Republican activity in Partry at first, but the Partry boys were caught drilling in a wood in Kilfoyle and were picked up early in the War of Independence. They were interned in Galway Jail and as a result not many people from Partry were active in the IRA in that period. Unfortunately, the War of Independence ended in a treaty which led to civil war in the country.

"I remember the Civil War. I remember hearing of six people executed in Tuam under the Irish Free State government. Happily, when the Civil War ceased we got down to real politics."

James Horan's recollections of World War I concerned its cause and the flu which followed it. "My grandfather said that the First World War was being fought for the freedom of small nations. It started, I suppose, because the Serbians and other small nations in the Balkans were fighting for their freedom. Ireland saw herself as a small nation in the same category.

"When the First World War was over the soldiers returned home, and they must have brought a flu with them from the Continent – the 1919 flu. Many people died from it, especially men, some of whom contracted pneumonia. The ninth day of the flu was considered crucial: if those who were ill survived the ninth or tenth day they would live, and those who were to die did so when the crisis struck on the ninth. 1919 was the first time that the word 'flu' was used by the people."

During James Horan's boyhood, tuberculosis (TB) or "consumption" as it was called, was a fatal disease, rampant in the West and elsewhere. The fear of TB was to stay with James even in later life as a priest. "I would like the youngsters nowadays to realise how lucky they are in regard to fears of sickness and ill-health. When I was growing up tuberculosis was rampant and all young people were afraid of it. When I went out to play football or perhaps went to a dance my mother was always worried that I would get a cold which might result in TB. I was terrified of it too because I saw a lot of my contemporaries die from it. I remember a family where a number died one after another. That experience had a terrible effect on me. One day they would be out in the garden; then they would disappear and die. A schoolpal of mine from Partry also got TB. On the way home from St Jarlath's I met him on the train and I got a fright because I could see that he was dying on his feet. It was a very lonely, lingering death.

"My mother was leaving me at the train one day in Ballinrobe; I was going to Castlebar to do an examination for the Irish College in Tourmakeady. On her way home she met a neighbour who said to her: 'I see you sent Jimmy away. I hope it isn't to a sanitorium he is going.' His remark upset my mother terribly; she felt that this man must have seen something in me that she had not noticed herself. She went home very sad. Of course, I escaped TB, although I found it hard to put up weight while I was at school.

"Later, one of my classmates in Maynooth got TB and was actually ordained on a stretcher. He was dying. Fortunately for many people in Ireland, Dr Noel Browne became Minister for Health in 1949. He worked very hard against TB as he himself or some members of his family had been victims of it. As a result of Dr

Browne's efforts the disease was almost conquered in this country; many people who would have died got better because of a new drug that came on the market."

During his boyhood James learned from his family and from others about conditions in earlier years, during the Great Famine of the 1840s. As he grew up he became a very keen observer of the living conditions around him.

"My grandfather often talked to me about the Famine. The potato crop had failed due to an early blight and it took a whole day to dig a meal for a family. When I asked him how the people survived he said they had a big field of turnips, about half an acre, which gave a marvellous crop that they shared with their neighbours. Nobody in the village died from the hunger during the Famine. If people got sick they would be sent to the workhouse in Ballinrobe which was controlled by the local landlords and the local authority. People had a dread of the workhouse because of the stigma attached to it; they would almost prefer to die rather than go. Indian meal [corn] was brought into the country during the Famine to save the people from starvation. Some of it came into Westport Quay and was transported on carts by some of my forebears and their neighbours to Ballinrobe where it was milled and refined. A lot of people died when they tried to eat porridge made from Indian meal; it was too strong and it seems they were unable to digest it."

The Great Famine which devastated the country in James's grandfather's time was still alive in the minds of the people, but by the turn of the century living conditions had begun to improve.

"During the First World War things were fairly good as regards food. The main dinner menu was bacon and cabbage. On a special day one had a *cáca phota* [a pot cake] which was put into a pot with bacon and cabbage. The 'Herring Man' came from Westport to sell herrings in Partry occasionally. I loved herrings, especially when they were grilled on the tongs on the hearth.

"When I was growing up people had great pride in their horses – the same pride as people have in their motor-cars nowadays. A good horse was a status symbol. The test of a good horse was if it could haul a ton of Indian meal on a cart. There were few veterinary surgeons at that time, but there were certain men – or 'quacks' – who knew all about horses. If the horses got some kind of illness the owner would usually send for a 'quack', or for a traveller. The travellers in Ballinrobe were experts with horses. My grandfather had a great rapport with them; anytime they met they discussed horses. The travellers then had a good relationship with the settled people, whereas nowadays the people do not seem to want to know them. During my youth when travellers came to the house they were never allowed to go away without getting something; usually they got potatoes or vegetables from the people of the house, but not money as there was not much available at the time. Travellers also sold tin-ware – tin cans or saucepans – which were widely used in the homes. Those were the days before the widespread use of plastic."

Farmers, travellers, country people and townsfolk all came together on the day of the fair.

"Going to the fair was very exciting, though I was only at a few. I remember one day being at the fair in Ballinrobe with my father. I was left minding our sheep while my father went into the pub for a drink, when along came a man who was interested in buying them. I sold the sheep to him and when my father returned he was very pleased with the deal I had made. I also remember going to the fair selling cattle. My father would graze cattle during the summer months on pastures around the countryside at so much a month or a week, because we had not much land of our own for grazing – maybe seven or eight acres scattered over a wide area. Then, at the end of the summer, he would sell the cattle at the fairs, where of course a bargain could never be sealed until the buyer would spit and shake hands. That gesture put the seal on the bargain. If you were selling, the buyer would put the point of his stick in the gutter and then on the animal as a sign that the deal was signed, sealed and delivered. He also spat on the money before he gave it to you, maybe hoping that it would come back to him in some other way. If the day was going to be good you would know it early on, as the jobbers would come out on the road to meet the cattle going to the fair. They were anxious to buy before their competitors might get in before them.

"At every fair you had the 'Cheap Jack' or hawker who sold all kinds of things. The farmers bought their clothes from the 'Cheap Jack', but they did not want to be seen doing so by their neighbours; they would approach him very quietly. If you did appear with a new suit and the neighbours knew you bought it from the 'Cheap Jack' they would not have the same respect for it. Yet the 'Cheap Jack' was a great institution in that it enabled people to get clothes they could not otherwise afford."

Against the background of underdevelopment and widespread poverty, emigration from the West of Ireland was very extensive in the early decades of the 1900s.

"The very sad thing about all the children who grew up with me was that most of them emigrated to other countries; it was simply accepted as the natural thing to do. They finished school at fourteen years of age as there was little chance of a secondary education, and soon afterwards they left. We were lucky in my part of the country because we had the Christian Brothers in Ballinrobe. The Brothers were pioneers in secondary education and did wonderful work, so much so that most people who got secondary education got it from the Brothers or from other religious orders. Had I not gone to St Jarlath's I could have gone to the Christian Brothers too.

"My father had almost emigrated to America in his youth. An uncle of his, Anthony Horan, a prosperous businessman and building contractor who had started out as a stonemason, thought that he would bring my father out and give him a job straight away. My father's passage had been paid and all the necessary preliminaries had been gone through to prepare for the journey but on the morning he was due to leave his mother became very upset: now there would only be one of her family left, my Aunt Mary. Fearing that his departure would break her heart, my father decided to stay at home. Then he started building on his own, as his father had done before him – building was a profession which went back a long way in my family. And from the day my father refused to go to America, his Uncle Anthony never wrote another line to Ireland.

"My uncle, James Casey, went to America to escape the threat of conscription during the First World War, and was a policeman in the New York police. The first time I saw a photograph of myself was when he came home on holidays and took a snap of me at the age of ten or eleven years outside in the yard beside a stack of turf. He was one of twelve children all of whom went to America, except my mother who got married at home. A few of them returned later and got married in Ireland. My Uncle Michael, the oldest in my mother's family, came home and married Lizzie Horan, the assistant teacher in Partry."

"It was the custom in my part of the country that all members of a large family would emigrate except one, a boy or a girl, who stayed at home to look after the father and mother. When the parents died the boy or girl who had looked after them would be of an age which made it very hard to get married. In later years I was always very conscious of this, as was a friend of mine, Fr Michael Keane, who decided to start the Knock Marriage Bureau to help combat the problem."

The Horan home was a traditional cottage with a thatched roof.

"There were several layers of thatch and as a result the house was very warm in winter and very cool in summer. Nearly every thatched house had a 'hag' or *cailleach*, a small room that was built on the side of the house with its own roof, usually made of flags. This room was near the kitchen fire and when anybody was sick they usually occupied the 'hag' so that they would be near the action in the kitchen. There was a wonderful religious attitude in all the homes of the village. Several rosary beads hung on the walls in our kitchen, and every house had a picture of the Sacred Heart with a certificate of consecration signed by the priest. You never had a home without holy water.

"We had a very happy village in Tooreen and especially at Christmastime the people had a wonderful system where every family had gatherings in their homes. I remember going to parties in my aunts' and uncles' homes: they provided tea, sweet cake, blancmange and jelly for desert, and there was music, set dancing and so on. But when I was younger my mother would not allow me to go around with the wren on St Stephen's Day. How I envied the lads who went out on the wren! When I got a little bigger I never failed to go hunting on St Stephen's Day. Some old friends of mine in the village, like Ned Carney, Davie Hennelly, Paddy Hennelly and some of my cousins, all went hunting for foxes, rabbits and hares.

"When it made very heavy frost all the pools and the water in the bogs froze over and we would have a marvellous time sliding on the ice. When Lough Carra used to freeze young men went hunting for fish. They brought mallets with them and when they saw fish underneath the ice they kept thumping the surface until the fish were stunned; then they bored a hole in the ice to gaff the fish and pull them out. My parents would not allow me to take part in this type of fishing because of the danger of the ice breaking. I spent my time in the ball alley. At the time, too, the bicycle was something new though more and more were coming into the village, and we youngsters enjoyed going out on cycling trips."

During his final year at the national school in Partry, James won a scholarship to the Tourmakeady Gaeltacht for the purpose of improving his Irish.

"My father brought me back to Tourmakeady on a side-car. It was a big excursion for a young lad of thirteen years. It was strange that though there was only a very short distance between Partry and Tourmakeady, yet, when you crossed the bridge at Derrymore you crossed from an English to an Irish-speaking area. We found 'digs' in the house of Mr Hughie Naughton where I was given VIP treatment for a month. The course cost £1 a week and £1 pocket money for going to *céilís* and other functions. Also on the course was a John Dominick O'Malley, from Kilmeena in Westport, who was later to become a classmate of mine in St Jarlath's and Maynooth. The majority of the students were teachers learning Irish because at that time, the summer of 1924, the language was becoming a subject in the national schools.

"The month in Tourmakeady was great. I was in a beautiful and scenic part of the parish with mountains surrounding it. There was a weaver there named Tom Coyne whom I visited quite often in order to practice speaking Irish. He played the accordion at the college *céilís*, and I also went to a few *céilís* in Jimmy Miller's house. Because I was only a small boy nobody would ask me to dance. People used to say: 'It is time for that child to go to bed!' Nevertheless, I thoroughly enjoyed my time in Tourmakeady, the *céilís* and the music and the atmosphere of the place. Ireland had just gained her independence and there was a kind of acceleration in the life of the country. The people had gone through very troubled times in 1916, 1921 and during the Civil War. All was quiet now and people had settled down to a peaceful life. There was a wonderful spirit and great enthusiasm for Irish, greater than I have ever experienced since. I was very enthusiastic myself; I loved the language and worked very hard at it. My natural flair for Irish came from the influence of my grandmother, who spoke the language with her neighbours and gave me an ear for it."

St Jarlath's College, Tuam

By the time he had finished his primary education in Partry, James had begun to look to the priesthood as a possible vocation. For that reason he entered for a scholarship to St Jarlath's Diocesan College in Tuam, Co. Galway. His parish priest, Canon O'Malley, encouraged the boy and gave him a letter of introduction to the president of the college. He had vivid recollections of his journey to Tuam.

"My Uncle Patrick, who was at home on holidays from the United States, hired a Model T Ford to take us to Tuam for the scholarship examination. We arrived there on the day before because the examination was to begin at ten o'clock on the following morning and we did not want to be late for it. On my first night in Tuam my father and my uncle brought me to a circus. It was a wonderful treat for me as I always enjoyed circuses.

"One of the compositions in the examination was 'My Journey to Tuam' which of course suited me down to the ground. I not only described my journey in the Model T motor-car but I wrote on my visit to the circus as well. I do not know what marks I got for the composition, but I could not have done too badly as I got my scholarship.

"My father wanted to bring me home after the examination so that he could buy me a suitcase. I had not brought any personal things with me, but the president of St Jarlath's, Fr Denis Ryder, said I had to do with what I had and that I must stay the night.

"That night I slept in a big room called a dormitory. One of the other lads there was feeling very sorry for himself and cried all night. On the following day my trunk was brought up from home in the Model T – from the very beginning the new invention, the motor car, had helped me out. I was now a college boarder.

"On my second day in St Jarlath's I stood back watching the older students and I was envious of them because they looked so confident, big and strong, and here was I just starting off. In the crowd I saw a lad I had met at the Irish College in Tourmakeady a year earlier, John Dominick O'Malley. We struck up a friendship. He was a bit of a character, a very lovable one. Tragically, he died young in life.

"During my first year I was very slow getting my collar and tie on in the morning, although I was always up in time. One morning I was late for prayers and myself and another lad were locked out of the oratory by the dean, Fr John Killeen. After prayers he came out of the oratory, brought the two of us up to his room and gave us two slaps each. That did us a lot of good as I made sure that I was never late for prayers again. I got on well with Fr Killeen while I was in St Jarlath's. He was a very fair man; he did not punish the boys very often and when he did he was never too severe.

"The boys in St Jarlath's came from various backgrounds; many were farmers' sons like myself, or tradesmen's sons. In St Jarlath's the fee was only £35 a year, out of which they had to pay the salaries of the professors and feed the students. This was only possible because the college had a fairly big farm on which they grew vegetables and raised their own sheep – we got a lot of mutton in St Jarlath's. All the same, £35 was a lot of money and my family would not have been able to pay that much were it not that I had won a scholarship. I belonged to a fairly big family and we could not sacrifice that amount of money on one out of seven. The lads who came from the national schools were, in a certain sense, at a disadvantage because the boys from the towns usually went for a year to secondary schools and had done the rudiments of Greek, Latin and other subjects before coming to St Jarlath's. But, apart from history, geography and mathematics, the boy going from the national school was starting all new subjects."

The different professors in St Jarlath's made an impression on the young scholar and influenced his attitude to the various subjects which he studied.

"For Irish I had Fr John O'Reilly, who was a lovely character. He made the class very entertaining by telling us all kinds of wonderful Irish stories. He would tell us a story and then ask us to write it out for him as a composition next day. I loved these stories; I think that the Irish have a great sense of humour and this humour came through in the stories. Fr O'Reilly was considerate and kind and never used the cane. When a professor was nice it gave you a liking for the subject. I regret very much that a professor who was tough on us gave us a dislike for his subject. I did not mind the cane so much; I objected more to a tongue-lashing as it can break young confidence at a time when it is most needed. I certainly liked my Irish professor and his subject, so much so that I took Celtic studies for my degree in Maynooth.

"Fr Jimmy Moran taught us Greek. He was an excellent teacher and a very likeable man. I liked Greek and got honours in it in the Leaving Certificate Examination. Mathematics was my favourite subject as my mind was bent on solving abstract problems. I got on well in mathematics in the Intermediate Certificate Examination but I did not, to my regret, do honours in the subject in the Leaving Certificate, because I was going to do the *concursus* examination for entry into Maynooth and in that exam mathematics was taken at pass level. Our professor of mathematics was Fr Delaney, who was a brilliant teacher.

"We had an excellent lay teacher, Sammy Doyle, for science. A lay teacher in Tuam at that time didn't have the same command or control over students as the priests had, but all of us admired Sammy Doyle because he was a kind and a very humane man. One day when the news spread that he had become the father of twins we demanded a free day. We got several free classes that week as we were celebrating the twins.

"We had another lay professor, Mr Cooney, who taught us geography in our first two years. He was a very warm character and had fairly good control over the boys, but nobody seemed to take geography or history very seriously, especially in the junior classes. One day when it was snowing one of the boys stuck a snowball on to the ceiling directly over the spot where Mr Cooney always stood at the top of the room. Just as class started the snow began to melt and dropped down on his head. He tried to find out who did it but, of course, he failed. Lay teachers always had a harder time than the priests in St Jarlath's.

"Fr Michael King was our professor of Latin in the junior classes. He was an excellent teacher and I got on very well at Latin, but, unfortunately, I did not have him for Latin in the senior classes where we had an old man, Mr Johnny Hession, who seemed to teach everything from Greek and Latin to Irish and English. I must say I loved my professors. Some of them were harder then others, but that was to be expected as everybody has his own character. I would not like to have been a teacher because I always felt that I would not have the patience – anytime I tried to teach my younger brother I found that I lost my patience very easily.

"Life in St Jarlath's was modelled on Maynooth College and the regime was very strict. You got up at half-past six in the morning, went down to the oratory at five minutes to seven for morning prayer, which was followed by Mass and breakfast. We had about three-quarters of an hour's recreation before starting classes, which went on until three o'clock in the afternoon. There was a break at twelve o'clock, and after school we played football. Usually we went to study at five o'clock; at half-past seven we had tea after which we returned to study for one hour. We had a prefect of studies who would walk up and down the study-hall supervising our work. We were usually fairly quiet, though sometimes he would find somebody reading a novel instead of doing his Greek and Latin. After study there was night prayer and then it was off to bed.

"St Jarlath's was a tough place, especially when you were a first-year. You were called a 'conner', and all 'conners' were to be 'barred'; in other words they were to be humiliated and kept down. In order to defend yourself you had to attach yourself to a gang or a *bodach* to be defended; if you were from Ballyhaunis, say, you would join the Ballyhaunis gang. Unfortunately, I was from the country and did not belong to any gang, so I had to pick out somebody under whose tutelage I could survive.

"When boys get together sometimes they can be very cruel to each other. Some of the boys who came to St Jarlath's were a bit easy-going; they were good boys who were harmless and innocent, maybe too innocent. Some of the other lads would get on to them and could be very cruel. That, of course, made life very difficult for the easy-going boys and I felt very sorry for them. Whenever I could, which was not very often since I was a small boy myself, I would stand up for them.

"Going to places like St Jarlath's gives you strength of character though; you have to be strong to survive there. It gets rid of that shyness and awkwardness of a young boy coming from a country school. You picked your companions during the first year; usually they became close friends and if you had any problems you could confide in them. It was good to have friends in college; we would walk around the grounds together during our free time. Boarding school gave a wonderful training to young boys. They were taken from national school, from their own homes, and brought to college. The experience hardened them and gave them the capacity to put up with things and to be patient. All in all it did a lot of good for the boys. The regime was demanding, and a lot of very fine young men who passed through St Jarlath's later became archbishops, doctors, surgeons, lawyers, or whatever. I always thought that there were others who should never have gone there because they did not have the academic foundation or else they did not have the ability to get their examinations. For every fifty people who went to St Jarlath's in my time, I would say about twenty-five or thirty finally got their Leaving Certificate. And it was not always the brilliant boys who did well afterwards in life.

"I enjoyed my time in St Jarlath's. Generally, the food was adequate and we were not hungry. Much was to be desired where games were concerned; we had handball, football and hurling, but we did not have competitions with other schools. We had college sports every year. I fancied myself at long-distance running and used to run around the grounds in a track-suit. I also fancied myself at the long jump. However, I never achieved very much in competition as I had a small physique; I was a late developer and I did not grow until I was eighteen. Even later, in Maynooth, I was fighting to put on weight; now I am fighting to keep it off.

"We slept in big dormitories which were each given nicknames. The dormitory where all the young boys were housed was called the Kip; opposite that was Heaven and under Heaven was Paradise. On the other side of the building were Hell and Limbo. Attached to Paradise was the Horse-Box, which usually housed the second-years. They were a rough crowd and fancied themselves a little having got through first year. During my fourth year I was the monitor in charge of Paradise and the Horse-Box. I had a lot of trouble with the second-years because in physique they were almost as well developed as I was, and I had to use my wits in order to keep control. It was the custom on the night of 'vac', the night before the holidays, to bar the door with trunks so that the dean could not get in. I remember one particular night when the dean tried to open the door and finally I had to get up and remove all the obstacles to let him in. Then, of course, there was a 'court' held inside to find out who the culprits were.

"It was always an important day when you had a visitor who brought a 'mag' with him. A 'mag' could be anything from a sweet cake to apples and oranges. If a student was a smoker the visitor might have cigarettes hidden in the 'mag'. Cigarettes were forbidden in the college and the dean often raided the toilets where boys smoked. Fortunately, I did not have that addiction so I had less trouble with the dean. This made me a likely candidate for the position of monitor and, later, I was put in charge of security. We all got a day 'on the bell' in our third year. That meant that you had to ring the bell for mealtimes and study. It made you stay alert all the time; I suppose it was a test of character to do the job well. When the priests' retreat came, about a week after the college broke up, monitors were called back to help out with the chores in the refectory.

"One night some of the boys were going out on the town but I refused to go and went to bed. They did not like this so when they came back and found me sound asleep they put a string around my big toe and tied it to the bed. Then they shook me awake; of course, I woke up with a start and nearly cut the toe off myself. That is the kind of thing that goes on where boys are concerned. You had to take it and offer it up. In St Jarlath's, and I suppose in all colleges, there was a kind of spirit that, no matter what happened to you, you did not report it. If you tried to get your own back by reporting it to the dean then it was too bad, because something else would happen to you."

Examinations were naturally an important aspect of secondary school life. The Leaving Certificate, the Matriculation and the *concursus* were the three examinations to merit particular reference in James Horan's recollections.

"I did six subjects in the Leaving Certificate: mathematics, English, Irish, Greek, Latin and science. The range of subjects was limited by the number of professors available to teach them, but I took the maximum. I think examinations are much easier now than they used to be. There was no prescribed course for the Intermediate and Leaving Certificate in our time; it was more or less general knowledge. In Latin and Greek it was all 'translations at sight': you were given pieces of text that you had never seen before and you had to translate them. That was quite difficult.

"The professors chose their own texts in English and Irish. They also chose the particular type of grammar that they would teach. You had to use your wits when it came to the examination in order to succeed in getting honours.

"Along with the Leaving Certificate we had the Matriculation examination, which was held in Tuam and also in Galway. We were so confined in St Jarlath's, for four, five or six years, that when it came to the Matriculation everyone always took the exam in Galway as we could go out on the town: there were always all kinds of stories told about the marvellous *craic* that could be had in Galway. I found the Matriculation so easy that though there were three hours to do the examination I had it finished in an hour and a half."

James also sat the *concursus*, the entrance examination for Maynooth.

"Twenty-one boys did the examination for Maynooth. There were only seven places and the boys who failed to get into Maynooth went to other colleges to study for the priesthood. There was great activity amongst the missionary societies who sent speakers to St Jarlath's quite often. I remember Fr Whitney of the Kiltegan Fathers and Bishop Shanahan from the African missions coming to speak to us. There were great efforts made to recruit students for the missions, and there were many vocations.

"When I was making up my mind in St Jarlath's to become a priest there was one other profession which I would have liked to pursue. I would have liked to become an engineer. I was inclined towards engineering because my father was a tradesman and so was my grandfather; that type of work was very much in the family.* Eventually, however, I decided that the priesthood was my vocation. I was successful in the *concursus* examination and got a place in Maynooth which I gladly accepted.

"My grandfather, James Horan, called me into his room when he learned that I had decided to become a priest. 'Are you sure that you want to go to Maynooth and become a priest?' he asked me.

"'I am,' I replied.

"'That's all right, but are you quite sure?'

"'I am,' I said again.

"That was the end of the conversation. He gave me a silver watch. He wanted to give me something before I left home.

"I think that a vocation grows in you gradually. I thought about it for a long time. I thought about all the consequences of going on for the priesthood, of all the lonely Sunday evenings when my pals would be going to dances while I would have to stay at home to mind the house. There would be occasions like that when I would make sacrifices. However, the sacrifices are all worthwhile; later on in life you appreciate this.

"Vocations are not as plentiful now as they were then. I often wonder why this is so. I think one of the reasons is that there are

---

His brother Pat and nephew James have kept the family tradition of building.

more opportunities for jobs when finishing school and there are more openings for jobs in the academic line. I suppose boys, not being able to make up their minds, go into these jobs and eventually stay there and make a career of them. I also think that the number of priests leaving the priesthood is a cause of a falling-off in vocations. In the past every father and mother would be proud to have a son as a priest, and naturally they would encourage the boy if he had a vocation or if he expressed a wish to become a priest, whereas nowadays they are scared to see their sons going on for the priesthood in case that they might leave and cause them heartbreak later on. This is a great pity. I think it should be accepted that a man who changes his mind gets a dispensation from his vows and returns to lay life. But he has given certain years of his life to God and that should be accepted as something positive and good."

While St Jarlath's became a preparation for Maynooth and the priesthood, the years of study were broken up with holidays spent working on the farm in Tooreen.

"There was great excitement the night before you went home on holidays. You felt marvellous going home; having been confined for three months, now you had your freedom again. My first journey on a train was when I came home on holidays from St Jarlath's. I got on the train in Tuam and came home through Claremorris. There was usually an hour and a half's delay in Claremorris before getting on the train for Ballinrobe, so I found my way down the town until I got to a little hotel at the corner of the Square called Cunnane's where I went and got a meal for one shilling.

"At home you got a little bit more petting and softness because you had been away for such a long time, but even so there was work to be done around the place. There were jobs that I liked and some I disliked. For some reason I hated 'stubbing' thistles. If you cut the thistles at the stem at certain times of the year they will not grow again. Thistles grew mostly where you had sheep grazing and one evening I was ordered by my mother to stub one of these fields. I had something else planned with some of my pals and told my mother that I could not do the job, but she ordered me to go, and when I was slow in going I got 'tally ho'. My mother must have thought that she had punished me too severely, for after I had finished the thistles I got a nicer tea than I had ever been given. I am sure that young boys have to stub thistles now and again but, if they do, they have my full sympathy.

"I spent many a day in the bog spreading turf. The first day I went to the bog I got so hungry on the way that when I reached the bog I wanted grub straight away, and they had to give it to me before I started work at all. Later on I went to the bog to spread turf, to foot it and turn it into stacks or *dúcháns*. I loved the bog because the air was good and the atmosphere absolutely uplifting. I led the donkey, which was harnessed with a straddle and cleaves, the four or five miles to the bog where it worked all day bringing turf from the bank to the side of the road. It was then loaded on to the horse cart or the donkey cart, and I drew the turf home sitting like all the other farmers on top of the load. Once I met a schoolpal on the road; I was a student in Maynooth at the time, and this schoolfriend told me that I was letting the cloth down in that what I was doing was really beneath my dignity. I did not agree and I continued to bring home the turf. I think that it was very important that I should work because we were a big family, seven in all, and it took a lot to feed all of us. I always felt guilty because of the fact that a little more money was being spent on me than on the others, though they never seemed to mind and they all got their chances afterwards.

"As a youngster I played handball very often. The handball alley was very convenient to us. It was built by the local landlord, Colonel Blas Lynch, and it was always maintained by the Lynch family. I also played football and I would have loved to own a football, but footballs in those days were expensive. The only time that you had some kind of a ball to kick around was when a pig was killed in the village and you got the bladder and filled it with air. It was only the very odd time that we had a football in the village and, when we had, we played ball on the lanes or *laontraois* in front of the village.

"I went to *céilís* in our local hall in Partry and took part in step dancing and set dancing in my own house at home and in the houses of my friends. I moved around with the boys and girls of my own village or parish. I had a wonderful relationship with them even though I was in college and leading a different kind of life from what they were living. Still, there was no difference between us as people and I communicated with them quite freely. I never got too far away from them. When I went to college and when I became a priest, I never had any difficulty in meeting them and they never had any difficulty in meeting me. Of that I am very proud because I feel that, in character, I did not change. The same goes for all the old people in my village. They could talk to me and approach me as they always did."

As a young man, James was introduced to the traditional religious shrines and pilgrimages of Co. Mayo. His early experiences of going to Knock are of special interest in the light of his later involvement with the shrine.

"I have very fond memories of pilgrimages that I made, both to Croagh Patrick and Knock Shrine. I climbed Croagh Patrick four times before I was ordained to the priesthood. On each occasion I cycled twenty miles or more to Croagh Patrick and then climbed the Reek, as it is called locally. I always left home in the evening and started to climb in the darkness of the night. One time I cycled to the Reek with my father. I got a puncture at Rossbeg just outside Westport on my way there and had to mend it in the light of a carbide bicycle lamp. However, I climbed the Reek, performed all the stations and prayers that were required, and came down in the morning after having got Mass and communion on the summit at six o'clock. Coming down I was very weary and my feet were so wet that I took off my socks and washed them in a mountain stream, squeezed the water out of them, put them back on and cycled home. I went to bed at around one or two o'clock that day and slept soundly until the following morning – I must have been really exhausted. I have never climbed the Reek as a priest. I was always occupied in my parish on the last Sunday of July, Reek Sunday, and could not get away.

"I went to Knock many times, too. I cycled there as a boy with a friend, Tommy Walsh. Again, we started cycling in the evening, and when we arrived in Knock we first of all visited the Blessed Sacrament and then went around the church, anti-clockwise, saying the fifteen mysteries of the rosary. After that we did the Stations of the Cross and when we had finished we visited the Blessed Sacrament again. Of course, we had to go to confessions and communion. There were priests hearing confessions all night and at six o'clock in the morning we went to Mass and received Holy Communion. Then we got our breakfast somewhere, got our bicycles and set off home again.

"I went to Knock earlier still as a child with my grandfather, my father and mother. We travelled by side-car, leaving early in the morning. My parents shortened the journey pointing out friend's houses and talking about people they knew along the way. I got to know the area very well after doing a few of these journeys.

"My grandfather was not a religious man but he was a man of great faith. When he started to plough the field in the spring he would always say, 'In the name of the Father and of the Son and of the Holy Spirit,' then he would give a smack to the horses and off he went. When he had finished a field he would say, *'Beannacht Dé le h-anamacha na marbh,'* (the blessing of God on the souls of the dead). He remembered all the people who had ploughed that field before him, his forebears or people who had been near and dear to him, and prayed for them all on that particular occasion. He would also invoke the Blessed Trinity on any work that was done around the house. Before starting out on the journey to Knock Shrine he would sprinkle holy water on the horse and car and bless himself. The prayer 'Welcome be God's Holy Will' was always on the lips of my grandfather and my parents. They said it perhaps when the cow died or when some disaster happened. They always believed that when God closed one door he opened another, or what he took away with one hand he gave back with another, and their beliefs gave them great balance in their lives."

St Patrick's College, Maynooth

I HEARD THAT I had got a place in Maynooth from the late Fr Tom Egan, who was passing through Lecanvey where I was on holidays. He met me on the road and told me the good news, and that I had got honours in the Leaving Certificate. I do not know whether I expected honours or not, but I certainly was not very worried about it; I did, however, expect my place in Maynooth. Seven of us got places and we all went to Maynooth College early in September 1929.

I remember carrying my bag from the station to the tall, impressive-looking gates of the college. We turned left to the Junior House and hung around for a while until we all gathered together in the prayer-hall where the dean addressed us and told us what was going to happen the next day. That evening we all got a bundle of items that we would need. These included some books, especially the Bible and a little prayer book which contained the prayers we were to say every morning for the seven years we would be in the college. We also got a meditation book called *The Imitation of Christ*, a book called *St Francis de Sales*, and a book called *Liber Usualis* which contained the Masses and the music for the Gregorian chant. We got a tablecloth and a few other small things; these items were added to our pension and we had to pay for them later on.

Our names were put into a hat and then drawn out; the draw determined one's seniority. I was drawn forty-eighth out of a class of seventy-four or seventy-five, and forty-eight was to be my number for the next seven years unless somebody opted out or "cut". "Cut" was the word used in the case of a clerical student leaving the college, though a student could also be fired if he was found to be unsuitable: he was told as much and then asked to leave. For misdemeanours a student could be "catted", which was a short way of saying "caveat" or "beware", and this warning was given by the council. If you did something like eating chocolate or reading the paper you were brought before the council and given a "cat". A student could not afford to get too many of these reprimands because he would be gone on the third one.

On our first day we wandered into the McMahon Hall, the *aula maxima,* a beautiful hall which was used as a theatre. We only got in there a few times a year for functions; sometimes there would be a play staged before Christmas or perhaps during Lent. There were also concerts held there and occasionally people would be invited in from Dublin, like the Rathmines and Rathgar Musical Society, to give a recital to the students. It was always a great break to go to a concert or to a film in the McMahon Hall.

At the centre of the college St Joseph's Square stood surrounded by beautiful Gothic buildings, including the Senior Chapel. The students' first two years were spent in Junior House and the last five years in Senior House; you went into Senior House in the third year, the year that you took your degree. In Junior House we had two buildings, "Rhetoric" which housed first-year students and "Logic" for second-years. They studied the subject, too; there was in fact a great stress placed on logic, which was studied in your first three years, because the strength of your arguments in philosophy and theology depended on your grasp of it. If you did not have a logical mind or if you did not know logic you would not be able to argue as well as you would if you were skilled in that art. Logic was the subject and it was also the name of the building! During the two years we spent in Junior House, we were completely cut off from seniors. Both juniors and seniors had separate lifestyles and sports facilities.

I was never strong enough or good enough to get on my class football team. Every class had its own team and there was great rivalry between them. Leagues were played during the winter between several teams from first and second year. There was a certain amount of money put on these league games, but the really big games were when one year played another. Later on, in Senior House, there were more classes or years, five in all, and the rivalry was even more intense. Everyone went out to the football pitch to cheer on the team and the competition made life more exciting when otherwise it might have been a bit lonely or dull.

Junior House was a bit confined – we even had our own infirmary. I remember getting the mumps and spending five days in the infirmary. It was not always a nice place to be; they took good care of you but you had to be as quiet as a mouse. If you did anything at all out of the way you were probably put out.

I had gone to Maynooth with an honours Leaving Certificate and I felt on top of the world. I felt that in First Arts I should do honours in Greek, Latin, Irish and English and take a pass in mathematics. The professor of Greek was Dr John Dalton, who later became a cardinal. At the beginning of our first class he said, "It is my custom to ask the students who are in this honours class what marks they got in the Leaving Certificate." I had got 250 or 260 marks out of 400 in Greek. So he began to ask the boys according to their seniority. The first boys to be called were people like Frank Cremmin, who was from Kerry and is now a professor in Maynooth: he had 400 marks. John Ahearne, who was also at the head of the class and is now Bishop of Cloyne had 400 too. McGuirk, from the North of Ireland, had 400; Thomas Brennan the same. Some other boys had over 300 marks. When I heard the others calling out their results, I decided to take my little bundle of books and disappear as quickly as I could. I went into pass class for Greek.

You had the cream of the country to compete with in Maynooth. After my experience with Greek I decided to concentrate instead on Irish, and I did Celtic Studies in my BA. I continued to do honours in the other subjects – Latin, Irish and English – in First Arts. Latin, of course, was very important as we would have to do all our theology through Latin. The lectures were in English but the textbooks were in Latin and you had to do your examinations in Latin also, which was a disadvantage to me. Most boys who meant to go on for big things in theology did classics – Latin and Greek – in their BAs so that when they went on to study theology they were already conversant with Latin. I would have had no difficulty with theology, had it been done through English.

Students in Maynooth were all asked to do a degree. In the past century all the ministers of other religions in Ireland usually had degrees and were trained in universities like Trinity College. It was important that the Catholic clergy should be well educated so that they would be able to take their place in society and become leaders. In Ireland in the past, priests were meant not merely to look after the spiritual welfare of their flock; they also had to be leaders, competent learned men able to stand up for the rights of their parishioners. So when Maynooth College was founded it was required that students should take degrees. This tradition had a great impact throughout the whole world; wherever Maynooth graduates went they were respected as coming from a very, very excellent college. They had an excellent academic background and as a result they won a certain amount of prestige amongst the people.

But one thing that I could not understand about degrees in Maynooth was that if you failed the First Arts in June you were not allowed to repeat in September, unlike Trinity College, UCD or Queen's University in Belfast. If you failed you had to stay back and do an extra year and, to make matters worse, you lost your seniority and became the junior in the First Arts class the next year. That I thought was too severe; it looked to me like a punishment. Yet anyone can fail an examination through no fault of his own. The student might simply be sick or worried about something, or there might be some other reason for it.

My professor for Celtic Studies was Dr Gerry Nolan, a very nice man and a great Gaelic scholar. He was associated with the Gaeltacht in Ballingeary and spoke Munster Irish, and I do not think that he thought a lot of Connaught Irish. However we got fair treatment from him, despite our Connaught Irish, and got good results. He did not push it too hard in class, preferring to let us study on our own. Irish grammar was one of his strong points – he had published many books on the subject and he was very insistent that you adapt to the forms that were given in his books. He was particularly interested in the word "is". Any scholar of Irish will understand all the complications that there are in regard to this verb "is". We also studied Welsh and Scots Gaelic. Scots Gaelic was very easy for anybody who knows Irish; differences between the languages are very few and you got into it easily. I came in contact with Scots Gaelic later on when I was stationed in Dumbarton.

I felt very tired after finishing my BA degree. My health was not great at that time and I felt that it might be too much to start studying Hebrew, which I would have needed for the Bachelor of Divinity course in theology. On top of that it was announced that anybody doing the Bachelor of Divinity in our class would have to do it at the end of that year, so that anybody who had not done Hebrew the year before would have had to do the two years study in one. I decided that that was too much. I thought it better to be ordained at the end of seven years than to kill myself, so I decided to skip the BD examination. However, I continued to attend the honours class in theology.

I have often wondered if I had the right attitude towards study when I was in Maynooth. I found out afterwards that a lot of students continued their studies when they went home at Christmas or in the summer. In fact, they anticipated the programme for the coming year and studied it during the summer holidays, or at Christmas they revised the work that they had done the previous term. I never did that and I regretted it later because the extra study gave these students a lot of advantage in competing for degrees or for prizes in the theology section. Mind you, I did work the summer before I took my degree in Celtic Studies.

During those years my health did not seem to be good. My health had not been very robust since my last year in St Jarlath's and one summer I got a very bad pain which I think now was due to my appendix. During all those years I was suffering from this appendix which came to a head later when I was a curate back in Connemara.

We always looked forward to the holidays, especially the first holiday. The idea of getting out after being confined for three or four months was marvellous and going home to the family atmosphere again was wonderful. We had three weeks holiday at Christmas, but we got an extra week if we had any kind of an excuse. If there was any celebration in the country or in the college, the monitors asked for an extra week which was usually granted. I am sure the professors themselves relished and appreciated this holiday bonus.

When it came to the last day before the holidays we all felt delighted with ourselves: we had done our examinations and were ready to take off. We had Mass at six o'clock and then left for the train. We usually went to Dublin on our way home and the first thing we did was to go to Vaughan's Hotel in Parnell Square for breakfast. That was the haunt of the students from the West of Ireland; we all gathered there and got a wonderful breakfast of rashers and eggs. Rashers and eggs were at a premium in Maynooth so on the morning of the first day of the vacation we did ourselves proud. We travelled West from Broadstone Station and came home to a wonderful welcome. My father or my grandfather, as the case might be, came with the side-car to the station and took me and my luggage home to Tooreen. I enjoyed my holidays and after three or four weeks went back to Maynooth refreshed in every way. It was marvellous to come home to see all the old faces again, and they all had a great welcome for me. It was unusual to have a clerical student in the village at that time so I got VIP treatment.

Of course, we had our recreation in Maynooth; it was not all work and no play. We enjoyed life and made the most of our free time. We had no radio, no newspapers or television as they have nowadays. We could not smoke except at a certain time during recreation. I did not smoke and never had any problem with smoking until I became a priest, when I became an addict, but I have not smoked now for the last twenty-three or twenty-four years and I am very proud of that. We played football, hurling, tennis, and also croquet. Croquet was the game played by the gentry, but it became very popular during the First World War and was not an expensive game.

The students from each diocese more or less kept to themselves. This was the rule in Maynooth. It was a preparation for future years when they would have to work together. You could pal with others but only casually; generally speaking you kept to your own diocese and fraternised with your co-diocesans. Every diocese had a special place where they gathered after lunch or dinner. There they stood around for a little while, had a smoke or a chat, and took some recreation either by playing games or just by going for a stroll. Looking back on it now I think it was probably a mistake to stick to one's own diocese and it would have been far better to move outside one's own very tight circle.

Usually we went for a stroll after breakfast and again after supper in the evening. While we walked we discussed various topics, like the subject-matter of our classes during the day or questions of theology or philosophy. Sometimes we would talk about games or little tit-bits of news that we got in letters from home. After dinner at three o'clock we usually played games. On ordinary days we began our studies in the evening at half-past five when we went to our rooms where we remained until we went to rosary and benediction of the Blessed Sacrament at a quarter-past seven. Afterwards we went to supper and had more recreation. After night prayers we had solemn silence which did not end until breakfast the following morning; we went very quietly to our rooms without speaking to other people. We also had to be silent at certain times in the refectory as there was a reader on the "tub" or rostrum who read all during the meal. The dean always said the grace before and after meals.

As students we were responsible for our rooms. In the morning, after getting up, we had half an hour to prepare and dress properly and go down to morning prayer, leaving our rooms in a respectable condition. That was regarded as being very important and the dean went around on occasions, during morning prayer or morning Mass, to check the rooms. I am not as tidy as most people and my room was not as neat or as well done up as other lads', but it was good enough to get by.

The food was very good in Maynooth. In the morning we got porridge which I always loved as I felt it was a very substantial part of my breakfast, and tea, bread and butter. We got a very substantial lunch which consisted of soup, meat (usually mutton or beef) and a dessert afterwards. At about half-past seven we had tea, bread and butter which was also substantial. On the whole, the food in Maynooth was very, very good.

The relationship between the students and professors in Maynooth was peculiar. When the professors met us on the corridor or in the grounds they did not speak to us or acknowledge us in any way – they simply looked ahead of them and walked past us. I could not pass judgement on that; perhaps it was the right thing to do, but I think law and order can be kept without going to such extremes. The professors were very kind and considerate people; they simply preserved this kind of attitude towards the students. The student never got near them or never got an opportunity of discussing his problems with them. Perhaps if you did ask a professor to see you or to discuss some problem, he might give you the opportunity of doing that but, generally speaking, you never had such a chance. That was general policy, intended to preserve law and order, so that the students would not get too bold or too brash. There was only one professor in my time who would speak to the students and that was Dr Michael John Browne, who was later made Bishop of Galway. He always spoke to the lads from the Tuam archdiocese, and if he met you in the corridor he would always say, "Good morning". The other professors never did.

We had two spiritual directors, Vincentians from Dublin who lived in Maynooth. When our course was finished and we were ready to go out to work as priests they gave us a series of lectures on how to deal with penitents in the confessional. We had all the theology and knew all the strict rules; it was their job to put a human face on the theological principles and give us some idea of how to deal with actual penitents with sympathy and love. We had three deans in the college: a junior dean, a dean for St Joseph's section and a dean for St Mary's section. Junior House, as I have already said, was separated from the Senior division, which had its own dean. Our first dean was the late Dr Michael Fallon who came from Galway and afterwards worked as a parish priest in Oughterard. He was very nice and, coming from the West, he seemed to like the western students. I certainly have very happy memories of him. He was a very practical and considerate man and a great success as a dean. The second year we had Fr Edward – or Ned – Long and I also found him very considerate and had no problems with him.

Study became more serious when we had completed our degrees and went on to do theology in our fourth year, i.e. our First Divinity year. There were several subjects. Moral theology taught the rights and wrongs of things; it taught about the commandments, one's duties and obligations, and so on. Dogmatic theology gave one the principles on which our religion was founded. It was a study which enabled one to prove the existence of God, the true Church and all the qualities of the true Church. In liturgy the student learned about the ecclesiastical year and the various Masses. Of course, there is only one Mass, but there are also Masses or liturgies in honour of the saints, Christ the King, Our Lady's assumption and Our Lord's nativity. Rubrics explained the ceremonies and the various ways to carry them out; for example, the way to walk around the altar and the dignity and the care to exercise. It dealt with the way that you looked and the way in which you performed all the ceremonies you had to perform in public before your congregation. It showed you how you should carry out the various parts of the Mass – the penitential service at the beginning, the scripture, the offertory and – the most important part of all – the canon of the Mass in which the consecration takes place with the elevation of the host and chalice for the adoration of all the people in the church. Ecclesiastical history was a very important subject also, because a priest should know the history of the Church from the very beginning. He should know all about the difficulties that they had in the Church and the solutions that they found for them; the priest should know all about the heresies.

Those preparing for the priesthood in Maynooth looked forward to the "call to Orders" at the end of their training. It was a time for anxiety for the students as some might be refused the call or have it postponed for one year. This vitally important day was called "Black Friday", "black" because there was a lot of disappointment amongst those not called to Orders on that day. The president came in and read out the list. If something had happened during the year, if you had somehow failed to satisfy the demands of your professors, the deans and your president, then you would not be called to Orders. Afterwards those not called had to go up to the dean to find out what was wrong, and he gave his opinion about their whole career in Maynooth. It was a great disappointment even though it did not mean that the student would not get Orders eventually, nor even that anything serious had gone wrong. Students were turned down for very trivial reasons sometimes, like being caught talking or going around in an un-tidy condition. Perhaps the student did not comb his hair properly or something like that.

Life was serious during our final years in Maynooth, when we got up to the higher classes and studied for the sub-deaconate and the deaconate. If you did not get them then you were made master of ceremonies, which meant that you had to spend your last year without Orders and only got to sub-deaconate and deaconate status at the end of your seventh year, the year of your priestly ordination. Then you had to get all your Orders at the end of that year, when you joined the rest of the class for the Order of Priesthood. The boy without Orders in his last year was called a master of ceremonies because of the part he played in ceremonies, where there was a celebrant, a deacon and an MC. It must have been a trying time for MCs because if anything went wrong they could be told that they were not suitable and that they would have to leave the college. I always felt sorry for them. In my particular class there were seven of us from Tuam and we all got Orders. We were fairly comfortable, but I always felt that the MCs, too, should have got Orders.

Seven years of training and study came to a climax the day we were ordained. The ordination ceremony took over four hours. My grandfather was old at the time, eighty years of age, and he found the experience very tiring. He was so weak at the breakfast in the refectory that I had to order a glass of whiskey to revive him. Thank God, he got over it and he lived for two years after that.

My ordination day fell on 21 June, the Feast of St Aloysius. In the sacristy we all got dressed in great excitement. We had been on retreat for ten days previously preparing for this day, the biggest day of our lives. You realise then the serious step you are taking; you realise that you are dedicating your whole life to God. You will no longer be a lay person, and in your new office you will have to be more restrained, more disciplined, more circumspect. Every year afterwards, on the Feast of St Aloysius, I prayed that God would preserve me and keep me in the priesthood.

On the Monday after ordination we had our first Mass in the college, a Mass at which a bigger number of people could attend. You were allowed to say Mass in the chapel of your choice and you could have your friends and visitors there, and arrangements were made afterwards for them to have a meal in the college. It was great to be able to invite some of your friends to Maynooth to see the college. Maynooth is known all over the world as priests have gone forth from its portals to work in every nation under the sun. All the priests who were ordained there and all the students who went forth from the college are proud of their Alma Mater; it is a truly wonderful place. The following day we had the Maynooth Union, a big dinner at which all the young priests attended. On our Maynooth Union day John McCormack came as a guest and sang for us after the dinner.

From Maynooth I went home and had my first Mass in the church of my native parish, surrounded by all my friends, neighbours and old schoolpals. That was truly a great day. After the Mass I was surrounded by friends offering me their good wishes, and I knew that I was home at last. They were so proud of me. In Ireland at that time and even, thank God, at the present day, the priest had a very high standing among his people.

I went back to the school where I had received my first education and I got great pleasure and satisfaction in meeting my former teacher. Going around to meet my friends I received countless invitations to call and visit, and I tried to honour all of them. It meant a lot of work and a lot of cycling, but on many occasions my father came with me. Cycling together made me recall that years before I used have to fit my leg in under the crossbar of his bike so as to ride it. Gone were the days, now, when I was not big enough to cycle my father's bicycle.

A Curate in Scotland

THERE WERE SEVENTY-TWO of us ordained in 1936. Now as I write, I think about forty are still alive. Thirty-two of them have died, many having spent their lives as priests in Ireland. But in the 1930s the majority of new priests had to go abroad for a short time because there were too many priests in the diocese and each had to wait his turn to come in. Nowadays it is quite easy to get into a diocese because of the shortage of vocations, but when I was ordained it was very difficult even in places abroad like Brooklyn or New York or other dioceses on the East Coast. A lot of my class-fellows went overseas, and when priests went away sometimes they did not come back. They grew to like the dioceses where they worked and, settling down there, they often decided to stay.

There were seven priests for the Archdiocese of Tuam ordained in my class and there were no vacancies for us there. The archbishop, Dr Thomas Gilmartin, asked us to look for temporary missions abroad. I applied to the Diocese of Leeds for a temporary mission and was accepted. However, the Bishop of Leeds died early in 1936 and that meant that no outside priest could be accepted into the diocese while the diocese remained vacant. I was anxious to get on the missions and get a taste of parish work so I applied to the Glasgow diocese and was accepted along with two other priests from my class. After ordination each of us had an interview with Dr Gilmartin to inform him of the arrangement that we had made. When we told him that we had got missions in Glasgow he did not seem to be very pleased; obviously there must have been problems in the past with regard to temporary missions there. In any case it was arranged that I take up duty in Glasgow in the first week of August 1936 and, as my sister was a trainee nurse in Manchester, I decided to visit her on my way. Many of my schoolpals from Partry had emigrated to Manchester also, and I longed to meet them and to find out how they had got on.

I started my journey to Dublin by train and then took the boat to Liverpool. It was my first time on a ship and my first journey out of Ireland; I was, as the Americans would say, "a real greenhorn". I arrived in Liverpool at about six o'clock in the morning, hired a taxi and asked the driver to bring me to a good boarding house. He took me to a place owned by two old ladies who showed me to my room. As I entered the room a black cat scurried past my feet and down the stairs. I was very tired and wanted to rest, but I looked at the bed and saw that I had lots of company: the fleas were jumping like racehorses all over the sheets. I put on my coat and went for a walk.

It was my first time on foreign soil. I had often dreamed of what it would be like. The air was the very same as in Dublin but a little murkier and more smoggy owing to the presence of industry. Red-brick buildings lined the streets. I could not help thinking that many of them had been built by Irishmen. Many of the Irish, fleeing from the Famine, reached Liverpool and had neither the money nor the energy to go farther. If they were lucky they got jobs; any kind of a job would do. It was a Sunday morning and the sun shone, or at least did its best to burst through the haze and smog. I made my way to the local church and presented my *Celebret*, a document signifying that I was a priest of good standing, to the priest of the local church, and was allowed to offer Mass. Then I returned to the boarding house and had breakfast.

I enquired about a train to Manchester and found there was none, but there was a train to St Helen's which would take me part of the way. I opted for the train as I was scared of the "racehorses" on the bed, and stayed in a hotel that night in a room which was clean and comfortable, though it was directly over the bar where there was merriment and carousing till the early hours. Sleep came fitfully. I was still feeling the excitement of starting my first missionary journey in a strange land. It could not have been as trying, nor as dangerous, as St Paul's journey. At about six o'clock in the morning my sleep was disturbed by the clatter of iron on the pavement: it was the iron soles of the clogs worn by the workers in St Helen's at that time. I enquired about Mass and was told that I could have Mass in the Notre Dame Convent not very far away. On the street I saw a young girl and I asked her to direct me; she said that she was going that way and she took me along to the convent gate. She was not a Catholic but I was impressed by her kindness and her friendly manner. I offered Mass there and afterwards came back to the hotel for breakfast.

At last I got a train to Manchester. The city was overpowering. It was a fine summer's day and the weather was beautiful. I knew the sun was shining somewhere, but not here; it could not penetrate the great black mantle of smog that enveloped the city. There was smog on my hands, my face and my clothes. I felt so hot and uncomfortable, my clothes clinging to my body with perspiration. Was I glad that Manchester was not my final destination! Compared to their brothers and sisters in Ireland, the young people on the streets seemed to be serious and unsmiling. You could read the stresses and strains of life on their drawn, pale faces. Perhaps it was the smog or the unhealthy conditions in the factories where many of them worked. This was in an era before communities and governments outlawed smoke and smog in the great cities of the world; nor had the unions enough strength and muscle to insist on proper working conditions.

I met my sister in Crumpsall Hospital and she took me out for the day. We went into Manchester to meet some old friends and neighbours. A few of her pals, who were Welsh girls, travelled with us and having studied Welsh in my Celtic Studies degree I was very keen to try out my Welsh on them. I met some of my schoolpals and neighbours in the city and thought that they looked well and dressed well. Most of them emigrated to the United States later – thousands of boys and girls went to England at that time with the intention of earning their passage to America.

After a few days I travelled by train to Glasgow, making my way finally to the presbytery in the Cathedral parish. There I met Monsignor Daly, the parish priest, and I dined with him and his priests for two or three days. I look back at those days and think that I was very brash and outspoken then. I had come from the renowned College of Maynooth and I was very proud of my Alma Mater and of all the great learning that I had acquired. At table I expressed my views and expressed them strongly. I felt later that my views and the way I expressed them did not go down well with the monsignor; I must have appeared to him as "My New Curate" in Canon Sheehan's novels. I was sent to a parish called Pollakshaws where the parish priest, a Corkman, was convalescing from an illness; the curate, Fr Coogan, was also an Irish priest. This was my first parish and the place where I was to carry out my first pastoral duties.

Many of the people in the Glasgow archdiocese had an Irish

background and an Irish priest was always welcome among them. In my early days in Glasgow I was given a full account of the rivalry between the Celtic and Rangers soccer teams; they represented the Catholic and Protestant communities respectively. I will never forget one New Year's Day I was leaving Celtic Park after a match which Celtic had won when a few Protestant youngsters whistled at me: "There he goes to phone the Pope!" They took these matches so seriously that I could well understand that they believed what they said. I had heard before going to Glasgow that I would find a lot of bigotry there, but I never found any real bigotry, and always felt that I was treated with the greatest kindness and consideration. I did not travel around Pollakshaws very much except to do the ordinary duties like sick calls. Visitation in Scottish parishes, as indeed in every parish, was very important. Each priest had his own district and was expected to visit parishioners in that district at least twice each year, and this work was carried out diligently by all the priests with whom I worked in Scotland. When the parish priest returned I was transferred to another parish, Cardonald, where the parish priest, Fr George Gilbraith, had taken ill. I was to stay there until such time as he got back on his feet again. I liked Cardonald and its people very much. It was out in the suburbs, a beautiful parish with a beautiful church. I was impressed by the great organisation in the Scottish parishes. They had very nice churches, often of wood, and they were kept spick and span. The sacristies and the vestments were everything that could be desired. It happened too that one of my class-fellows, Fr John Jennings, was stationed in Cardonald and that made my sojourn there all the more pleasant. I quickly felt very much at home.

    I spent a month in Cardonald and when the priest was due back I was changed to a new parish, Dumbarton. I was told, before I went there, that I was going to a very strict parish priest, Monsignor Hugh Kelly. I grew to like and admire Monsignor Kelly. He was fairly strict and some priests perhaps thought that he was too strict; however, I got on well with him and I had no reason to complain. He may have been strict but he was fair and kind. He kept a beautiful presbytery and I certainly got a great training under his leadership. I was stationed there for the rest of my time in Glasgow, a period of three years.

    The rules were firmly applied at that time in every Scottish presbytery. We had to be in for supper at nine-thirty, and if you were out after that it was just too bad: the doors were locked. I was never locked out; I kept the rules. Monsignor Kelly did not approve of priests spending too much time at soccer matches, not even at Celtic or Rangers matches, and for that reason he always made sure that the hours for children's confessions on Saturday afternoon coincided with the time for soccer matches.

I play golf, and of all the hobbies I have had in my lifetime I got the greatest satisfaction and pleasure from golf. I think that it is a most suitable game for priests: if I were a bishop I would almost make it obligatory. It is a great game for keeping fit, mentally and physically. I played golf quite often in Cardross Road Club with another curate who was a fellow-student of mine in Maynooth, Fr Denis Lucy. The parish priest did not approve of golf and did not like us to indulge in it, but we had to do something on our free day. We were far from home and we had no friends to visit.

When we went off for the day we always had a car put at our disposal by Paddy Cleary, a Catholic garage-owner in the town. Neither did we have to pay fees at Cardross Road because, unlike Ireland, a priest got free admittance. Despite all of the music-hall jokes about the Scotsman being tight or mean I found the Scottish people very generous and hospitable. There was a chemist's shop owned by a Protestant situated across from the presbytery in Dumbarton, and he supplied me with razors, razor-blades, soap and shaving-cream free of charge. No matter how I protested he would not accept a penny. God be with you, Scotland! In Ireland they would spot a Roman collar coming a mile away and the prices would shoot up immediately!

There was an old tradition in Dumbarton that St Patrick came from an area near by called Kill-Patrick. There may have been some truth in the story because, after all, he was given into the hands of Milchu to herd pigs on Slieve Mish, Co. Antrim, a short distance across the strait from Scotland. I had another experience of the closeness of Scotland and Ireland when I was sent one weekend to an island called Dunoon to do duty for a priest who was sick. I tried out my Gaelic on the islanders and was surprised that I was able to understand them, to some extent.

Dumbarton was not far from Loch Lomond and every Friday and Saturday evening hundreds and hundreds of young people cycled through the town on their way to the Loch. It seemed that all the young in Glasgow took to their bicycles in summertime, cycling up to Loch Lomond and camping around the lake. They lined the roads for miles on their way back on Sunday evening, returning to the city for work on Monday morning. I learned the words of "Loch Lomond" and I have been singing it ever since. I always associate Dumbarton with this song.

There was a beautiful church in Dumbarton and it was immaculately kept; it was well furnished and had a beautiful organ. There was sung Mass every Sunday at twelve o'clock, the last Mass of the day; the altar boys were well trained and well dressed and everything was in good shape. It was a wonderful place for a young priest to train because once he grew accustomed to that kind of standard he would feel very uncomfortable with anything less. I felt fortunate to be under this wonderful if rather strict parish priest. Monsignor Kelly was a great worker and a man of stature in the archdiocese. Deeply interested in education, he was a member of the Education Committee in Dumbartonshire, and went to Glasgow quite often to attend to diocesan affairs in the Chancery Office. He was a great administrator and in preaching he always called a spade a spade and did some straight talking. The parishioners took it well and they certainly carried out his wishes.

I attended the three hospitals in our parish regularly, one of which corresponded to what we would regard as an old people's home. In this hospital I often met Irishmen who had emigrated to Scotland from places like Donegal, Connemara or Achill. They were men who never married, who did not take care of themselves. They lived on the "bru", which at that time amounted to twenty-seven shillings a week for a single man. They had their abode in a lodging house where they got bed and board for the night at the cost of one shilling.

The occupants of the model lodging house, which was known locally as "the doss house", drank heavily. As their cash was so limited they could not afford ordinary beer or spirits so they had to resort to a red wine of a high alcoholic content called "Red Biddy". They lived aimless and careless lives. They were homeless, far away from friends and relations. They lived from day to day, week to week and year to year, until at last, worn out from neglect, they collapsed on some back street. Then they were taken to the home, where the matron, who was a Protestant, informed the priest immediately. Many a time I attended them in the home and gave them all the rites of the Church. Sometimes they recovered and more times they did not. If they recovered they had no option but to go back to the lodging house.

One day in the park by the Clyde I met an Irishman who was obviously down-at-heel. I stopped to chat with him and asked where he came from. He said he came from Donegal. "What age were you when you left Donegal?" I asked him.

"I left when I was seventeen. I was one of a big family," he told me.

"What youthful ambitions had you when you left dear old Donegal?"

"To tell you the truth," he answered, "the only ambition I had was to earn as much money as I could and drink it; what I have done ever since."

He was in his sixties. I could not understand why he had never had any ambition. That sad tale was only one of many that I met, lovable characters, but oh, how unfortunate. One day he, too, would die a lonely death, far from the friends and neighbours who loved him.

You would meet many Irishmen of that kind in Glasgow, as indeed in many other cities in Great Britain. I felt so sorry for them, but I also felt a kinship with them. They were Irish like myself. On the other hand there were hundreds of Irish men and women in the parish who were happily married and raised wonderful families. They were proud of the land of their birth and, in their lives, were a credit to Ireland.

When I went to Dumbarton I was given special duties, one of which was to act as chaplain to the League of the Cross, the temperance association. The League of the Cross promoted all kinds of social evenings and provided entertainment – concerts, black-and-white minstrel shows and card games – all organised mainly by people who had previously had problems with drink, although they also got help from other teetotallers.

On my first Sunday in Dumbarton, after I had said Mass in the parish church, an old woman came to the sacristy and told me to go and see her husband, Mick, who was drinking very heavily. I went down later that day. I asked directions to the house and was told that I would have to enter by a back-way. I climbed up a rickety stairs with the aid of a rope. I went in and there was my bold Mick in bed, well under the weather, a bottle of Red Biddy beside him. Red Biddy was a most deadly drink. A five-naggin bottle could be bought for 2s 6d and if you got drunk on it you could remain in a permanent state of intoxication for twenty-four hours by drinking water or any other kind of liquid at intervals.

"Mick!" I said, "you will have to pull yourself together and join the League of the Cross." I asked him if he would take the pledge and he said "Yes". I looked at the bottle of Red Biddy and said: "What should I do with this?"

"Throw it in the ashes, Father."

I poured what was left of it into the ashes and Mick promised me that he would attend our next meeting. Mick kept his word, took the pledge and kept it during my years in Dumbarton.

The visit to the home of Mick and Anne was my first visit to a home in Dumbarton. It was a poor home but neat and comfortable. Both Mick and his wife were from the North of Ireland. They were a very happy and devoted couple, especially when Mick was sober. Mick had no job and they lived on the "bru". Thank God that I was able to help them and bring a little happiness to their home.

The years 1936-39 were a time of poverty and recession in Scotland and, indeed, all over the world. The problems then were similar to the problems in Ireland in the 1880s. Because of the unemployment and poverty there was great unrest, especially amongst the young. The communists tried to take advantage of the situation to gain more followers amongst the poor; they gave themselves the harmless name of the "Independent Labour Party", which deceived many Catholics and lured them into joining the party. The majority of Dumbarton men worked either in Denny's shipyard or in the erection of a huge distillery for the making of Scotch whisky. The unemployed received unemployment benefit – a single man got about £1 7s and I suppose a man with a family got a pound extra or more. Amongst the unemployed were many Catholics from the parish. It was a very difficult time for them.

Many people in the town owned their own homes, especially families which had been living in the area for a long time and inherited their houses. Usually private homes were owned by the middle or upper classes while most people lived in flats in large tenement houses. Each tenement had an entrance through a passageway called a "close", inside of which stone stairs led up to the flats. The rents were reasonable and did not seem to cause too much concern. The welcome was always warm and sincere. New housing estates were being built in places like Bruce Hill and Newtown and the families from the tenement buildings were being moved there, but in all the older streets in Dumbarton tenement buildings were still the norm.

All through the depression years people from Aran and Achill came over to Scotland for the digging of the potatoes, or the "tato picking" as they used to call it. They came over in springtime after they had sown their own seeds and went home again after the harvest. They came in large numbers and lived in very poor conditions.

It was during my time in Scotland that the terrible disaster of Kirkentillock took place. On a farm near Kirkentillock, where a large group from Achill had come to work, the boys were living in a kind of bothy, the girls in an adjoining two-story building. The roof of the bothy where the ten boys slept was made of pitch or tar; a stove was positioned just inside the door. The door of the bothy was bolted on the inside and once the bolt was released the door slid back on its railings, but the young boys from Achill had never seen such a door before and did not know how to operate it. Another door led from the bothy into the house where the girls were sleeping and it was always kept locked. Bags of straw lay on the floor where they served as mattresses for the young workers. When the fire started the building was quickly consumed by the flames. All of the boys died in the conflagration. The girls, thank God, escaped.

It was hard to judge on whom the blame for the conditions should be placed. The farmer had a contract with the gaffer who was to dig and pick the potatoes at a certain price; he hired people from his own parish at home in Achill or perhaps people from other parts of Connemara. This was how the work was carried out. The farmer obliged him, as it were, by giving the workers a roof over their heads. That is literally all they had, because there was no accommodation or comfort whatsoever.

The remains of those who died in the tragedy were brought to Westport, then taken by rail from Westport to Achill. The Achill line was still there but the train with the cortège was to be the last one which ever ran. This train was especially put on to take them to Achill even though the line had been out of use for a time. The event seemed to fulfil a prophecy which had been made in regard to the Achill line. It said: "The first train and the last train will carry coffins; they will both be sad occasions." When the first train went to Achill there had been twenty-one coffins on it, the corpses of those drowned when their boat capsized in Clew Bay.

Those unfortunate people had set out so that they could ride on the first train to travel from Westport to Achill; instead, their remains were carried on it. When the bodies of those who died in Kirkentillock were brought home the prophecy was fulfilled.

News of the Kirkentillock tragedy was widely reported in the world press and created much concern and dispute in Scotland. The Archbishop of Tuam sent a priest, Fr Thomas McEllin, curate of Achill, to investigate the conditions in which the immigrants lived and to make recommendations as to their improvement. He visited various farms and saw the bothies which housed the immigrants, then reported back to Dr Gilmartin who sent a copy of the report to the British government and the local authorities in Scotland. As a result the government in Westminster, together with local authorities in Scotland, laid down new rules and regulations for the housing of people who came to work on farms.

I often met the Achill people who were over "tato picking" because they came to Mass and confession in our church at Dumbarton. Many of them were Irish speakers and it was only then I realised that there was an area in Achill where Irish was still spoken as the everyday language of the people. After the Kirkentillock disaster I went to the funerals of the victims, ten young boys aged between thirteen and eighteen. I am always haunted by the vision of the ten coffins ranged in front of the altar during Solemn Requiem Mass.

There were many societies in the parish working with the poor, among them the Children of Mary, the Boy Scouts and the Third Order of St Francis. We did not have a Legion of Mary as the parish priest did not believe in it; he defined the Legion as "the invention of a lazy curate". He had little tolerance for laziness and it was most extraordinary the strict rules that he laid down for the members of the parish associations: they were forbidden to go to the movies, pubs or dances. They observed these rules faithfully – I knew young girls and boys who kept the rules thoroughly and I was awed by the tremendous sacrifices they made. They certainly were model youngsters – they had the faith and they had it strong. Dumbarton was the most Catholic parish in Britain and it produced scores of vocations, both while I was there and afterwards. The regime was very strict but where you have a strict regime vocations flourish. After all, what does joining the priesthood or the religious life mean but to renounce the world, to sacrifice the things that the young people of Dumbarton were asked to sacrifice?

We had two convents in the parish and the curates had to act as chaplains to both of them. You had to get up very early to offer Mass in the Carmelite convent at 6.30 a.m. but that was good for a young priest – it gave him a good long day with lots of time to attend to his other duties. The Sisters of Notre Dame ran excellent primary and secondary schools and gave a wonderful education and training to the girls of the parish. These schools were completely paid for and maintained by the government, and still the Church had complete control of them. It was a system that had been offered to the whole of England many years previously, but the English Hierarchy had been afraid to accept it as they were apprehensive of too much state control over the schools. However, the Scottish Hierarchy accepted the deal and it worked out very well – there was really nothing that you could complain about in the way the national schools were run. There was also a large secondary school for boys in the parish which was run by the Catholic church. On the whole the Dumbarton people were well served in the line of education with the result that many of their sons became priests and many others entered the professions.

One of the heartbreaks for a priest in Scotland was mixed marriages between Catholics and Protestants. The parish priest was loath to ask the archbishop for a dispensation in such cases and without a dispensation the marriage could not take place in the Catholic church. Some of the boys and girls in the parish found their own solutions to the problem; when they could not get a dispensation for a mixed marriage in their own parish they went off to the next one, the Renton, where it was not so difficult. The heartbreak came when the Catholic boy or girl ran away and got married in a registry office or even down in Gretna Green, a place where they could get married at a moment's notice. I do not know the details of the ceremony but I do know that it had something to do with parading around a blacksmith's anvil – perhaps he welded them together with the blacksmith's hammer! Looking back, one of the hardest things to bear in Scotland was to see a good faithful Catholic go off and get married in a registry office – that was a real problem and it was very hard to cope with it. Yet many did come back and were reconciled to Mother Church, and sometimes too the Protestant might decide to become a Catholic. In that case the Protestant entered the converts' class for six months and was eventually received into the Church.

I was put in charge of the converts' class, which was very interesting. I remember a Protestant girl who was to marry a boy who had fallen away from the Catholic faith. It was a most extraordinary case. She refused to marry him until he came back to his religion and was willing to attend the converts' class with her. She attended the class and became a Catholic and a very good one, while he became reconciled and did everything that was asked of him to make reparation for any scandal that he may have given. One of the things he had to do was to hand over a pile of anti-Catholic literature that he had been passing around among his friends. He brought in a cart-load, and the books were duly burned in the presbytery furnace. The couple were married in Dumbarton Catholic Church and lived happily during my time in the parish. I certainly would wish them well and I hope that they have grown in faith and love for each other and for God.

During my third and final year in Dumbarton, in 1939, the parish priest asked me to act as chaplain on the Anchor liner, *California*. I told him that I would be delighted; I welcomed this opportunity to go to America and meet all my relations. I had two uncles in America and several first cousins, and of course many of my schoolpals had emigrated to the States also. My schedule was to sail to New York in July, which gave me a chance to visit the World Fair. All the arrangements were made: my salary was a nominal one shilling, I was given a first-class cabin and a special cabin to hear confessions, and I was to say Mass every morning in the lounge.

I dined at the Purser's table with the Purser and two others. One was a German businessman who spoke continually about the German army, boasting about its efficiency and strength. The Purser, an Englishman, argued with him about the relative strength of the German and British armies while I sat between them, with no idea that a world war was around the corner.

The *California*'s first call was off the coast of Donegal where it took on passengers who arrived by tender from Donegal, among them Americans and Canadians returning home after holidaying in their native county. We arrived in America in the middle of July and lay at anchor in New York harbour for some time before we berthed. It was hot and humid and I really suffered from the heat. On disembarking I was met by my two uncles, Patrick Casey, who had brought me to St Jarlath's in a Model T Ford, and Seamus Casey. I stayed with Patrick for the first few days in Long Island and then I alternated between his house and Seamus's in Brooklyn.

In America they were very worried about communism. They blamed Mrs Eleanor Roosevelt, the President's wife, for being a little too soft on the communists, especially the Communist Youth Movement. This was the thirties and America was just getting back to normal after the Depression when the banks had closed on people's money and many people had been left penniless and unemployed. Years later I met another cousin of mine, also called James, who lived in Philadelphia. His father was a contractor and stonemason who had had a big business and beautiful home but fell victim to the Depression and lost everything. Jim walked the streets of Philadelphia for a whole year at the time, without a job, although he had just qualified as an engineer. Thankfully, he got a job eventually with the Philadelphia Authorities as Borough Engineer.

I spent two weeks in New York and thought it was a regular fairyland. I met all my cousins and schoolpals and went from place to place attending parties. America, I thought, was an absolutely beautiful place. The standard of living was high and my friends, who had had no work and no future in Ireland, had found a beautiful life here.

Alas my sojourn in New York passed very quickly and I had to rejoin my ship as chaplain. This time we sailed on the *Columbia*. Some of the people who had travelled to New York with me on the *California* were now returning to Europe, too, and I also made many new friends. There was a happy, holiday atmosphere on board and we had beautiful weather on the trip. These people, full of joy and expectation on their way to Europe, did not know what was in store for them. On 3 September England declared war on Germany, and in the first days of the war the *Athenia* was sunk by a German submarine off the coast of Ireland. Many of the bodies were washed ashore along the west coast and twenty people were buried in a common grave in a cemetery at Rahoon, Galway. I attended the funeral because I knew a number of the people who had lost their lives in that disaster. I remembered, then, the arguments that had gone on between the Purser and the German on the *California*. The *California* itself was to be torpedoed during the war, and so was the *Columbia*.

Back in Dumbarton I was soon at work among my parishioners. After my break I could see anew what wonderful people they were. They looked on the priest as their leader. They rallied around him and had great respect for him, as indeed do Irish people, but they also went to him in all their troubles and trials. Even the children loved the priest. When I walked down the street in Dumbarton I often had nine, ten or twenty children trailing after me. In Ireland, on the other hand, the children were shy. If they saw you on the road they would almost be inclined to turn down the boreen rather than meet you. I think the reason was that when their children misbehaved parents sometimes threatened the priest on them. They might say, "We will bring in the priest" or "The priest will put horns on you". All that was bad for the child psychologically. From the beginning children should be told that the priest is his friend, that he is kind and does everything possible to help people: that is the priests's vocation. It can be disastrous to threaten the priest on children. I have preached against it and I hope, please God, that people have given up a habit that can be so harmful. Later in life, if that child gets into trouble he should be able to approach the priest without any inhibition and know that he is approaching somebody who is kind and considerate. That is the priest's vocation and if he fails in that he is not following the example of his master, Jesus Christ.

There is no country in the world where there is such respect and reverence for the priests as in Ireland, but for some strange reason that respect creates a barrier between the priest and his people. They place the priest on a pedestal but in doing so they seem to isolate him. I must say that all that has changed in recent years and the relationship between priest and people is now very natural and very normal, but in 1939 I noticed the difference immediately when I came back to Ireland. People were slower to speak to me, slower to start a conversation. I had to work very hard with both adults and children to create the kind of relationship in which they would talk to me and trust me, and regard me as a friend.

One of the important things that I learned on the mission in Dumbarton was that visitation of the homes was one of the best ways to relate to people. I never had any trouble walking into a house, sitting down and having a chat. The people before me might be complete strangers but I could always sit down and start a conversation. I did not seem to have any inhibitions in that way as I was well used to visiting when I was a young boy back in my own village of Tooreen. It is a duty, of course, for a priest to visit his people and get to know them and I could never relate fully to people in a new parish until I had gone around, met them all and got to know them personally; then you can relate to them quite easily. After all a priest, like Christ, must be a good shepherd. The motto of Christ, the good shepherd was, "I know mine and mine know me." People may get the wrong impression of a priest if they just see him in the pulpit, preaching and laying down the law as it were. A priest is also a friend who visits the people in their homes, who is interested in their families and their welfare.

I liked Scotland and often wondered whether I should stay there or not. I had the option of staying in Glasgow but then I would have had to break my connection with my archdiocese and Ireland. It was something that I thought about and considered but seeing that my parents were in Ireland I decided that I should come home for the time being at least. I did come home, but I never returned to Scotland.

Curate in Tiernea

Two weeks after coming back from America I got a letter from my archbishop, Dr Thomas Gilmartin, asking me to return to Ireland. I told my parish priest that my archbishop was recalling me, and I was back in Ireland by the end of August.

I went immediately to see Dr Gilmartin at the Archbishop's Palace in Tuam. I was ushered in by his secretary, Dr James Fergus, who later became Bishop of Achonry. The old man was sitting on his chair with a stick in his hand; he had not been well. He was, however, very gracious and kind and presented me with two books, a copy of the *Diocesan Statutes* and the *Provincial Statutes*, which set out the rules and regulations for the priests of the Tuam archdiocese and the ecclesiastical province of Tuam. As you might imagine, rules and regulations were important in those far-off days, more important, anyway, than they seem to be now.

The archbishop told me to go to the Franciscan Monastery in Ballyglunin. I went there on the appointed Friday – all priests were changed on a Friday so as to be on duty for the weekend. I called to the parish priest, Fr John A. Burke, and presented my credentials. I will never forget the interview. He began to pose leading questions to me, weighing up my answers with careful deliberation, looking right through me, or so I felt. Later I found him to be a real gentleman and we became very good friends but he never lost that acute, inscrutable expression, especially at the card-table. Some time afterwards I met him when he was about to go to America to raise funds for a project in Abbeyknockmoy. I gave him the benefit of my own experience, all the advice that I possibly could and all the names and addresses at my disposal, and he made a great success of his mission. He was a very efficient person and a very efficient parish priest. Sadly, after returning from America he fell into ill health and spent the end of his life in hospital.

Ballyglunin was not a curacy, it was a chaplaincy; I was chaplain to the Franciscan Brothers. The monastery church was public, however, and I celebrated two Masses on Sunday and preached the homilies, and I had the usual confessions on a Saturday. The work there, in fact, was similar to the work that a priest would have in any curacy in the Archdiocese of Tuam. I did not know why I had been sent there even though, when I was recalled from Scotland, it had seemed to be very urgent. I heard later that a Fr Thomas Jennings, a professor of Irish in St Jarlath's, had applied for the professorship of Irish in Maynooth. If he had got the chair perhaps I would have been sent to St Jarlath's College to teach Irish as I had a first-class honours degree in Celtic Studies. Whether that was the case or not I do not know, but it really makes no difference; in life, man proposes and God disposes. Providence decreed that Fr Jennings would not go to Maynooth, and so I remained in Ballyglunin for another month or two.

Ballyglunin church had been built by an old aristocratic family from the area, the Blakes, and when they attended Mass, they sat in a special place in a small tribune beside the sanctuary. The Blakes belonged to the old landlord class and being a chaplain in Ballyglunin, I was, I suppose, also regarded as a chaplain to this very old Catholic family. I was invited once to their house; since then, both John Blake and his wife have died and the place has been sold. It is now in the possession of the Opus Dei Society who run a number of seminars and retreats there for priests.

Ballyglunin gave me my first taste of pastoral work in Ireland, though my stay there was very short. After only two months I was changed to Tiernea, in the parish of Carraroe. Archbishop Gilmartin, who had looked so frail when he interviewed me in August, died early in October and shortly after his death his successor, Most Rev. Dr Joseph Walsh, sent me to Tiernea.

I was now in a district of my own, with churches to serve, one in Tiernea and one in Lettermullen, and I was also chaplain to the Presentation Sisters in Tiernea. My area of pastoral responsibility consisted of the island of Tiernea which was connected by bridge to the mainland, and Lettermullen which was joined by a bridge to Tiernea.

I had a house of my own for the first time in my life, and I liked that very much. It was a new challenge to furnish and maintain it. I began to go to auctions, especially the auctions of deceased priests because when a priest died there was usually an auction on the occasion of his Month's Mind Mass and you could pick up furniture and books at a reasonable price. As well as making my home comfortable I also had to build up a library of my own.

Nowadays, in our archdiocese, the archbishop has made a rule that the priest's house should be furnished by the diocesan authority. Then, when a priest is changed from one parish to another, he does not have to haul his furniture across the country with him. That, of course, does have the disadvantage that the furniture may not be to the new priest's liking, as we all have different tastes.

With the advent of World War II household commodities began to get very scarce, and I had to watch the housekeeping bills with an eagle-eye. In those days the priest depended entirely for a living on the generosity of his parishioners. A priest had three collections – one at Christmas, one at Easter and one in the autumn – and he depended for a livelihood on these and the few pounds that he might get in the form of Mass offerings. I was just about able to make ends meet. There was also in Connemara a unique form of collection which was not found in any other part of the Tuam archdiocese. This was called "*Altóirí*" and consisted of offerings given by people on the occasion of a funeral. The size of the collection depended on the status of the deceased person in the community and was taken up at the wake; its purpose was to have Masses offered for the soul of the deceased. I always felt squeamish about this collection and was pleased when it was abolished.

The method of collection today is quite different from what it was fifty years ago. We have now four collections, at Christmas, Easter, June and in the autumn. In the old days the collection was taken up at the church door, the amount noted and announced publicly later. The amount of the collections is now a matter between the person concerned, God and the priest; it is simply placed in the parishioner's envelope and is never published. From every point of view, and particularly from the priests' point of view, the result is more satisfactory. Another change was introduced later by Archbishop Joseph Cunnane who set up a system by which part of the collections from the richer parishes is transferred to the poorer parishes and every parish priest and curate is guaranteed a minimum salary.

I liked Connemara. It combined a bare, barren and rocky countryside with rolling hills and valleys and inland lakes. Tiernea and Lettermullen had a beauty and charm of their own. Tiernea was in a very isolated and backward area, thirty-two miles from Galway. The people were poor and found it difficult to eke out a livelihood for themselves and their families. The families were usually large and the population was increasing. They had the sea all around them and every opportunity to fish but they did very little of that; they fished for their day-to-day needs and salted some fish for use in the winter time. The land was strewn with rock and bog. They had cut turf in Connemara for generations, and the only fuel left on the cut-away was *scraitheacha* – they dug these scraws from the surface of the bog, the green grass and heather coming away with the turf, and even after it had been left to dry it made a very poor fire on the hearth. If they wanted good turf they had to import it from other places, even from outside Connemara. Much of the turf was brought in through the quay at Ballyvaughan in boats called *pucáns*. The *pucán* was a sailing boat, a fairly large craft suitable for carrying cargo.

The principal livelihood of the people was through seasonal emigration to England and Scotland: they emigrated for six months of the year and stayed at home for the other six. They worked on various jobs abroad but usually on farms, and many were at a great disadvantage as they had very little English. I knew an oldish man who went to England each year though he spoke no English. He had to wear a label with the address of his destination pinned on his coat, and when he was lost he had to enquire for directions by pointing to the label. He strayed once into an American camp during the war. When he spoke in Gaelic the Yanks thought they had a Russian on their hands, but fortunately some workmates rescued him and explained the position.

The food was ample, and I would say nourishing. The people were able to bake their own bread and of course they had a supply of fish as most families had their own currachs. They did not use very much meat as they could not afford it.

The people were well dressed. Women wore red petticoats with a black apron over it and a woollen cardigan, and the older ladies wore the old-time bonnets on their heads. The men dressed in lovely *bréidín* suits made from yarn woven by the local *fiadóir* on his loom and made up by the local tailor. As head-gear they might wear an ordinary cloth cap, woollen cap or tweed hat. The hat was the exception rather than the rule. At sea the knitted woollen cap was popular and protected head and ears, and it was also very practical as it could not be blown off very easily by the wind. The knitted cap was particularly popular with the young children. By 1939 dress had become very modern in most parts of the country and was becoming modern in Tiernea and Lettermullen also, as there was closer contact with the outside world through emigration. But in many respects Tiernea and Lettermullen were different from other parishes, and so was Carraroe for that matter. They had no dance-halls, no picture-houses, and I am sure that there were people there who had never gone to a dance or a cinema in their lives. They held dances in the neighbours' houses with a local musician playing the accordion. These dances referred to as "timeanna". The expression came, I suppose, from the word "time", and they coined the more Irish-sounding "timeanna" to mean that they had a good time. These homely social events brightened the peoples lives, and they were at all events a happy and good-natured sort.

Naturally I started to visit the families in Tiernea and Lettermullen almost immediately. I visited the country homes, sat by the turf fire and spoke to them in their native tongue. In Tiernea you had nothing but Irish; it was in the very air. It seemed like a new world, and I was delighted with it because I now had a chance to become really fluent, which I did. I picked up the Connemara *blas* which was a little different from the *blas* that I had known in Partry and Tourmakeady. I found that the women spoke more clearly, fluently and grammatically than the men. I remember one old woman in particular who spoke the Gaelic language superbly. She lived in Trá Bhán, near a beautiful white sandy beach. It was a wonderful place to be on a fine summer's day when the sea was inviting you to swim, and over the years I took full advantage of it. Afterwards I would visit my friend; I could listen for hours to this old woman speaking her rich musical native tongue. Her grammar and articulation were perfect. I could not explain why she spoke the language so clearly and beautifully compared to her neighbours. Perhaps it was a tradition in her particular family.

In the district, or half-parish, we had several schools: one in Tiernea, one in Drim, one in Lettermullen and one in Cnoc, or Knock. The children were bright and friendly, well dressed in homespuns and woollens. They wore clogs or boots in the winter and went barefoot in the summer, as did children in all rural areas at that time. Irish was their spoken language. It was only on entering national school that they began to learn English, though there were exceptions, of course, among the better-educated families. As a consequence, though the standard of education was high, the standard of English in the schools was lower than in other parts of the country. The Connemara children did gain a good grasp of English from school, but they needed to practice the language before emigrating. Many of the girls got jobs as domestic helps in various places in Ireland and in this found an opportunity to improve their English. It was also an experience that helped them when they emigrated to England and America.

The people of Tiernea and Lettermullen, like people in other parishes throughout the country, had to emigrate. Families were large and only one or two of the household could hope to find a livelihood at home, and even for these seasonal emigration was a fact of life. I noticed that very few emigrants came back. An occasional emigrant did return, having found life abroad too lonely, but these were few and far between. From my travels in England and America later on, I found that the boys and girls of the area got on well in their adopted countries. They were nice friendly people, a credit to their parents, teachers and to the parish of Carraroe. When I visited the USA in 1949 I found that many people from Connemara had settled in Boston. They continued to speak Irish in their own family circles and still loved their native tongue.

With the advent of the Kennedys to political power in the USA in the early sixties a restriction was put on emigration from Ireland to America. This was a big blow to the people in places like Tiernea and Lettermullen. There always has been and always will be some emigration, and the practice of seasonal migration continues to some extent even now. In the last twenty years, however, the people leaving the area got jobs in other parts of Ireland. Young people now get secondary, and in some cases third-level education, and are, therefore, better equipped and better able to compete for jobs in their own country.

Emigration drained the life from the land, but even so it was as nothing compared to the plague of TB. TB, or "consumption", was a dreaded disease in that age. It was rampant in our area; adults and children alike fell victim to it.

The death of young people was heart-rending. It was very hard to reconcile a young person who was dying of TB to the reality of approaching death. I remember attending a girl in Tiernea who was suffering from the disease: I have never met anyone who clung so desperately to life. As she lay on her bed, her life ebbing from her, she asked me to stay with her and her family during the night. She died in the early hours of the morning. If only I could have saved her! But then, it is only a matter of time before the bell tolls for each and every one of us. TB was especially prevalent among the young, and more so among girls than boys. There was a common belief, too, and one I subscribed to though it might not be entirely valid, that the Connemara people were more vulnerable to TB because they ate more fish than fresh meat. However, there was a great deal of ignorance about the disease. It was called "consumption", a word that struck terror into the hearts of people. It meant that a person literally melted away until death ended the agony.

I was called one day to a house where an old man was sick; another brother and sister lived in the house with him. I heard his confession, gave him Holy Communion and anointed him. As was my usual practice I went back every day to see him, and after a day or two I grew suspicious that something more serious was wrong. I had a chat with the doctor who eventually diagnosed typhoid. Twenty years previously there had been an outbreak of typhoid in the same house and, as often happens, it had broken out again. The alarm was raised and the sick man and his brother and sister were brought to the fever hospital in Galway. The sick man died and his brother died shortly afterwards. Eventually, the house was burned down to prevent any further outbreak of the disease but an occasional case of typhoid was inevitable because there was no public water supply in the parish and it was quite possible for a well to become contaminated.

Despite the many hardships I was full of enthusiasm and energy for the work in Tiernea, Lettermullen and Carraroe. The people had very little of the world's glory and I felt that I should do something to brighten up the winter by providing some entertainment. One Christmas I decided to put on a Nativity play with the children. We had no hall but my eye caught sight of a shed owned by the shopkeeper in the village. I asked him for the loan of the shed for the night, put up a stage and prepared the children for the play. We had great expectations when the night came and even though the weather was bad people arrived in big numbers. This was I believe the first time that any such play had ever been staged in Tiernea village. But this gave rise to one slight problem: some of the young people felt that they should be admitted for free. To charge for any kind of entertainment had never been known in the district; it was always given for nothing.

Movement was never restricted and life was as free as the wind that blew over the island. When they were not admitted, well, they had to do something to pass the time so they gave in to the common temptation of throwing stones. Unfortunately the temptation was made all the greater by the fact that the roof of the shed was made of galvanised iron.

I had a certain amount of sympathy for the lads who threw stones because it was one of the predominant passions for youngsters in Tiernea at the time. Stones were everywhere, and what could one do but throw them? On the other hand, admittance cost sixpence. And so stones rained on the tin roof at intervals as the birth in the stable was being acted out. I was fearful for the safety of the children and the Sisters, who had done Trojan work in preparing the children and the costumes, and I'm afraid it dampened my enthusiasm for such ventures in the future. I know that that was a cowardly way to look at it, but then I felt that more appreciation should have been shown for this particular type of work. Nonetheless, we had our Nativity play and it was a great success.

The people of Tiernea and Lettermullen could be very suspicious of strangers. Strangers to them were "*daoine iontu féin*", literally "people in themselves". I could never understand whether this peculiar attitude to strangers arose from some kind of groundless fear, or more likely perhaps from some inferiority complex. The same phenomenon had existed in the relationship between the peasants and the gentry in times past, but all that had passed into history. The strangers in the area happened to be the teachers, the Gardaí, public officials and even the priest. No priest in living memory was ever known to have been ordained from that particular area. I suppose the reason was the lack of funds and educational facilities; the fee in the local seminary at that time was only £35 but that was a large sum when a labourer's wage was just five shillings a day. Later on scholarships were granted by the county councils and the government departments, and students from that area were able to attend secondary schools. I had the pleasure of meeting a priest, a native of the area, who worked in the Archdiocese of Tuam after his ordination. In the same area a girl had joined the Mercy Order and worked as a teacher. This was a very welcome change of which the people of the area can be proud. They were a very intelligent people yet, as I say, they had this suspicion of outsiders. You had to work hard to win their confidence, and I may say that I felt I succeeded.

Soon after arriving in Tiernea I became the proud owner of a car for the first time. A Tubbercurry dealer who had a sister married in Lettermore heard of the new curate coming and, having an eye to business, he pounced on the poor fellow immediately. He knew that I would need a car to travel long distances and recommended a new Ford Anglia at a cost of £139. That Anglia lasted me ten years, until well after I had left the parish.

Petrol was rationed during the Emergency and sold at 1s 6d a gallon. At first the ration was generous, some twenty-four gallons a month, but eventually it was cut down to eight gallons. Only certain classes of professional people were given a petrol ration: the priest, doctor, vet and various government officials. However, the priest was not allowed to use his car outside the parish. I had a friend in Lettermore who owned shops there and in Lettermullen. His name was Richard O'Toole and he was very good and kind to everybody and especially to priests. If ever petrol or benzine was washed ashore the local people brought it to him and he paid them very generously for it. If he had petrol he always shared it with the priest on the condition that, if he shared the petrol, the priest would occasionally share the car.

I visited Aran with my mother and my brother to see how life was lived on other islands. Aran is a beautiful place, with its old-time cottages and all the people speaking Gaelic. They wore their own native dress, the red petticoats with the black apron over it, and bonnets and shawls were much in evidence while the men had their own suits of *bréidín*, nicely tailored. Most of the people in Aran wore pampooties, a kind of slipper which they made out of hide. The islanders, like the people in Tiernea and Lettermullen, were lovely unspoilt people with a tradition and culture of their own. Being a group of islands, the Arans were protected against the evil influence of the outside world. Similarly, the language in Tiernea and Lettermullen and Carraroe protected the people to a certain extent from the contagion of a very permissive press and radio.

After a very pleasant day on the island we started back to the mainland and everything was going well until suddenly there came a great calm. There we were, stranded in the middle of Galway Bay until a favourable wind should come to take us back home to Tiernea. It was quite serious for me because the next day was a holy day of obligation and I had to be back for Mass at 8 a.m. in the convent. However, the Lord eventually directed us ashore – and in good time for my Masses!

I visited the Arans again when I was invited by the archbishop, Most Rev. Dr Joseph Walsh, to attend Confirmation on the islands. The lifeboat came into Rossaveal Harbour to pick up the archbishop and his entourage and transport us to the islands. Off Aran we transferred to a currach to take us ashore. Just as we got off the lifeboat to get in the currach a big wave came along and swept right over us. I was drenched to the skin from head to foot, and as I had no change of clothes I had to go to the little guesthouse where I was to stay and go to bed until my clothes dried out.

While the Confirmation was on the priests heard confession out on the rocks surrounding the church. The rocks are plentiful on Aran. A number of priests had been brought out so as to give the people a *copia*, a choice of confessors. It was very important to do this occasionally because otherwise the people of a parish might come to know their priest so well that they could find it rather embarrassing to go to confession to him. If complete strangers were brought in then they had every opportunity to go to the confessor of their choice. It is very important that people have a choice of confessor.

As we travelled to the three islands, Inis Mór, Inis Meán and Inis Thiar, I realised what a tough place it must be for a priest to live, especially during the winter months when he could be stranded for weeks without ever being able to got to the mainland. The priest in Inis Thiar had to travel across to Inis Meán each Sunday to celebrate Mass, and sometimes he had to take risks in very bad weather. A priest might be left on the island for four, five or six years, so it was really a tough time for a young priest. It was always the young priest who was sent out there, and almost immediately after his ordination. Whether that was a good thing or not it is very hard to say. I suppose that a young priest, fresh on the mission, might find it easier than somebody who had already worked in less difficult parishes.

Illness and Recovery

One Saturday I woke up in pain in the middle of the night. I found that I could not turn with the pain. The only way that I could get relief was to lie on my back. I did not panic and eventually slept a little, but when I got up in the morning I almost fainted and had to sit on the bed to rest for a few minutes. I shaved and headed to the convent to give communion to the Sisters before proceeding to Lettermullen church to celebrate Mass at nine o'clock. When I was entering the convent one of the Sisters said to me: "Father, you are not looking well this morning."

"No," I said, "I have a cold in my stomach again." For many years my stomach had been giving me trouble. I had not gone to the doctor and I did not know exactly what was wrong; I just got attacks now and again. Now it seemed to have caught up with me.

I went on to Lettermullen and said Mass and by the time I got back to Tiernea again to say the eleven o'clock Mass I was feeling pretty faint. I was afraid that I would not be able to get through the ceremony and I told one of the altar boys to bring out a little armchair to place beside the altar so that if I had to sit down I could do so.

It was a day in June and Galway were playing a match in Croke Park. Some of the local boys came to my house to listen to the broadcast on the wireless but I could not join them. I walked around the church and eventually came back to the house and went to bed. I sent for the local priest, Fr John Philbin, the curate in Lettermore. Fr Philbin came and saw me that night and he began to blame me for imagining things. He said I looked well and that there was nothing wrong with me, and that I must be a bit of a hypochondriac. At that stage I was feeling very tired and I said to myself, "OK! Maybe I might sleep."

I did not sleep. During the night I had severe pain, but by morning the pain had eased and been replaced by a temperature of 102 degrees. I sent for the doctor; immediately he suspected, as I did myself, that I had appendicitis, and that my appendix had probably burst. There was an ambulance coming out for a woman in the village but they directed the ambulance to me as my case was more urgent. I was brought into Galway and as soon as the doctor arrived I was taken to the operating theatre. I was placed on the table where everything was in readiness for the operation and as I lay there I heard Dr McDermott discussing some new theory with the doctors present. I do not know what experiment he had in mind or what he meant to do with me.

They put something to my nose and asked me to sniff it. They told me to count or say the Our Father. I said the Our Father and by the time I had finished I was passing out; my last thought was that I had died. They told me afterwards that the feeling came from the fact that I was struggling all the time – they had actually had a lot of trouble trying to keep me on the table.

I woke up late in the night. The nurse on duty told me my operation was over and that I had tubes in my stomach to drain away the poison – it seemed that the appendix had burst and they had a very big mopping up job to do. The operation had taken about three or four hours, as they had to try and drain as much of the poison as possible from the system.

I was six weeks in bed recovering. As that time penicillin had not been discovered so the chances of survival after a burst appendix were not as high as they are now. However, they had M&B or sulphathizine tablets that were developed during the war in the treatment of the wounded. The great danger after an operation for burst appendix was peritonitis, but the M&B tablets did not allow this condition to develop. The matron told me afterwards that my case was very critical and that gangrene had set in before the operation had taken place.

While I convalesced in St Bride's Nursing Home I was delighted to hear a request being played for me on the "Hospital's Trust" programme; it was a song calling home somebody who had gone away from a little fishing village. I would like to think that the people of Tiernea had missed me and wanted to see me back among them again. I spent six weeks in the nursing home before I was allowed to get out of bed, and when I did I was not able to stand. It took me three days to find my feet again and walk, but from then on my health improved.

It felt great to return to Tiernea, crossing over the bridges that linked the islands and the mainland. Perhaps because I had not seen them for so long I was struck anew by the peculiarity of the arrangement. These bridges were the only bridges I knew in which the water flows one way in the morning and another way in the evening, according to the ebb and flow of the tide. There was a story told that the bridge between Lettermore and Tiernea was built by Arthur Balfour, Chief Secretary of Ireland from 1886-91. Local tradition held that he visited the islands and partook of the local beverage – poteen. I thought, when I heard it, that the story was just a local yarn and I certainly did not believe it. The story about the poteen was just too much to swallow, and it was hard to believe that the Chief Secretary had ever visited an area so inaccessible in that age.

Later, I decided that I would do some research on the matter. I discovered that Arthur Balfour was the scion of a landed family from the Scottish Lowlands. He was reputed to be a philosopher and writer of no mean intellectual calibre. He was a social reformer and almost a radical as far as land grievances in Ireland were concerned. While all this was true, he was regarded as being "as relentless as a Cromwell" in the enforcement of law and order. He was successful in restoring order and that encouraged him to carry out social and economic reforms, not only at the official level but in a private capacity also. He toured the West of Ireland with his sister so that he would experience life there at first hand and he was shocked by what he saw. The wretched conditions of the people left an everlasting impression on him. It is reasonable to assume that he was in that kind of mood when he put his hand deep in his pocket to aid development in the West. Norman Atkinson, author of *Irish History 1848-1950*, claims that Balfour gave money of his own to build a bridge in the West of Ireland and there is no doubt that this is the Tiernea bridge.

I had no trouble in accepting the story after I read up on it. Arthur Balfour was a philosopher, an enlightened man and above all compassionate, and I am certain that he did not need the stimulating effect of poteen to make a decision about the bridge. He was the man, more than any other, who implemented the land reforms for which Michael Davitt suffered so much and campaigned so hard.

Back in Tiernea, with my health improving all the time, I returned to my work with vigour. We had missions in Tiernea every three years. The popular missioners were the Redemptorists and among the most popular of the Redemptorists was Fr Ó Conghaile, a native of Aran. Anytime that we had a mission he was on the team. The big abuse at that time, as far as the mission was concerned, was the making and selling of poteen. Before the mission ended everybody in the church had to take a pledge against drinking poteen and, of course, against making it. The poteen-makers were asked to leave their equipment at the church before taking the pledge; this was necessary if the pledge was to be administered to the people concerned.

At one mission in Lettermullen a man arrived at the church with a barrel tied on his back with a rope. He left it and some other equipment down at the sacristy door, came in and told the missioner that he was ready to take the pledge. When the mission had ended the mission cross was erected as a sign that the people of the parish had taken the pledge against drinking or making poteen and that everything would be well henceforth. However, a week or two after the mission the poteen-maker was back in the sacristy. "*Cé mhéid ar an mbaraille?*" – "How much for the barrel?" – he wanted to know. Was his good resolution weakening? Did he intend to start distilling poteen again? I don't know whether he did or not, but I did nothing to help him anyway.

Poteen was a great abuse and it seemed that anybody who got drunk on poteen went a bit berserk. It was the root cause of a lot of rows and unpleasantness amongst people and families in the area, and the missionaries were perfectly right in trying to stamp it out. Poteen is still going strong, especially at Christmastime, and thousands of pounds can be made from distilling it. The poteen-makers are getting more sophisticated as time goes by; they no longer make it at home but travel long distances to find some island or other lonely place. When I was in Tiernea much of the poteen that was brewed was made on an island called Inisherk. There were just four or five families living there and one of them had the name of being a poteen-maker. It was very hard for the Guards to come on them unawares, so they could make poteen with impunity and the only thing the Guards could do was to raid and try to find and destroy the poteen-making gear. Of course, in places like Tiernea and Lettermullen and Inisherk there were so many rocks that looking for the equipment was like looking for a needle in a bundle of straw. They say of this family that they made so much poteen that they always had a bucketful inside the door so that anybody could help themselves when they called. I do not believe that story! But they do say that one of the islanders got a holding of land from the Land Commission in Co. Meath but he got tired of life there and came back home to start making poteen again.

Fortunately, people nowadays have a more mature outlook on poteen; they take it perhaps for its novelty on special occasions like Christmas. I have been a pioneer all my life so I do not know what poteen tastes like – they tell me that it has a burnt taste and that it is not very nice to drink. People drink it for the effect it produces on their personality and physical condition. They do say poteen is good for a cold but I never tried it for that purpose either.

After some time in Tiernea I thought that it would be a great idea to bring my brother, Bartley, to live with me for a year or two. He could finish his primary school here and at the same time learn Irish from the young boys in the area. The principal in Lettermullen school, Eamonn Goggin, took a great interest in him and gave him special tuition so that he could sit for the scholarship examinations. He got on very well. He picked up the Irish very quickly and made friends with the local boys.

My parish priest was the Very Rev. Andy Moran, a very pleasant man and a fluent Irish speaker. He had served for a number of years as curate in Cornamona before coming to Carraroe. He liked the people of Carraroe, as indeed he liked the people on the islands, Tiernea and Lettermullen, and soon made himself at home. He stayed in Carraroe as parish priest until he died. He was a great patriot and very Republican in his outlook, and always blamed England for being an obstacle to the unity of Ireland. When the Stations were being held on the island Fr Moran always came and stayed in my house. The Stations have their roots in the Penal Days when the Mass was outlawed and had to be celebrated in the deep valleys and mountains and in the humble dwellings of the poor. When better times came with the Emancipation in 1829 Stations were still kept alive by the priests, who visited the villages and townlands celebrating Mass for the people in their homes. The Stations were regarded as a privilege for the household, a tradition handed down to us because of the faith of our forebears. Fr Moran enjoyed the Stations as he was a man of the people.

My own house was a nice little presbytery, built by one of my predecessors, Fr Thomas Concannon, but unfortunately its walls were very damp. I consulted a friend of mine who found that the blocks that were used in building had been made of sea sand, and of course salt in the sand prevented the cement from setting properly. Indeed, if you rubbed your fingers against the block the sand would come away quite easily. After I had left the island a new house was built, and the church was saved by plastering over the walls with good sand and cement.

I spent most of the war years in Tiernea. I bought myself a bicycle and when I was unable to travel to Galway by car I would cycle the thirty-six miles to the city, setting off in the morning and coming back that evening. I often arrived home at one or two o'clock in the morning after cycling the seventy-two miles. I loved to go to Galway because, as well as being an opportunity to visit some of my parishioners in hospital, it was also a break from the work in Tiernea. I would have a meal or perhaps go to a film; I liked films, especially if there happened to be a good one on the programme.

The war was on and even if we had not read about it in the newspapers we would have known about it from the remains of men and cargo washed up by the sea. When the bodies of some German airmen were washed ashore we gave them a Christian burial in the local graveyard. The island community reaped foodstuffs and timber from the sea when ships went down off the coast.

While the population was declining in most areas of the West it was increasing in Tiernea and Lettermullen; in fact it was increasing in the whole parish of Carraroe. Families were large and there was less emigration from the islands than from any other part of Connemara. One reason for this was that Irish was the spoken language; many of the older people had no knowledge of English, and even young people who wished to emigrate often came to me to help them find jobs in domestic service or labouring in various parts of Ireland so that they could practice their English before leaving the country. People also stayed at home because it was so easy to get a site for a house. There was a lot of commonage in the district and it seemed that anyone could build a house on the side of a mountain or hill without leave or hindrance. They dug a garden for potatoes and vegetables and later other land was reclaimed for the pasture of a cow. The cottages they built were usually very plain and had roofs thatched with wattles and straw, but they were comfortable and many fine families were raised in them. As in Achill, the families did not emigrate permanently but went to England for the "tato picking" and harvesting; they spent the other half of the year at home, including part of the spring when they sowed their own crops.

Life on the islands has changed completely in modern times because of transport facilities but, paradoxically, I think that people can feel themselves more confined on an island in an age of greater mobility. In my young days a motor-car was a novelty and everybody stopped work to watch it pass by; to see a car parked outside a house always gave an impression of prosperity whereas nowadays you may see two or three cars on a driveway. The young, with better education, set their sights on far-away places and the advent of television in nearly every home stirs a wanderlust and curiosity to see and savour lifestyles in other countries. The gap between lifestyles on the islands and the mainland has closed in recent years. The dress, both for men and women, the food on the table in the country house, all have completely changed and, thank God, for the better. The people of the West also have their own radio station, Radio na Gaeltachta, on which all the local events are broadcast.

I love to return to Tiernea and Lettermullen and see how my former parishioners are getting on. I often wonder how the Gaelic is faring since I ministered there many years ago. I think that more and more English is creeping into the hearths of the Gaeltacht. This may be inevitable as all homes have radio and television at their elbows and because of better communications the boundaries of the Gaeltacht are being pushed back. It is often asked if the media has damaged the status of Irish. While I cannot answer that question, I can say categorically that the media has certainly not improved it. However, I am not discouraged. Through the teaching of Irish in schools everyone must surely be able to speak and understand some Gaelic.

It is ironic to think that when more and more people go to the Gaeltacht to learn Irish, the end result may be that the people of the Gaeltacht turn more and more to English. One day I was passing through the Tourmakeady Gaeltacht area when I met a man on the road and spoke to him about the position of Irish in the homes. Irish had been spoken in his village but he told me that the young people no longer spoke it. That was a great surprise to me and brought home the sad truth that Irish is on the decline, even in the Gaeltacht.

When I went as curate to Tiernea you had nothing but Irish in the parish; it was in the very air. It must have been hard on priests who did not have a good command of the language. I heard a story about one of my predecessors who had gone out on his first sick call. In the sick room they did not have the necessary items on the table for him – one of the things missing was holy water. He started asking for *uisce beatha* –whiskey – which he thought was the word for holy water. I am sure that the people of the house were stunned, or perhaps they saw the joke. The word for holy water in Irish is, of course, *uisce coisriche*.

I was delighted to be in Tiernea and Lettermullen, which seemed to me like a new world. I studied Irish with enthusiasm and I knew that I became really fluent in it because on going to Galway I found that when I spoke English, Irish words were always popping up. I was thinking in Irish rather than English. That is the sure sign that you have become fluent in a language and that the language has become part of you.

A Curate in Tooreen

In July 1944 the postman called at my door. When he handed me the letter I recognised the official markings: it was from my archbishop, Dr Joseph Walsh. It was the season for changes so my heart gave a few leaps as I opened the envelope. As I pulled out the message I realised that it was not an ordinary letter but an official form giving me instructions to leave Tiernea, post haste, and to report to the Very Rev. Michael Carney, Aghamore, on Friday 29 July.

When I looked more closely at the document I found that the archbishop had changed his mind three times. He had put a stroke through the word Aghamore, re-written it and drawn a line through it again, then finally written Aghamore once more. That was it. Aghamore was my destination. I will never know whether it was that God had changed his mind three times or whether he found it difficult to get the archbishop to make the right decision. In any case, I regarded the bishop's will to be God's will for me. After all, I had taken a promise of obedience to my bishop before ordination.

I arrived bag and baggage in Ballyhaunis, in the parish of Aghamore, to my new parish priest, but I found that he was not at home; he was in fact in hospital for a check-up. I was referred to the senior curate, Fr John Concannon, and stayed in his house that night. I was told that my destination was the village of Tooreen, a namesake of the village I had grown up in.

Bright and early the next morning I set off in my Ford Anglia to inspect my new district. The digs arranged for me were a long distance from the church but I spied a very nice house much nearer to it and went in search of accommodation there. I was received with open arms by Pádraig Forkan, his wife, Winifred, and their family. That was to be my home for the next fifteen months.

As I was walking out to Mass on my first morning in Tooreen I found the landscape very strange indeed. I was so accustomed to the sea and the rolling of the waves that I found it odd to be confronted by green fields and golden corn and the tang of new-mown hay in the air, while the farmers were making their way in donkey carts to the bog. But the greatest jolt I got in my new surroundings was the fact that I was now amongst people who spoke a different language. Tooreen had a different culture from Tiernea; in fact, I felt at first that I was living in a completely new world. It was the difference between the Gaelic world and a world which had adopted a new language and culture. For some time I was inclined to address everyone I met on the road in Gaelic, forgetting that I had left that world behind me. My greatest difficulty arose in preparing my sermons as I had been preaching them in Irish for four years; now I had to find English phraseology and idioms to express my spiritual and pastoral themes. However, I need not have worried. In a short time I settled down and became acclimatised.

I was the first resident priest in Tooreen and they revelled in the opportunity of studying me at close quarters. The first people you meet in a new parish are usually teachers and shopkeepers; they make the community's approach to find out what the new curate is like. To save them all this trouble I decided to visit all the homes in the district as quickly as possible; I always felt at a loss, anyway, preaching on Sunday to people I did not know. When I had visited the people and understood their circumstances I was better able to assess their pastoral needs. I found them very lovable and friendly people, just like those in my native village of Tooreen. On the whole, they had small but comfortable holdings and were able to make a frugal livelihood for themselves and their families.

I wrote to my father and mother to tell them how much I liked this second Tooreen in my life, and found that I had to travel six miles for a stamp and the nearest pillar-box was two-and-a-half miles down the road. I knew at once that my flock needed a new Post Office and before you could say "Jack Robinson" I found myself facing an array of post-office officials in Dublin's GPO, and I did not mince my words in describing the backward state of the postal services in my church area.

I know of other priests who worked themselves to the bone in order to help people to get postal services, electricity and group water schemes. They even built and roofed houses for the old and the poor with the aid of state grants and voluntary labour. One of my pet aversions is to see a "Johnny-come-lately" on television, pouring scorn on our priest-ridden society, when priests in this country have always been the champions of the people. They were the friends of the poor and the underprivileged and if they were friendly with the landlord or the gombeen man it was merely to use that friendship for the good of their parishioners. The priest acted as a liaison between landlord and tenant. The priest in my era was a man like his master, concerned not merely with spiritual work but also with corporal works of mercy. He kept his parishioners informed of their rights and privileges under the law. He took all necessary steps and completed all the necessary documents in applying for grants and benefits on their behalf. Whenever his parishioners were in any kind of stress or difficulty they came to him as their pastor and father. He consoled the sick and the sorrowful, the mother with the handicapped child and the bereaved, the person in difficulty with the law, the oppressed. As St Paul summed it up, he had to be "all things to all men".

I was instructed by my archbishop to build a new house for myself in the parish. I set about looking for a suitable site and almost immediately I got one from the owner of the local grocery store. These were the halycon days when one could buy a site for £100. World War II was not yet over and building materials were scarce. With some difficulty, the contractor succeeded in getting the materials and the contract to build a bungalow was signed at a cost of £1,300. The parish priest gave me authority to collect money throughout the whole parish. I collected small contributions, mostly of £1 or perhaps £5 from the wealthier people and made up the balance with the aid of concerts, plays, quizzes, *céilís* and an occasional fancy-dress parade in the local school. I moved into my new house fifteen months after my arrival in the district. I was proud of the achievement and the speed with which it had been accomplished.

I found that the life of the people in Tooreen and Aghamore was much the same as the life of the people in my own native village of Tooreen, Partry. They were simple people, very intelligent and skilful, and they lived fairly comfortably. They had nice holdings of land, not big but enough to give them a fair standard of living according to the standards of the time. I did my best to improve their lot and pioneered projects such as electricity and group-water schemes, afforestation and even road-works and drainage schemes.

I pioneered the ESB scheme in the whole of the parish of Aghamore. I travelled round the parish, visiting each house several times, convincing people that electricity would be an asset to them and would bring a brighter and better life. I found the campaign quite difficult because the people at that time were very conservative in their thinking and were always suspicious that I was doing this for some purpose of my own – perhaps light and power for the new Tooreen hall! I had to convince them that I stood to gain nothing more from it than they would themselves.

I was not surprised to find that people were afraid of the bi-monthly rent they would have to pay. There is an in-bred fear in the Irish of rents and rates because they suffered so much down the years from rack-rents and evictions under British domination, and there was still a terrible fear in their subconscious of hunger and famine that had come down from another age. People had a very real fear that they might not have the ESB rent when asked to pay and, consequently, they did not want to have anything to do with the ESB. I failed at first to get a sufficient percentage of householders to justify the scheme. I got around sixty per cent and the ESB authorities would not entertain the project until I had over seventy. I visited all the homes again, and after I had been round the parish two or three times I got the amount I needed. When I presented the results to the ESB they agreed to initiate the project. That was a very big day for the parish of Aghamore because the ESB was about to revolutionise the entire lifestyle of the area.

The scheme got underway but immediately there was trouble with people who had signed the agreement but now refused to accept the electricity. When they were presented with the agreement by the ESB official they would say: "Sure, *a ghrá*, I would not have signed at all but I did not want to offend poor Fr Horan." Back I had to go to persuade them that electricity would be of great benefit to them. Then there were the people in each village who sold paraffin-oil and made a little profit on it, and naturally they campaigned against the ESB development as it would hurt their pockets. The paraffin-oil "barons" were usually the self-appointed spokesmen for the people; the head-men of the village you might say. They played their part in history as the champions of the peoples' rights and that was good and useful; now, unfortunately, they were an obstacle in the way of progress, and that was bad and misguided. There was also a fear amongst the old people of the dangers of the electricity system. They had heard of tragedies or read about them in the newspapers but we convinced them that, with a little care, there would be no danger. In the end we succeeded in our campaign and got light and power in our parish. The people who had refused to take the electricity initially were afterwards pleading to have it installed when they discovered how useful it was in the home.

In my experience I got more co-operation from women in the various parishes in which I worked than I did from the men. Somehow the women seem to have more time, as housewives, to work in the various committees and organisations in a parish. Were it not for the women it would not be possible to carry on the work that is being done in many parishes. They are very efficient and very unselfish, and I had experience of their great work in the Legion of Mary.

I was first introduced to the Legion through Fr Carney, my parish priest, who had a praesidium in the Aghamore area. I started my own praesidium down in Tooreen, and later became chaplain to the Claremorris curia of the Legion of Mary; when the Claremorris curia was amalgamated with the Tuam curia I became chaplain of the combined curias. The women were very dedicated, though I hasten to add that I had nothing but the greatest admiration also for the men who worked in the Legion of Mary. They did marvellous work, but their numbers were few compared to the women. Women had tremendous scope for their gifts in the Legion of Mary; they carried out great pastoral work in the parishes, visiting homes and, without being intrusive, inculcated Christian values by their kindness and obvious love for and interest in people. They trained schoolchildren and teenagers in the Junior Legion, encouraging them to care for the old, the sick and the disabled, and putting them in charge of old people living alone. The youngsters ran messages and carried fuel and water, and turned the parish into a wonderful caring community. Aghamore parish would have been a much poorer place without the Legion of Mary.

If you take the Legion of Mary as an example, then you can say that there is great scope and potential for women in the Church. The Church needs women in its pastoral mission. However, I could not favour women priests because I feel that if Our Lord wanted to ordain women then he would have ordained them from the outset. We do know from the Gospels that he founded the Church on his twelve apostles; there was no woman included in that number and surely, if Our Lord had wanted to ordain women, His own mother would probably have been the first to be ordained. Jesus did many things that the ordinary Jew would not do with regard to women. He gave them their rightful place in society. We can see his attitude in his dealings with Mary Magdalene, the sinner; in his dealings with the woman taken in adultery; in his dealings with the woman at Jacob's well. A woman was the first witness to the resurrection, even though according to Jewish law a woman was neither worthy nor capable of being a true witness to anything. Our Lord gave women the first news of the resurrection and sent them to the apostles to deliver the good news. Our Lord went against all the Jewish customs and the Mosaic law in His treatment of woman, and if He had wished to ordain them then He would have had no hesitation in doing so. We must conclude, therefore, that it was not his wish to ordain women as priests.

However, apart from ordination, there is a tremendous role for women in the Church and I hope and pray that they will continue to play that great part. There are women in the Church like Mother Teresa of Calcutta who exercise an enormous influence for good all over the world. St Teresa of Avila and St Catherine of Sienna have been raised to the highest ranks, having been declared Doctors of the Church. There is enormous scope for women in the Church even without being admitted to the priesthood.

I was appointed to preach in the cathedral in Tuam on Good Friday, 1948. It was always an ordeal for a young priest to be asked to preach in the cathedral during Holy Week. He had to give a formal sermon with the archbishop on his throne, all the priests from St Jarlath's College and the surrounding Deanery in the choir, and a huge congregation in the pews. The sermon was delivered at Wednesday evening Mass or Holy Thursday morning, or at the Good Friday morning ceremonies, but no matter which occasion it was a great ordeal. But I prepared it well, I worked hard at it and gave it everything I had got. On my way to Tuam that day I could think of nothing but the sermon. I arrived half an hour beforehand, went into the cathedral, placed myself in front of the Blessed Sacrament and offered myself up. I said: "Here I am. I have done my best and I want some help."

I am sure that God and His Blessed Mother did help me during the sermon because I felt that I did fairly well. I am the kind of person that may be uneasy before an event but when I am on the spot I seem to forget everything and get on with the job. I am the same today; I have not changed. A few days before the big event I might be worried or uneasy but when the occasion arrives I am quite cool, calm and collected. Having offered myself to God I am resigned to everything, even failure, and when you do that it become quite easy.

There was an infallible test of success or failure for the priests in Tuam cathedral. If the archbishop asked you to his house for a cup of tea you had passed the test; if, on the other hand, you were relegated to one of the convents near by he was not impressed. I was invited to tea and was happy.

Nowadays, the times and the liturgy have changed. The preaching ordeal in Tuam has ended and the examinations for young priests have been discontinued. When I was curate in Tiernea I had had to do an examination each year. The exams were based on the programme of studies at Maynooth so that over a period of four or five years you covered the whole programme of theology, scripture and canon law again. It was a good practice as it kept one up-to-date in theological studies. You also had to submit a certain number of sermons, and they had to be of a good standard. I was glad that we had such discipline as it kept one alert. It helped the young priest to fight lethargy and boredom in a country parish, and taught him to take care in the preparation of sermons. It is a pity that this discipline was discontinued. I was also one of the last group to sit the special examination for prospective parish priests. When you were twenty years ordained you were eligible for this examination, and everybody with twenty years' service was very anxious indeed to sit for it because, if you did not, you might not be offered a parish when your turn came. The examination was discontinued after Vatican II and I think that was a great pity. The programme for the examination covered practically the whole course for clerical students in Maynooth.

In Tooreen I also had one of the best Sacred Heart sodalities that I ever had anywhere. The Tooreen men were particularly proud of their sodality because women's sodalities were usually better attended than the men's. In Tooreen the men were certainly as good as the ladies in attending their religious duties. After I had left the parish I met a man who challenged me: "I bet the sodality in Cloonfad is not as good as the Tooreen sodality," he said.

"Well the sodality in Cloonfad is very good," I answered diplomatically, "but I would not like to make comparisons because that would be rather invidious."

Tooreen has given a number of fine priests to the Church. One of my illustrious predecessors as parish priest of Knock was the Very Rev. John Canon Greally. A native of Shanvalla, a village within half a mile of Tooreen church, he was parish priest of Knock from 1932-47. He was a generous benefactor of Knock and indeed of Aghamore church; he built Shanvaghera church in Knock parish from his own personal resources. With the dedicated backing of the Knock Shrine Society he promoted devotion to Our Lady of Knock and provided facilities for pilgrimages at the shrine. He also bought two portions of land in the village which proved to be of strategic importance in the development of the shrine grounds. He bought a field in front of the shrine from Thomas Henry Byrne and the Knock Shrine Calvary grounds from Mrs Mallee, mother of the late John Mallee. When he died Canon Greally was himself buried in the church grounds, *Go dtuga Dia aoibhneas na bhFlaitheas d'á anam*.

Right Rev. Monsignor Hugh Curley, former parish priest of Claremorris, is a native of Crossbeg, Tooreen. His brother, Fr Mark Curley, was also a priest in the Archdiocese of Tuam. He was a lovable and friendly character, but unfortunately he was called by God at an early age. Monsignor Curley had a very distinguished career in the archdiocese and has now retired. He always took great interest in Knock Shrine. He spent many long days at Knock in the confessional when he was parish priest of Claremorris and even after his retirement and he gave me, as parish priest of Knock, great moral support in all my undertakings.

Raising Funds for Tooreen Hall

The idea of building a community hall in Tooreen came from my parish priest; he had had the idea away back in 1938 and had started a campaign to raise funds. He raised some £300-£400 locally and in America, a substantial sum at the time.

Now that the war was over emigration had reached new heights. The great cities destroyed in the conflict had to be rebuilt and there was no problem in finding employment in any of the English-speaking countries. As a result thousands upon thousands took the emigrant ship to England, Australia and the USA, or sometimes spent a few years in England to earn their passage to the USA. There was a certain glamour and adventure for young people in emigrating. They were going over to friends and to meet their old schoolpals. The fine clothes and prosperous air of display put on by returned "Yanks" enticed many to follow them abroad.

The media was decrying emigration from the rooftops and blaming it on a lack of entertainment and social life, especially in country areas. They said that young people were leaving the loneliness and boredom of the countryside for the bright lights and glamour of the cities. Fr Michael Carney and myself were fired with a great enthusiasm to build a community hall to provide entertainment and games for the youth. I was young and understood the rigours and loneliness of exile in a foreign land, so I was especially keen to do something for young people. Without my knowledge the parish priest consulted the archbishop on the matter of a fund-raising trip to the United States and both archbishop and parish priest decided that I should go to America to raise funds for the community hall. I got all the necessary documents and papers from the archbishop and prepared to go.

The prospect of a second trip to America appealed to me greatly. I made my way to Southampton where I boarded a liner bound for the USA. It was a very fast ship, one of the most modern, and the conditions were certainly luxurious. I travelled tourist class and shared a cabin with two others, one an American Jew who was on his way from Rome to New York and the other an American industrialist on his way home from a holiday in Europe. The Jew had gone to Rome to seek interviews with cardinals and other Church dignitaries. He was a publisher based in New York and was gathering material and photographs for a new book on the Holy Year, 1950. He praised the Roman dignitaries and spoke highly of the Holy Father, the cardinals and the Curia when he was sober, but when he had a few drinks taken his tune changed and he became very critical. Obviously, he had not got everything he sought from the cardinals and the Church authorities and this left a sour taste in his mouth. Still, we got on well although I did not agree with all his views. The American industrialist seemed fairly prosperous but he had a problem with his health. He was suffering from some kind of nervous tension or strain. His doctor had recommended that he take a holiday for the sake of his health.

He had a romantic problem which he confided to me. He had met a very nice girl on board the ship and liked her very much; however, he was upset because she would not allow him to pay for her drinks. She explained to him that on arrival in New York she wanted to be in a position to say goodbye and end the friendship. He had fallen hard for this girl and told me all his troubles – me, a Catholic priest, even though he was not a Catholic! But, unfortunately, having no experience in such matters, I was not much help to him.

On board ship you meet people with all kinds of problems. I met a girl whose husband had been shot in New York by gangsters; he had been a policeman and she was very depressed and downcast over his death. I met others who had gone home, perhaps to see a mother who was very ill or to attend the funeral of a father, and now were returning to the USA. One had to listen to all their problems with a very sympathetic ear and naturally when you celebrate Mass on board a ship the passengers all look on you as their pastor. In many ways the journey felt like being at home in my own parish.

When we docked in New York I was met by my two uncles, Jim and Patrick Casey. I went to stay with my Uncle Jim, who lived at the junction of Troy Avenue and Avenue D. My Uncle Patrick and his family lived in Maspeth or Middle Village in Queens. Both had beautiful children who were brought up very well. They took schooling very seriously and were very keen on education; the children were now in their teens and the older ones attended

St John's Catholic University. Education was very competitive; the time was long past when jobs came easily. Yet the Irish emigrants got jobs and settled down very quickly – they seemed to have a monopoly in the building industry in particular and gave jobs to their fellow countrymen. All of the children of Irish parents got on well at school and most got third-level education. Some of my cousins attended the University of Brooklyn, which at that time was called the "Red University" because a lot of the professors seemed to have leanings towards communism, but it did my cousins no damage as they were very staunch Catholics. Of course, they had the benefit of a wonderful home training and had the support of prayer in the home.

I arrived in the USA in Irish-style clerical dress. Even though I had got a new outfit for the trip my Uncle Jim did not think it was up to standard and the day after I arrived he took me to a store on Fifth Avenue where I got an American-style outfit. The distinctive feature of my new dress was the stock and collar. The American collar was narrower and neater than the Irish, and the jacket of the suit was shorter and more stylish. It was bought off the rack and adjusted by the tailor, and when I tried it on I was assured that I looked the spitting image of Bing Crosby in *Going My Way*. Having been dressed I was now ready to start the work for which I came to America, to raise funds for a social centre in my parish.

I carried out separate campaigns in Brooklyn, the Bronx, Queens, Woodside and Manhattan. I perfected my campaign strategy in New York and used it to great advantage in other cities.

Before leaving home I had made films of people and events in Aghamore and Tooreen so that their friends and relatives could see them in the flesh. I filmed a fancy-dress parade, a sports festival and some horse-racing. I filmed the scenes after Mass on Sundays, when friends and relatives got together in groups to exchange the latest news or gossip and took the time to have a smoke and a chat. This piece of film in particular was very popular with Irish Americans as they were able to see old neighbours and familiar scenes and savour once more a lifestyle that they had almost forgotten. It brought a tear to the eye. I also had the good fortune to get the loan of a beautiful film from Dr Lyons of Kilkelly called *The Four Seasons*. It showed every possible scene in Irish country life through the course of a full year. It showed the farmer ploughing in the spring and harvesting in the autumn. It dealt with the details of rural life such as the feeding of calves, hens, ducks and chickens. It brought back memories of pastimes in the winter months, dancing, music, card-games. It gave a picture of the housewife in the home and the many chores that she performed. It was truly a wonderful film and gave a lot of pleasure to the emigrants who saw it.

I organised all the boroughs, holding functions in various parts and then ending with one great rally at the end of my campaign. At the film-shows I got contributions from the people present and those who could not come sent gifts. All the Irish people and their non-Irish friends were very helpful and generous; they sold tickets for the final dance and chance-books, which are the equivalent of our raffle tickets, and all of which helped to fill the kitty.

I received a wonderful reception in New York and now I moved on to other cities. I went to Philadelphia and then to Boston, and in each city I arranged ten or eleven venues to show the films and then finished up with a big dance. I also accepted any invitations to speak at functions where I could explain the conditions we faced in Ireland and our need of support. In my travels in America I focused on cities where there was a concentration of Irish people. New York was my prime target as there were four boroughs, all with big contingents of Irish, but Chicago was a city where I had many friends, relations and acquaintances. Many of my schoolpals were there, along with others from the Gaeltacht areas in Connemara. Like other ethnic groups they spoke their own language in their family circles; indeed, I found many second-generation Gaelic speakers. Once when I was on Radio Boston I greeted my listeners in Irish. I remember the comment of the interviewer: "Rare but not extinct, a Gaelic speaker on Radio Boston."

I visited Jersey City, Newark and all the Oranges, and discovered good friends everywhere. I went on to Springfield, Mass., and from there to Worcester, a small city with not many Irish around. In the spring of 1950 I turned my face to the west and visited Cleveland and Chicago. In both cities I found that the Irish had kept their Irishness and even their soft Irish brogue. It sounded beautiful to my ears.

In Cleveland I found that Irish social life centred around St Patrick's Cathedral. The Irish in the city were well organised and formed a tightly knit ethnic group. I had the pleasure of residing with a Tom Joyce and his wife in West Ninth Street and they were as kind as a father and mother to me. They both hailed from the Joyce country near Tourmakeady. One of my principal organisers in Cleveland was a Mary O'Laoghaire who was very active in Irish social circles. I also met an old friend, Thomas Walsh of Carrineragh, Partry, who helped me raise funds and introduced me to a number of people. One day he took me off to Youngstown to visit his sister. We stayed the night as her guests and while I was there I visited another friend of mine, a priest from Ballyhaunis, Fr John Lyons, who worked in a parish in the area. I will always remember Youngstown as the place with black snow. Along the Mississippi River stood rows and rows of steel and chemical factories, and the snow which had fallen heavily in December and January was now covered with coal-dust. I understand that there is black snow there no longer as the factories have all closed down.

An important part of my preparation for America was to get as many names and addresses as possible from friends in Ireland; with these I could call on people for help with my campaign. I also had addresses of people with whom I would be welcome to stay. It was very useful before going to a city like New York or Philadelphia to know that you had a place to stay. It was necessary to have all these arrangements made before leaving home; of course, one would make other friends along the way, but it was best not to leave anything to chance.

Chicago was the place where all my old neighbours from Partry settled. I felt very much at home there as I could claim many of the Chicago folk as cousins – if I were to count them I suppose I would have more cousins in America than I have in Ireland. My first stop in Chicago was with a cousin, Willie Staunton, who had been a next-door-neighbour of my family when he lived in Tooreen, Partry. He and his daughter Marion were the principal organisers of my campaign in Chicago. They had run a successful function for me even before I reached them. I was to have gone to Chicago before Christmas but I could not make it until late spring, and when I reached the city there was a wonderful campaign afoot. I had a very easy week in Chicago as a result. We had a number of small gatherings of relatives and old neighbours, and then a wonderful function in Carpenter's Hall. I was very relaxed as it had drawn near the end of my campaign, and I was delighted to be with old friends and neighbours once again.

I had a few more functions to attend in New York State and I arranged to have a short holiday at Easter. I flew from Chicago to New York via Washington. I had only a few hours' stay in Washington so I had to make the most of it. I hired a taxi to take me to the White House and the Capitol. I could only view the White House at a distance: the President did not know I had arrived! I gained admission to the Senate and listened to some speeches on education. The speaker was complaining about some material in schoolbooks that he felt was no more than political propaganda for the government – politics are the same all over the world. I was amazed that there was no protective screening between the visitors' gallery and the senators in the chamber beneath; in Dáil Éireann there is a wire mesh to prevent visitors throwing missiles at the TDs. A few years later a gun-attack was made on the representatives in Congress from the same gallery and a few people were wounded. One should never take a chance where security is concerned.

Of all the cities I visited I was most successful in Philadelphia, and not surprisingly as most of the people who emigrated from Aghamore headed for Philly. I raised more money there than in any other city except New York, and I also had a success of a different kind.

I had a grand-uncle, Anthony, who had emigrated to Philadelphia many years previously. A stonemason by trade, he became a very successful building contractor. During the War of Independence he sheltered and entertained many Republican supporters when they went to the United States to raise funds for the campaign in Ireland. He met people like Éamonn De Valera, Mary McSweeney and others of the Republican movement, and his home was open to anybody from Ireland who wished to call there; he was a very staunch Irishman of Republican sympathies. When my father was young Anthony had invited him to America. He got his ticket and was ready to go but on the morning of his departure he baulked. This change of heart upset Anthony with the result that, when I was young, there was no trace of my uncle. All was silence; he never wrote another letter. I presume he blamed my grandfather, James, for the change of plans.

When I arrived in Philadelphia I stayed with friends from Tooreen, Aghamore. My grand-uncle had a son named James, and I wanted to see if I could find him. I got out the telephone directory and looked up "James Horan". Then I thought of a second name which I guessed might be "Anthony", so I looked up "James Anthony" and, sure enough, I found "James A. Horan". There was only one "James A. Horan" in the whole list and I phoned the number. James Horan's wife answered and quickly confirmed that I had found my cousin. They immediately came to meet me and as soon as possible I went to stay with them. They lived in Jenkinstown where my grand-uncle had lived in his lifetime.

My mission had involved much travelling from city to city. I travelled by train to cities that were near my base in New York, such as Philadelphia and Boston, and by air from New York to places like Cleveland and Chicago. It was easy to travel in America as the transport system was well organised; the services were excellent whether by train, bus or air. I also spent a good deal of time visiting various friends and relations of my own. I had to visit many people from the parishes where I had worked in Ireland because they were all very anxious to get the latest news from home. It is a pity that I cannot mention the names of all the good people who helped me, but that would be impossible. I stayed in numerous houses of friends who were most hospitable, and countless numbers of people helped me in organising my fund-raising campaign. I always felt very tired after attending a function, dance or concert. At each function courtesy demanded that I would go around and meet everybody, and everybody was anxious to meet me. They were all ears to hear the latest from the old country, as they called it, and I did my best to give them any information that I had. They were glad to meet the priest and have a heart-to-heart chat with him.

Irish emigrants remained fond of Ireland and looked back with nostalgia on the days of their youth. It was a pity that they had to leave their own country to make a living elsewhere, yet, on the other hand, I was delighted to find my old schoolpals from Partry doing so well. When Irish boys or girls emigrated to America, they usually started with any type of job they could get and went to night-school at the same time. Having received only primary education in Ireland they had a lot of leeway to make up. I am glad to say that they did that and more. Some went on to get university degrees and secured good jobs, and for that reason Irish people were highly respected in American society.

Irish people are gifted; they have wit and a sense of humour. Good looking and fair skinned, they stand out in any crowd. In

America the Irish followed one another into areas where a Catholic school and church was near at hand. The schools, both primary and high school, were privately run and not subsidised by the state, and wherever Catholics went schools and churches were organised for them. There was also a few Catholic universities, like Notre Dame or St John's, Brooklyn, run by religious orders. The many Irish priests in America did wonderful work for Irish Catholics but unfortunately, when emigration started in the last century, the priests did not follow their flock with the result that many Irish people lost the faith. When there were no priests available they joined other Christian communities and you can find Irish names amongst the congregations of other churches like the Baptists or the Quakers. This was more likely to happen when emigrants settled in remote areas as many early settlers did: it was of course easier to keep the Catholic faith when one was among one's own kinsfolk in cities like New York where priests and churches were near by.

The Irish Americans were well organised. They were organised on the basis of religion, and the various church groups helped them to keep their Irish identity, and there were the county organisations such as the Mayo Men's Association or the Galway Men's Association, with an "umbrella" organisation such as the All-Ireland Counties' Organisation over all. There was also the Knights of Columbanus, which embraced all of the United States, and the Ancient Order of Hibernians, a powerful body with widespread influence. The Gaelic League was also very strong in all the big cities; it organised Irish dancing, *céilís* and Gaelic classes. I also met many Irish priests during my visit, including a few who had been at school with me. I found priests very kind and courteous but a few pastors might have been too officious; it was in that age before Vatican II when we all took ourselves a little bit too seriously. I helped priests in their pastoral work whenever they called upon me because I was anxious to have that experience in the United States.

The big difference between the Irish in the USA and in Great Britain was that the Irish in Britain were assimilated into the community in which they lived, while in America they formed ethnic groups which stayed together down the years and found strength and influence within their own society. The Irish were respected and loved by all other ethnic groups; it must have been their wit and humour as well as the "old blarney". I did find great anxiety among the Irish at the prospect of coloured people moving into their area. The Irish had nothing against the coloured people; in fact, the Irish in America were ready and willing to co-operate with everybody, but they were afraid that their homes would be devalued. If the coloured people moved into an area then the value of property would drop almost immediately and for the Irish who had worked hard and long for their homes that would be a financial tragedy. In New York some Irish had sold their homes and moved to areas such as Queens or Woodside.

In the eyes of the Irishman, an unusual feature of American life was that a husband always helped his wife in the kitchen. In Ireland men did the outdoor work and women performed the indoor chores. Both departments were separate: only very rarely did an Irishman help out in the kitchen and regarded that kind of job as beneath his dignity. Anyone who took on such domestic work was dismissed in a very derogatory Irish word – *piteogach* or effeminate. I admired very much the help given by husbands to their wives in the cooking and washing-up in the American household and thought that it was a practice that would be very desirable in Ireland, all the more so because I knew from experience that Irish women helped in the fields, especially in sowing and reaping. The work-practice in the farm and in the home should be shared by husband and wife.

America was always looked upon as the land of opportunity and freedom, and it certainly proved to be all that: the very atmosphere instils confidence and trust in one's self. It is a big country and one does not find the parochial and insular attitudes that are prevalent in Ireland. Ireland is often described as a nation of "knockers" and "begrudgers" and unfortunately I think this is absolutely so. The media lead in this negative attitude to progress. If anyone shows initiative or drive he is bashed immediately. Neighbours are envious of anyone who advances himself in any way. Anonymous letters are despatched to departments and newspapers – anonymous because "the begrudger is always a coward". But America is a big country and the Irish seemed to thrive in the more open society. They have scope for their intelligence, initiative and drive and they avail of the many opportunities which America presents. The Irish have advanced in business, politics and entertainment; they have the wit and the humour that charms.

On the occasion of President Reagan's visit to Ireland I thought of all that America had done in the past for Irish men and women of every class and creed and I was disappointed with the outcry in the media against the visit and the proposals to stage protests while the president was in Ireland. There may have been some dissatisfaction with America's foreign policy in regard to Nicaragua, El Salvador and the Philippines, but I felt then and still feel that any grievance or misunderstanding in that regard could be cleared up by the leaders of our country in private consultation with the president. I put that point of view forward on nationwide television and the same view was expressed by many retired Irish Americans living in Ireland. There should be no public protest on the occasion of a visit from the leader of a friendly state to our country. I am very grateful for what America has done for my schoolpals, friends and relatives all down the years. We may not have liked what was happening in El Salvador but private parley would be better than public protest. With the best intentions in the world, public protests do not attract the better elements in our community – I was certainly not impressed by the look of the public protest which took place near Dáil Éireann on that occasion.

America is a country that encourages initiative and the Irish in America have developed great confidence in themselves and a belief in their own ability. This is the kind of spirit that is needed to achieve anything in any walk of life. My trip to America was a great experience for me, too, and did much for my personality. I had the opportunity to address very distinguished gatherings and to give lectures on aspects of Irish life. The experience hardened me and got rid of a lot of the shyness and nervousness common to young people, even young priests. It helped to take the corners off me and to instil self-confidence in my own ability and initiative. My mission was a great success all told. In those nine months I had raised about £8,000.

I came home and gave the money to Fr Michael Carney and gave an account of my stewardship to the archbishop. Nothing more was heard about the hall for more than a year; the idea seemed to have died. People began to grow impatient and a rumour swept Tooreen that three local men had purchased a site to build a hall. When this came to the ear of the parish priest he was very concerned. He discussed the matter with the people involved and gave a guarantee that he would build a parochial hall. That satisfied them and kept them quite for a while.

Eventually, when he did decide to build the hall, Fr Carney could not decide in what part of the parish it should be built. I told him that I had no strong views on the matter: the choice was between Tooreen and Aghamore, and I suggested that he should consult the archbishop on the problem. Unfortunately, Fr Carney dallied between one place and another, but at last he consulted the archbishop at a conference in Claremorris in 1951 and they decided to build it in Tooreen. I travelled home from the conference with Fr Carney that day and as we drove he told me of the decision and explained that there were two reasons for it. The first was that there were no pubs in Tooreen and they wanted the new social centre to be at a distance from pubs. The second reason was that they wanted me to build the hall and run it. I would have liked a change from Tooreen as I had already spent seven years there, but now it seemed that I was going to spend seven more.

A site was purchased from Pádraig Forkan at around the same time that we heard a new parochial hall had just been completed in Ballyjamesduff. Fr Carney and I went to inspect it and met the architect; we found we liked the plan and engaged the same architect to draw up ours. Before we had time to proceed any further a new commercial hall opened in Ballyhaunis. It was obvious that this new and unexpected development would create many problems for us. The Ballyhaunis hall was big and we decided that, if our hall was to be viable it must be built on a fairly large scale also or it would not attract the popular bands who worked on a percentage basis. It would also have to be an extensive building to accommodate the youngsters who wished to play games such as badminton, table-tennis and basketball. Finally the revised plans were completed, the site prepared and work on the construction started towards the end of 1951.

Naturally there was disappointment in Aghamore at having lost out on the hall, but with the approval of Dr Walsh I decided to give half of the funds raised in the USA to Aghamore for the erection of its own hall. It turned out to be a satisfactory arrangement and everyone was happy with it, though the move left the Tooreen hall with a fairly substantial debt. This was later paid off by various fund-raising functions: I organised concerts and card games, *céilís* and dances, and with much hard work and heartbreak the money was made up. When I left Tooreen the hall had a small credit balance.

RAISING FUNDS FOR TOOREEN HALL

To attract the patrons I engaged the best of artists and bands and no hall in the country was as well run and as strictly supervised as Tooreen. I supervised the hall personally on all occasions and there were never any rows or trouble of any kind. There was no drink to be had locally and therefore we had no drunks unless perhaps one would stroll in on passing. We did everything possible to make the place a success and a model for all parochial halls. We wanted it to provide entertainment for the young people so that if they were dissatisfied with living in the country through boredom or lack of entertainment they could see that we were at least trying to do something about it. A very decent and select crowd danced at Tooreen and it became known as the pioneers' hall because there were no pubs near by nor any drink sold at the dances.

I had a wonderful group of young people working with me in running the hall. A big committee was formed with members recruited from all parts of the parish and I found them very loyal, reliable and discreet. They were firm and strong and at the same time always friendly and reasonable; they never provoked any of the patrons and did their best to make people feel at home and at ease. The committee organised the sports side of the social centre which had table-tennis, basketball, badminton and boxing.

Though we had started out fairly successfully I was disappointed by the fact that people who had been criticising priests for not providing entertainment for young people were now criticising them for organising dances in the parochial halls. It seemed that no matter what a bishop or priest did he was criticised: if he did not build a hall he was criticised; if he built a hall to provide entertainment for young people and help stem the tide of emigration he was criticised even more. It was said that it was neither part of a priest's job nor his vocation to organise dances.

This criticism of parochial halls was voiced particularly by the owners of commercial premises. They formed an association and petitioned the bishops to make a rule limiting the hours of dancing for all halls to midnight. It was quite obvious that the Dance Hall Owners' Association had no intention of observing the twelve o'clock rule themselves – they just wanted to gain an advantage over their competitors. Some bishops knew that commercial halls would not observe the rule, yet if they did not make it they would be criticised for it seemed such a sensible idea. They might have replied that it was not their duty to make laws governing the hours of dancing but that of the state, yet in the event they made the rule. From the beginning the commercial halls took no notice of the rule, and, not surprisingly, it damaged the parochial halls' business.

One extraordinary thing happened during the running of Tooreen hall. A Redemptorist priest wrote a pamphlet with a weird title, "The Devil At Dances", and on the very first page he told a fictitious story to illustrate his theme. The story was of a girl who went to a dance one night and was asked to dance by a very good-looking, debonair young man. They danced together, but when they had finished she noticed that he had cloven feet. In the twinkling of an eye "he vanished in the midst of a cloud of sulphur smoke. The smell of sulphur permeated the air in the hall."

It was a silly pamphlet and should never have been published. Written by a priest it gave Catholic teaching a superstitious flavour, and I am sure the writer did not think it would be taken seriously. It is incredible that any newspaper correspondent should report the matter yet a few – who had long ceased to believe in things supernatural – pretended to take the rumour seriously. Almost immediately the story was tagged on to a few halls in the Limerick area. It spread from Limerick to other halls around the country and eventually it came our way in Tooreen. We had a high profile and a reputation for procuring popular bands.

The hall was so successful that it created some jealousy in the surrounding areas and it might well have been due to the scheming of some begrudgers that the story of "the devil at dances" was circulated. If so it did not succeed: everybody took it for the crude joke it was. Indeed, it disgusted people so much that they came in their thousands to support us.

As time went on the hall progressed and became a great success; it certainly gave enjoyment to many, many young people who danced there. They came up and talked to me and even in later years they loved to meet me on social and festive occasions to talk about "the old days". Tooreen hall also gave me an opportunity to have a relationship with young people. If you do not join young people in their sport and recreation then it is very difficult to get to know them well. A priest discovers when he grows old that he does not have the same opportunity to meet with young people in their recreation. Usually the young priest in the parish is the man who takes charge of the youth; it is good pastoral work and indeed a duty for priests to organise entertainment and sport for the young people. It is good to meet them, relate with them and influence them for good, and it gives the priest a much better image in their eyes. They will not look on him as an old fogey who is against everything that they enjoy if he joins in their activities.

I certainly had the best of intentions in regard to the hall and I have no apology to make for my association with it. I still think that the hall was a very good idea from a social and even from a religious point of view; it certainly was a great idea in the circumstances in which it was built, a time when the life blood of the West of Ireland was being drained by emigration. I hope it helped to make life more enjoyable for young people, and that in some small way it worked to achieve the purpose for which it was built.

Acting as master of ceremonies gave me great confidence both on the stage and on the pulpit. I seemed to be a natural entertainer and always felt at home on the stage – I feel happy and satisfied if I can help people to enjoy themselves. Having organised and MCed concerts, question-times and *céilís* in order to raise funds for my house in Tooreen, I continued to act as MC for years afterwards and the people seemed to enjoy it. It gave them a different image of the priest from the one they saw on the pulpit. On the pulpit they might see him as stern and even severe at times, whereas at a concert or social they can see the priest as somebody very human who enjoys life, a joke or a song. By running these little concerts I got to know people better, and to know the people is an advantage whether you are dealing with them in their own homes, talking to them from the pulpit or listening to them in the confessional.

Afterwards, in other parishes, I continued to run concerts for the purpose of getting people together. I thought it very important for country people to have some form of entertainment or an opportunity for a night out. It was traditional in Ireland for the men to go to the pubs but it was not customary for women to be seen there so that, to give the women a break from their chores you had to have something like a concert, a question-time or even a card-game. It gave them an opportunity to meet neighbours and friends. There was always somebody needed to act as

MC or organiser for these events and I was always there to help. That gave me great confidence in public speaking, preaching and in giving after-dinner speeches; I also found it most helpful later when asked to speak on radio or television.

I loved to mix with people in their daily lives. In Tooreen, as indeed in Tiernea and Lettermullen, I loved to go into their houses, sit down by the fire and have a chat. I knew and loved country people and I regarded myself as one of them. As a student I had done every kind of farm work, from digging to ploughing the fields, from cutting the harvest to saving turf. To empathise with people, to understand them and to help them, it is an advantage to have shared their lifestyle. If country life is a hardship, and I do not think it is, then I was able to sympathise with them, and I was welcome in every home.

My next-door neighbour in Tooreen was Affie Feeney. He lived with his brother, Paddy, who has since gone to his reward. Affie was very kind to the priests stationed in Tooreen and kept the presbytery supplied with vegetables from his own garden. One day he was annoyed because the local boys went into his fields playing football, so he went out and chased them and came to report the matter to me – he thought that I should be able to keep law and order in the area. "Why didn't you scold them yourself?" I asked.

"Ah, Father," said he, "I didn't get the chance. They ran out, got on their bicycles and made off. What can you do when the youngsters are mechanised?"

My other next-door neighbour, Margaret Mulrennan, was a remarkable old lady of some eighty years of age. It was common knowledge in the area that she had prepared for her death many years before God called her. She always kept a Franciscan habit in her home ready for the big occasion, and seemed to have no fear of death but looked upon it rather as another event in her long life. She was like the wise virgins who had bought oil for their lamps so that they would be prepared when the bridegroom came. This is not the end of the story either, for when the fatal illness did come she actually had her coffin brought to her bedroom. Death or the thought of death held no terror for this woman who was preparing for a far happier life with God. It was typical of the faith of many old people of her era. I would love to have her outlook and faith: her strength of faith and trust in God would put me to shame.

I have always been overwhelmed by the simple faith of ordinary people. I would say to myself: "Here I am, a priest. I had secondary education and was trained in the biggest ecclesiastical college in Ireland. Yet I feel small and deficient when faced with the extraordinary faith of ordinary people." I could have knelt down and kissed their feet. They had such strong faith that they seemed to be living saints, and so it was with this old lady.

While I was stationed in Tooreen I visited the home of Willie Scally many times. Willie Scally, of Cummer, had been deeply involved in the War of Independence when his house was a "safe house" for Republicans and those engaged in the struggle for freedom. Many raids were made in the area by the Royal Irish Constabulary and by the Black and Tans who were stationed in Ballyhaunis, but, Willie told me, the Republicans had a friend amongst the British forces in Ballyhaunis who kept them informed of impending raids and searches; he also gave them information in regard to any intelligence work being done for the British by local people.

A raid was made one Sunday morning on Aghamore church when the curate Fr Pat Garvey was about to celebrate Mass. As he vested for Mass Fr Garvey got word that the British forces had surrounded the church. It was an old ploy by the army and one that the local people resented: they were going to screen all the people at Mass in the hope of netting some wanted men. Fr Garvey delayed Mass as long as possible without arousing suspicion while word was sent to Pádraig Forkan and other wanted men in the church. Pádraig Forkan, whose name will always be linked with the Republican movement, was the most wanted man in the congregation. They decided to take him to the gallery and work on disguising him. They found a lady about his own size, borrowed some of her garments and shoes, and dressed Pádraig up as an old lady. They put a pair of glasses on him and he walked out of the church on the arm of a younger woman. On the way out he was confronted by a policeman from Ballyhaunis who knew him well. Pádraig thought that the policeman recognised him but he did not let on; he gave Pádraig a chance. Forkan was lucky – he would probably have been shot if he had been discovered. On another occasion when the army raided his house in Tooreen, Pádraig took to his heels out the back door and ran into an adjoining field which could not be seen from the road. There was a hidden well in the field and he climbed down and remained there until he got the all-clear. The Black and Tans searched his house and not finding him they withdrew. The well saved Pádraig's life.

A man known as Captain Boland was shot when the British forces raided the village of Derryvaughna, however. A lorry-load of police and a lorry-load of Black and Tans searched the Nolan home in Derryvaughna but there was nothing or nobody found there. They withdrew, but half an hour later they returned. There had been a man working in the bog named Boland who had watched the first raid from the safety of the bog but then he went into the Nolan home to find out what exactly had happened, and when the British forces returned they captured him in the house. They took him outside for questioning, and after they had questioned him they told him to go into the field and keep walking. He did what he was told and as he walked away they shot him in the back. In that way the verdict at the inquest was bound to be that he was shot while trying to escape.

Stories such as these still raised bitter memories even though the time of the Troubles had passed and our strife had been overtaken by the much greater conflict that was World War II. The war ended in 1945 but the effects were felt in the countryside for a number of years afterwards. There were shortages of food, petrol, building material, cattle fodder and all other imported goods. At the beginning of the war there had been a great influx of young people from England to avoid conscription; now that the war was over and many English cities had to be rebuilt there was plenty of work for young people in England and elsewhere and the great exodus of our young people began. Thousands upon thousands left each year and continued to leave all through the 1950s. There was little opportunity for secondary education except for the middle classes, upper classes and holders of scholarships – though there was secondary education for rich and poor alike if they were fortunate enough to be within cycling-distance of a school run by a religious order. But by and large the young people who emigrated were badly prepared as they had not got the education or training that would qualify them for good jobs. Our girls had to take menial jobs as domestic servants and the boys had to work with the pick and shovel. The boys got work on buildings sites and were also recruited in teams for road building and the construction of airports. They left their own country to improve the economy and lifestyle of other places.

Many priests in that era, too, were living from hand to mouth. There was a great myth amongst people in the 1930s and '40s about the priest's salary, though his total salary for the year in some parishes was something around £250. One could barely exist on that income. It was essential to have a housekeeper; she could only be paid £1 a week and her "keep", but taking as little as that out of such a salary still left you with very little to spare even in those days.

When I came into the Tuam diocese in 1939 I had to buy a car because a priest was dependent on a car to get around in Connemara where long distances were involved. I bought it for the sum of £139 and I was a long time paying off the debt. Strangely enough, I was better off as a curate in Tiernea than I was when I came to the parish of Aghamore. There was a parish priest and two curates in Aghamore at that particular time and the whole revenue had to be divided between the three of us. To give an example: at the autumn stations a half-crown had to be paid to the priests by each householder. Out of that half-crown a shilling went towards the cost of a bell that was erected in Aghamore some time previously; 6d went to the clerk; 6d went to the parish priest and there was 3d each for the curates. That situation was changed later on when it was pointed out that a shilling of the priest's revenue should not be going to pay for a parish bell which should be paid for from some other source. In any event, I hope that these figures will explode the myth of the priest's salary.

It was very hard to get people to raise their contributions. I remember well the effort that was needed to raise what was called the "Oats Money" at harvest time. "Oats Money" derived from the time when priests travelled in a horse and trap and that particular contribution paid for the priest's transport. People were asked to raise it by one shilling and there was much grumbling even about that amount. I think that the people did not really understand and perhaps there was a lack of communication between priests and people. Nowadays people are given the facts and they are very generous indeed, but people at that time had an innate fear of bills. They had a dread of anything that had to be paid on a regular basis. It was a fear that came down from another generation when a family might be evicted for not being able to pay the rent, and whether it was a question of paying ESB bills or paying "dues" to the priest, the same feeling persisted.

Curate in Cloonfad

After fourteen happy years I left Tooreen in July 1959. Just a few weeks before I was changed I had passed through the village of Cloonfad on my way to Galway. As we drove down the long and dreary hill leading out of the village we passed the local curate walking along the road. I said to my companion, Jim Ganley: "I know that I am going to be changed soon and I would not like to come to Cloonfad. That curate looks a very lonely figure indeed."

Two weeks later I got my letter of transfer and, sure enough, Cloonfad was to be my new mission. I went immediately to meet the curate and get all the details of my future pastoral duties in the area. Shortly afterwards the same Jim Ganley called to see me. "Well you have come here after all," he said.

"Yes, indeed!" said I, "and if it is not the place that I would have liked, perhaps I can turn it into something." That I did, because I spent the four happiest years of my life in Cloonfad. I did more work in those four years than I ever did in any other parish. And there was ample scope for good work, because Cloonfad was a very depressed and neglected area.

Straight away, the week after my arrival in the parish, somebody came and told me that a married man in the area was in desperate need of a job. He had been drinking heavily, his only cow had died, and the man's neighbour asked if I would try to get work for him. The neighbour also explained that his little girl, an only child, had been sick for a few weeks and hinted that it might be due to malnutrition.

The most likely possibility for creating employment was in forestry, something I had been thinking of for some time. There had been an afforestation scheme initiated in Cloonfad some years previously by Fr Eamonn O'Malley, who later became parish priest of Kilmeena. I got in touch with the Forestry Department and I was told that the only obstacle in the way of further progress was the acquisition of land. I called a meeting of the people in the area and told them of my plans and how they could be achieved. I explained that if afforestation was to succeed in the district, then the farmers would have to sell waste or unused land to the Forestry Department. We formed a committee and sent two men to each village to persuade the local farmers to make their waste land available to the Forestry Department so that they could develop it and plant trees. However, the price per acre offered by the department was very low and there was no great incentive to sell. There was another big obstacle in the shape of a farmer on top of Cloonarkin mountain who was not willing to part with any of his land. He was the key to the whole place because he owned a big portion of the mountain, and without his co-operation it would be impossible to drain or develop the area. Though I had appointed working parties in the various villages I could not get anybody to do Cloonarkin, so I decided to do it myself, and asked Michael Eaton, Ballyroe, to join me.

One Monday afternoon we went to Cloonarkin to do the job. We went from house to house and got on very well, finding the farmers willing to commit some land to the project, and we were now ready to face the man who seemed to be so sticky. I decided that I would not press my luck that evening but would let the matter rest for a few days so as to think it through and be very sure of making the correct approach. But before I had the opportunity to return to Cloonarkin the man called on me and said that he was very disappointed that I had not visited him when I had called on the others. I explained that at our meeting in the school everybody had felt he would not sell. He said very angrily: "They had no right to say such a thing. They had no authority from me on the matter."

There must have been a guiding hand behind the scenes. That farmer gave us his full support and with no further problems to hamper us the afforestation went ahead on schedule. We had up to twenty people employed in afforestation during the following years. The scheme certainly solved the difficulty of the man who had been drinking and had lost his cow. Some years later I met his daughter, and I was delighted that she had got on well and that everything was in good shape at home. With that success behind me I set about working on further community improvement schemes.

I co-operated with the Dunmore people in promoting afforestation in that part of Dunmore parish adjacent to Cloonfad. I attended meetings with TDs Mark Killilea and Mick Donnellan in Dunmore and spoke to the farmers about the advantage of afforestation both for beautifying the countryside and for giving employment. Great progress was made and the results can be seen clearly today: a drab and dreary landscape has grown green and beautiful. Districts can only benefit from more co-operation between parishes in regard to projects such as afforestation, drainage and other activities.

Cloonfad was a very low-lying, boggy area and needed a lot of drainage. I organised many drainage schemes, making use of the Minor Employment Scheme to do the job initially, but that grant only provided about £600-£700 each year. The amount depended on the number that was unemployed in the district on a particular date the previous year, and when I went to the department for more money I was told that there could be no further grant under that particular scheme. I was informed, though, that they had millions of pounds under a Rural Improvement Scheme, and it was also explained to me that I would have an advantage under that scheme because people in Cloonfad had very low land valuations – about £5 per farm on average. So I promoted projects under the Rural Improvement Scheme and for all the work that we did – on by-roads, drainage and various other projects – we got a 90% grant. At the same time I persuaded the local workers to take £1 less per day in wages so as to make up for the 10% shortfall in the grant. They may have been getting less than a County Council worker but they were improving the roads and land in their own villages, and on the strength of their efforts an incredible amount of work was carried out in a short time.

When the County Council elections came around the people of Cloonfad and Ballinlough realised that the more councillors they had from the parish the better chance they would have of getting grants for local improvement, so they decided that they would try to have two councillors elected, one from Fianna Fáil and one from Fine Gael. They succeeded in that: Michael Mitchell from Ballinlough was elected as a Fine Gael member, and Pat Moylan of Ballinlough was elected for Fianna Fáil. We had a foot in both camps and the Roscommon County Council was very good to us subsequently.

I had a great relationship with the county engineer, Mr Earner, and with Dan O'Rourke, chairman of the Roscommon County Council. Through our efforts we persuaded the council to renovate the road from Cloonfad to Dunmore; winding through the bleak hills and entirely open to the elements, it was in a poor state of repair. Roscommon County Council was one of the first councils in the country to use gravel as the foundations for main roads. The gravel proved to be a more stable foundation than stone; while the stone would often sink in one area and remain solid in another, the gravel formed a kind of a bridge across the foundation to keep the road level and uniform. Gravel roads were also fifty per cent cheaper and could be built at twice the speed of other roads. When the Cloonfad–Dunmore road was completed work began on improving the steep hill leading from Cloonfad village to Ballyhaunis. The road was shaded from the sun so that in severe frost it remained very slippery and dangerous for most of the day and cars and other vehicles en route to Ballyhaunis could not negotiate it. It caused much inconvenience but after the council's work the traffic problem on the hill was solved.

While in Cloonfad, of course, I lobbied politicians as I have always lobbied them for the good of my parishioners and for the good of the people in the West generally. Mr Brian Lenihan, who became a very big man in politics, was then a senator. More than twenty years ago I made representations to Brian and the results were good. He and Harry Boland helped me to get a grant for a new school, the building of which was left in the capable hands of my successor, Fr Jarlath Canney. I had a great friend, too, in Jack McQuillan, an Independent TD for Roscommon. He seemed to be all-powerful and the government departments gave him anything he asked for – local people believed that the governments departments were afraid of him and his word was law. He eventually married and gave up politics – maybe he was a wise man! I had a wonderful accord with all politicians in those far-off days. I claim to be a "bread and butter" politician and someone of that ilk must have a good relationship with politicians of every colour. That kind of relationship is, of course, more difficult nowadays: I think that I should know!

The Cloonfad people backed me in all the things that I wanted to do; they knew that I was doing my best for them and that anything I had in mind was for their good. I found that the whole atmosphere of the place changed once things began to happen. Our progress gave Cloonfad great courage and renewed spirit, and a marvellous feeling of community grew amongst the people. I was delighted with the excellent relationship I had with all the parishioners. I had been warned that I might have trouble with one or two villages that seemed unco-operative; however, I always made up my own mind in every situation, and the outcome was that I got the fullest co-operation from those particular villages. One should never make a judgement on hearsay!

The church in Cloonfad was a very beautiful building and served the people of the district well. I had 340 families, over 2,000 people, in my spiritual care. They were a very religious, good-living people and tremendously loyal to the priest. During my time in Cloonfad I installed new Stations of the Cross in the church; I also built porches at the side-doors to prevent draughts and make the building more comfortable. To raise funds for landscaping around the church and in the presbytery grounds I organised concerts in the local hall owned by the Burkes. They gave us the use of the hall for a nominal sum and we always made £40 or £50 per function. The people of Cloonfad were very talented and provided the entertainment, and they always gave a good performance.

I loved visiting the school and meeting the children and the teachers. The children were talented, intelligent and well behaved. I tried to get them interested in music and dancing, which they did. I always believed in sharing the joys as well as the sorrows of the people. In that way they get a chance to know the priest better and, seeing him as a sociable, good-natured person, they will be more likely to seek his advice and guidance in any kind of trouble. The quality of the teachers and children in Cloonfad school was superb. In one particular year nine of the girls competed in a number of scholarship examinations and all nine won scholarships to different convents. They were all very successful in later life and distinguished themselves in their different professions; some entered nursing and teaching, others the civil service. They were really a credit to their school and to their teachers. That was also true of the boys in Cloonfad, though they were not as spectacular as the girls.

Some years later I was in the Department of Education and making no progress with the problem which I had on hands. I had been speaking to one of the secretaries of the department and was waiting for him to return with a decision. I was surprised to see a young girl coming over to talk to me. I said to her: "Did he send you down to persuade me to accept something that I am unwilling to accept?" I wanted a certain decision and I was determined to get it; I felt sure that I had right and justice on my side.

"Oh, no," she said. "I came down because I know you. I was a pupil in Cloonfad school when you were our curate." Straight away I remembered her name and I remembered that she was one of the nine brilliant pupils who won the scholarships.

I am glad to relate that I got good news from her: I got approval for an extension to the primary school in Knock. For fourteen years I had had a prefab classroom that was in dreadful condition, so cold and damp that I was fearful for the health of the children using it. I had a very good case but I was grateful, too, that she should have brought me the good news. Even when you have right on your side it is nice to have friends in high places. This happened at a time when we had a very tight economic situation in the country and the government was trying to practise "fiscal rectitude".

My work in Cloonfad was made very easy with the help of a wonderful parish priest, Fr Michael Malone. I benefited from his help and advice from the first day that I called at his house in Ballinlough until the day that I was transferred from Cloonfad to Knock. I found him to be a gentleman in every way; he was my parish priest and my good friend. He helped me with every project that I undertook in Cloonfad and his curate, Fr Tommie McEllin, who later became my colleague at Knock, was equally kind and generous. When there is a team of priests in a parish that pull together and co-operate then marvellous things can happen.

I was anxious to act as chaplain on a pilgrimage to Lourdes so I offered my services to Shannon Travel, a company based in Dublin. I had been to Lourdes previously and had experience of all the spiritual exercises carried out by pilgrims. My application was successful and I was duly appointed chaplain to a group. My duty was to lead them in the shrine, celebrate Mass, conduct holy hours, perform the Stations of the Cross and lead them in the rosary and Blessed Sacrament processions. There was also a courier who as well as organising accommodation arranged daytour to places of interest in the vicinity of Lourdes, usually places that had an association with the life of St Bernadette. It was a big occasion for me because I also booked my father and mother on the trip; it was their first journey outside Ireland and they were very excited about it. They had heard so much about Lourdes and its shrine that they felt privileged to be part of the pilgrimage. My brother had just got married and had taken over the home farm, so they were relieved of all responsibility and they could afford to take a holiday; their children were now settled in life. The old people had done a very good job and deserved a break. The pilgrimage was very worthwhile, especially for the sake of my father and mother. We made a return trip the following year, and now my father had to be taken around on a wheelchair as he suffered from arthritis. It was difficult to persuade him to sit in the wheelchair: he was a very proud man in that respect and had been very active all through his long life. There is that same reluctance in all of us to accept the disabilities that come with old age, but though he did not like it he had to face reality.

In my last year in Cloonfad I wrote to my archbishop, Most Rev. Dr Joseph Walsh, to ask permission to go to Lourdes once more. Again I had decided to bring my father and mother on the trip. I got no reply. I met his secretary a week later and said, "I wrote to the archbishop about a trip to Lourdes but I got no answer."

"Well, I wrote the letter and handed it over to the archbishop to sign," he said, "and I do not know what happened after that."

I decided to write again, an identical letter to the one I had already written. This time I got an answer by return post. It told me that the archbishop was delighted to hear that I was making a trip to Lourdes but he assumed that it would be part of my annual holidays. I had got away with it the previous year and I suppose he felt that it was time to call a halt to my gallop. Now that I am much older and wiser I know that I blundered badly by insisting on getting a reply. He had wanted to let me away with it, unofficially, by leaving my letter unanswered.

In Cloonfad I was very active also in the Legion of Mary and chaplain of the diocesan curia. The praesidium in Cloonfad was made up of both men and women and we always travelled together to the curia meetings. The Legion of Mary did marvellous work and did everything pertaining to both spiritual and corporal works of mercy. It is still doing a terrific job in the archdiocese and I hope that God and Our Lady will help it to achieve even greater things.

I was delighted with my change to Cloonfad after spending fourteen years in Tooreen. It is a good policy for a bishop to change a curate every seven or eight years. It is better for both priest and people to have a change. A priest takes stock of his own spiritual life; he makes a better effort at serving the people and preparing sermons; he reviews his commitment to his parish and to his flock. Generally speaking he makes a fresh start. I was able to work very hard in Cloonfad for the four years I spent there. They were the four happiest years of my life because I had scope for doing the things that I like to do. I had the opportunity to do social work. I helped the farmers and the people, old and young, in every possible way.

Nowadays I feel proud every time I pass through Cloonfad. It is such a tidy village with the streets and houses so neat and done up in great taste. Once the people began to take an interest in their village and gained confidence in their own ability to achieve things, they never looked back. A village that once looked bleak and barren is now a place of great beauty and grandeur. When I drive up the hill to Cloonarkin the windswept village on the side of a mountain now seems to have acquired the beauty of Killarney, with 1,500 acres of forest on every side. What a transformation! How I wish that the millions of acres of wasteland in Ireland could be used for the benefit of all the children of Caitlín Ní hUalIacháin.

James Horan receiving his BA degree.

James's parents, Bartley and Catherine.

With his Aunt Mary and mother after his ordination.

In Tiernea. The girl on the right is Miss Goggin.

With his uncle, Jim Casey, in New York 1939.

The young curate in the 1940s.

With his mother and father on pilgrimage in Lourdes, 1962.

The day before the Pope's visit. Standing: Mr McGuinness, assistant county manager, Mayo; Mrs Catherine Horan; Monsignor Horan; Archbishop Joseph Cunnane; Miss Nancy Horan. Seated: Mrs Margaret Finnerty and Mrs Bridie Fannin, who are also sisters of the monsignor.

Joe Malone, Bord Fáilte, Archbishop Cunnane, Gay Byrne and the monsignor.

The Basilica of Our Lady Queen of Ireland.

Monsignor James Horan with Pope John Paul II at Knock.

Monsignor Horan with Charles J. Haughey TD, on the occasion of the inaugural flight from Connaught Regional Airport.

Monsignor Horan and the Minister for Transport, Albert Reynolds, having a chat.

Connaught Regional Airport: inaugural flight, 25 October 1985.

Members of the parish committee, with the parish priest of Partry, Fr Jarlath Waldron, at the celebration of Monsignor Horan's Golden Jubilee in June 1985. He was presented with the rocking chair on which he is sitting.

Enjoying a joke with his nephew, Declan Horan.

The remains of Monsignor James Horan at Connaught Regional Airport, August 1986. Members of the monsignor's family are in the front row; the celebrant is Most Rev. Dr Joseph Cunnane, assisted by Fr Dominic Grealy.

James Canon Horan.

The Observant Traveller

During my years in Cloonfad I always took my holidays abroad, travelling with a priest-friend, Fr Dominic Grealy, to the Continent and the Middle East. It was a time when air-fares and accommodation were very cheap, especially in places like Spain and Italy – I remember staying at a *pension* in Tarragona where bed and breakfast cost just 3s 6d.

We made one trip to London, Paris and Rome. In London we spent our time on conducted tours through the city and visited the Tower of London, the House of Commons and the British Museum, and many other places of historical interest. We strolled in Hyde Park on a Sunday afternoon and listened to preachers, agitators and Gospellers at Speaker's Corner. They spoke on every subject under the sun, each with his own hobby-horse. I had the feeling that if the buildings and stones of London could speak they would tell many tales of Irish men and women. That story would tell of the great successes of those who reached the heights, and it would include many tales of woe and misfortune.

We left London for Paris and found that the "City of Light" lived up to its reputation for beauty. Being there brought to mind all we had learned in story and song about the charm of Paris, the mecca of artists, scientists, painters and authors. Along the streets all types of musicians performed at street corners, artists sat painting at the city's famous bridges. We had studied French in Maynooth College under Fr Louis Rigal and brushed up on it for the trip, but found that the French generally were not very tolerant of people speaking their language badly. Of course, we visited the famous churches, Sacre Coeur and Notre Dame. We climbed the Eiffel Tower and drank coffee looking out over the majestic city. We loved those Parisian cafés and restaurants where you can listen to light orchestral music and enjoy your meal and although prices in Paris were dearer than in other cities they were not prohibitive. One could sit for hours outside a café and watch the whole world go by. Paris must be one of the most cosmopolitan cities in the world: everybody everywhere wants to see Paris. Still, it would not be my choice to live there. Architecturally the city is very beautiful. The French are very proud of their language and would like it to be recognised as the great international language of the world; French cuisine is world-famous, French culture renowned, but give me the simple fare of Ireland any time.

From Paris we flew to Rome and landed in Chiampino Airport. This was our first trip to the Eternal City and it was so exciting: of all the cities in the world Rome has a special appeal for the Catholic priest. This is the city of the Vicar of Christ, the Pope of Rome.

On our trip we did not usually arrange bookings in hotels as we did not wish to be tied to any particular place; we preferred to come and go as the spirit moved us. We just took a taxi at the airport and asked the driver to take us to a hotel that happened to be advertised in the tourist brochure, usually a two-star hotel as we had to keep a close watch on our budget and the two-star cost £1 for bed and breakfast. So at Rome airport we hired a taxi to take us to a hotel. As we arrived an electric-storm thundered overhead and I was in so much of a hurry to get shelter that I left a small briefcase containing my passport, traveller's cheques and other essentials in the car. I felt so stupid, as one always does after a silly mistake of that kind. I was upset and sleep did not come easily that night. I phoned what corresponded to a taxi-drivers' association headquarters but got no tidings, but next morning the taxi returned with the case, at a fee of 1,000 lire, the taxi fare for the return journey with my belongings. I was delighted and admired that taxi driver's honesty; I had prayed to St Anthony and he did the needful. We spent a week in Rome, staying for the most part in a hostel run by an order of nuns. We visited the famous Coliseum and the ruins of ancient Rome, and went to see the catacombs of St Callisto on the Appian Way outside the city.

Another year we took the Orient Express in Paris bound for Switzerland and Montreux. The Orient Express suited us perfectly because we could get on and off wherever we wished. We reached Montreux, beautifully situated on the shores of Lake Geneva at the foothills of the Alps. It was, of course, a tourist resort, geared to make the visitor's holiday pleasant and enjoyable, and kept clean and free from all litter. I was very impressed by the profusion of flowers everywhere; I even saw flowers growing on the pier-walls by the shore of Lake Geneva. The Swiss are a very thrifty and industrious people. To make the mountains fertile they created terraces by building a series of retaining walls on the slopes which prevented the erosion of soil that might otherwise have been caused by rain or melting snow. Literally every inch of ground was cultivated. What an example for Ireland where you see thousands and thousands of acres of wasteland, land which could be made useful.

We could not leave Montreux without paying a visit to Geneva. After a cruise on the lake we visited the city. We found it very beautiful, so steeped in history that we got the feeling as we walked the streets that history was unfolding before us. We returned to Montreux that evening and, with only four days in Switzerland, we had to continue on our way. We got on the Orient Express bound for Milan, hoping to attend a performance at the city's famous opera house. Our journey took us through the Alpine Tunnel into Italy and then, unfortunately, when we arrived in Milan we discovered that the opera season – which runs through the winter – was over. We hadn't expected that. We had heard of the famous soprano, Maria Callas, and were anxious to hear her performance, but it was not to be.

We stayed just one night and then we were on our way to Venice, the city with canals for streets. It was not so romantic, after all, to ride on the famous gondolas: the canals were a bit smelly and probably suffered from pollution, as do many of our waterways in modern times. It strikes me as ironic that an age of such industrial progress and wealth should spoil some of the beautiful things that God has created. During our two-day visit we spent some time in St Mark's Cathedral, marvelling at its spaciousness and emptiness. Only one large chapel had seats and that was where Sunday Mass was offered; for big ceremonies there was just standing-room with no seats whatsoever. I gazed open-eyed at the beauty of the cathedral's architecture and its works of art. St Mark's contains a history of great art and culture which held us in thrall.

Outside on the spacious square in front of the cathedral was the Doge's Palace, formerly the house of the Chief Magistrate of Venice. We viewed the Bridge of Sighs attached to the palace, which was trodden by criminals being led to execution in the cruel old days. In those far off times crime did not pay! On St Mark's Square thousands of pigeons were the guests of thousands of tourists each day. We went on a boat trip of the bay and saw the "playa" or beach which had become the playground of the rich and mighty of this world. I was happy to have seen Venice, the scene of many films and plays including Shakespeare's *Merchant*.

From Venice we went to a seaside place called Rimini on the Adriatic coast where we stayed in a German-owned hotel about five minutes walk from the sea. The sea was very pleasant and much warmer than the Atlantic waters in the West of Ireland. As Catholic priests we were the objects of much curiosity at first, especially from the German tourists, but as usual, when they found we were ordinary human beings we were accepted and became quite popular. The week passed very quickly and soon we had to re-board the Orient Express for Paris. We tried to book a sleeping berth on the train so that we could have a night's rest but found we could not do so until we reached Milan. At Milan we were told that we did not qualify for a berth without first-class tickets; we had only a third-class ticket as that was all we could afford! There was to be no berth.

We boarded the train and found there was worse to come: all the carriages were full so it seemed that we would have to stand in a very crowded corridor. We got so tired, moving along the corridor, dragging our suitcases. Finally we stopped at an empty first-class carriage and decided, for better or worse, to take it. We did so and pulled the curtains so that we could sleep. Several people opened the door during the night, bowed, apologised and disappeared. I presume that they were weary travellers doing penance in the corridor. Eventually an inspector called, rattled his money-bag, and we paid up. We were not disturbed again until we reached Paris the next morning at ten o'clock. Although we may have been tired and weary we were absolutely delighted with the trip; we had enjoyed a wonderful holiday, one that we would always remember. We kept a strict account of every penny we spent on the trip and the total cost was £81 each. It was marvellous value for a three-week holiday.

Another wonderful trip we made was a cruise on the Mediterranean. We flew from Gatwick to Venice and there boarded one of the Greek touring ships. We sailed all around the Mediterranean calling at different ports, including the Port of Piraeus. When we arrived in Athens we toured all the historic sites; on another stop we went by bus to Turkey and to Ephesus, the place made so famous by St Paul in his letters. The site of the city of Ephesus has been excavated and one could see the remains of houses and streets. Then we went to the house on a bare deserted mountain where Our Lady is said to have lived with St John and his household after their departure from Palestine. The building was old and dilapidated, ancient and holy. On our return to Athens and the Port of Piraeus we boarded ship again and set off for Cyprus, Crete and Rhodes. In each case we anchored at the port and then took a bus which brought us on a tour of all these places so rich in history.

When we were in Cyprus some of the Irish army were serving on a peace-keeping mission under the auspices of the United Nations, trying to preserve the peace between the Turks and the Greeks. We went to Rhodes, which was a very beautiful island indeed, but of course the highlight of our trip was the Holy Land.

We landed in Tel Aviv. From there we had two days in the Holy Land, returning each evening to the ship. In those two days we saw Nazareth, Cana of Galilee, Jordan, Jerusalem and Mount Tabor. We saw all the famous shrines except Bethlehem and Calvary; these we could not see because at that time, before the Seven Days War of 1967, the area was held by Jordan, as was part of Jerusalem, and one could not go there from Israel. We were saddened at not being able to visit Calvary or Bethlehem. We could view Calvary from a hill in the Israeli-occupied part of Jerusalem, but we could not see Bethlehem.

In all my travels, all over the world, no attempt was ever made to rob me – except once. Lo and behold, on this hill overlooking Calvary it nearly happened. On the hill there was a little shop in which we bought some postcards to send to our relatives and friends. I began writing the postcards using the roof of a car parked near by as a table, when a young boy came by on a bicycle. I felt something peculiar behind me and turned round. There was another young lad with my wallet in his hand ready to pass it to the boy on the bicycle. Surely, it would have been ironic to be robbed on a hill looking down on Calvary.

Parish Priest of Knock

Throughout my priestly life my destiny has been completely directed by providence. It was always the will of God and the decision of the archbishop that decided my fate. As I now look back on life I would not have it otherwise. I never asked for any special assignment and never grumbled at what God sent me. I may not have liked the parish to which I had been sent, but with God's help I prepared to do my best for it.

But I think that if I had had a choice I would have chosen Knock, because it presented a special challenge. There had been many problems in the parish that had caused frustration and disappointment to parish priests, administrators and curates down through the years; this state of affairs presented a great challenge and I was prepared to take it on. In Cloonfad I got a hint from a senior cleric that I would not be left too long there. I had a hunch that I would be sent to Knock Shrine and I was absolutely right. I got a letter transferring me to Knock as curate, and I arrived there on Thursday 12 September 1963. At that time there were only two priests in Knock, a curate and an administrator, and the usual pattern of events was that the curate would succeed the administrator after a number of years.

I had gone to Knock frequently in my youth and, of course, as a young priest I went to Knock very often on the day of the diocesan pilgrimage. At other times, when Yanks would come home from America, we always brought them to the shrine, or when my father or mother was sick or when we had a special request to make we went to Knock to pray to God and His Blessed Mother for our request to be granted, and I think we were always fairly successful. Of course, if we did not get our wish, God's holy will was welcome.

Knock was an entirely ordinary village. In the thirties and forties some old thatched houses had been knocked to make way for new buildings, but beyond that nothing seemed to have changed since the time of the apparition in 1879. We have an outstanding record of Knock as it was in the nineteenth century from a contemporary, Daniel Campbell. Campbell was living in Birmingham at the time of the apparition, and when he read about the event in various English newspapers he was inspired to write down his memories of the parish. He had been born in Eden, Knock, in 1825, and lived there until 1849. He survived the Famine of 1844-48 but when his father died in 1849 he emigrated with his mother and brother to Birmingham where he lived for the rest of his life. Fr John Baptist Byrne, CP, gave me a copy of Campbell's manuscript, which throws much light on the life and conditions of the people of Knock from 1800-79. He begins by situating Knock and explaining the placename.

It is in the Barony of Costello on the Estates of Lord Viscount Dillon. It is built on elevated ground. The parish takes its name from hill or Knock on account of its elevated position, "*Paróiste an Chnuic*" or "Parish on the Hill".

The present church was built in 1828 by the Revd. P. O'Grady, P.P., on the site of the old thatched house where his predecessor, Fr. Henry Bourke, officiated. I remember when the Church was consecrated by Archbishop Kelly, and I was confirmed by Archbishop McHale on his first visitation to Knock, on the very spot of the Apparition. I remember his Grace asking me what Confirmation was, for I believe I was the youngest confirmed that day. I answered him in his own Catechism or in his abbreviation of Butler's Catechism translated into Irish. I sat next to His Lordship that day and attended on him at Church before the Altar of the Apparition. If I was to know then that the Church would become so famous I would take note of everything that happened. I would keep an account of every Mass I served and my fellow-servers. I would keep an account of every priest that said Mass there too; of the Stations of the Cross that I assisted at and read in my turn when a boy, for my father always conducted the Stations of the Cross, which were performed every Sunday before or after Mass by most of the congregation.

I may as well state here that the chapel of Knock is dedicated to Saint John the Baptist for he is the patron of the parish for the pattern, as it is called, is held on the 24th June, and I have seen many cut heads and bleeding noses on the occasion; it was the only day at Knock for a spree. The pattern was always held about 40 yards north of the Church, for the parish priest would not allow any tents to be erected or a stand of any kind to be near or opposite the Church. There were but two inns at Knock in my time, but that was sufficient, for every house, from the by-road at Lecarrow to the Crossroad of Ballyhaunis and Kiltimagh, sold whiskey and tobacco – without a licence. So there was no shortage of drink at Knock in my time. But now the second inn-keeper of Knock, I was to say a few words about him, as recent proceedings at Knock brings him to my memory. He married a Miss Bourke, a daughter of Mr Tobey Bourke, who held the chapel farm and who was nephew to Fr Henry Bourke, predecessor to Fr Pat O'Grady. ... I would not go into the family history of the Bourkes, Hills and Byrnes, but for the information of people who are unacquainted with the first witnesses of the Apparition at Knock.

The first witness given in the *Universe* was Patrick Hill of Claremorris, a boy who said he was at his aunt's house at Knock, Mrs Byrne, at the time the first Apparition appeared. Mrs Byrne was a sister to Mrs Hill and mother to Mary and Dominick Byrne, who were interrogated by the correspondent of the *Dublin Weekly News*. ... The above witnesses left the chapel yard while the Apparition was visible there. They went to see an old woman that was dying. The old woman was my aunt Mrs Campbell and I did not hear of her death until I saw it in the *Universe*.

I went sometimes to school to Mr Thomas Waldron who lived in a little house about 40 yards from the Church. ... Mr Waldron's school was a long low-roofed thatched house with no windows and no light but what the door admitted. I think there was a window or hole on the western side. We used to bring two sods of turf under our arm to make a fire, and if we did not do that we would not be let to the fire and would be caned if we did not bring our two sods of turf. Though we were rude and unmannerly enough on other occasions, we were obliged to call Mr Waldron, Master, so he went generally by that name. He had scholars varying from 3 years to 22 and ... I believe some of them were older. I knew three young men that came from near Claremorris, namely, John Brogan, John and James Concannon, a distance of 5 or 6 miles, to finish their education, for they were to be schoolmasters themselves and the town of Claremorris could not boast of a schoolmaster at that time that could cope with Mr Waldron. ...

Now for some of its traditions – for Knock like other places had its stories and fairy tales and fairy women which I will relate hereafter.

One particular saying which I heard when a child and never can forget it; that was, that no plague or cholera should ever rage on Knock, that is, between Ballincostello bridge and the bridge of Ballyhowley. The reason why I will tell as I heard it related many years ago. A holy pilgrim was travelling and met a man who was driving a horse and cart and the pilgrim or holy man asked him for a ride or lift which he cheerfully granted. I cannot say whether the traveller met the carter at Ballincostello or Ballyhowley, but the parish of Knock extends from one bridge to the other, a distance of four miles. The holy pilgrim prayed and prophesised that no plague or pestilence should ever enter Knock.

The writer of these lines saw the prophecy partly fulfilled, for he lived at Knock the time cholera was raging on every side of the Parish, when hundreds were dying in the surrounding towns and parishes. Still Knock was free from the plague excepting one solitary case and that was I think the name Mrs Follard of Ballyhaunis; she was a native of Knock, sister to Charles and Pat Forde of Knock. The cholera was raging in Ballyhaunis and to shun the danger Mrs Follard left Ballyhaunis where she lived and came to her brother's house, Pat Forde of Ballyhowley, but she was not many hours at Knock when she died from the cholera, but no other person took it and so the cholera ended without any more victims at Knock. So that was the part of the prophecy fulfilled.

I remember Pat Egan of Cloonteriff coming to our house in a great hurry and leaving a straw drawn from the thatch of another house, and the family so served was to say three Hail Marys I think for the cholera to cease. And the occupier of the house had to do likewise in three more houses on the same condition. Some had to travel miles before they could meet a house that was not served. I remember the words Pat Egan used when he left the straw at my father's house. He said: "Oh John make haste. Bishop McHale is coming down the road with his coach full of straw." We were so excited that my father would hardly wait to say the three Hail Marys until he was on his errand serving the straw as above stated. ...

Now I must give a little account of Mary, the fairy woman, of lower Aughtaboy within a half a mile of Ballinacostello. She was the fairy woman of the district and I knew different people came to her from different parts of the country for the purpose of keeping the fairies away from themselves or their friends. It might be perhaps to cure some person "overlooked" by the evil eye; a red-haired man or a black-eyed woman or as the case might be to restore the butter that was stolen from the cow's milk on May Day by some evil-disposed person; or it might be the sow did not take to the litter of bonaveens as she ought to do; or perhaps one of the hens began to crow or the cock crew at the wrong time which would be a sure sign of bad luck. A stitch in time saves nine.

So Mary was consulted in time about these things and her salary or fee was 2s 6d to 10s according to the case. And before she commenced, a bottle of whiskey was requested for she would not undertake any difficult case without a drop of whiskey to help her to encounter the fairies. This looks like a romance.

Fr Pat O'Grady being parish priest, often denounced her from the Altar of Knock. Still she carried on her old game, but when she had a child to christen, or herself to be churched, she would promise faithfully never again to be guilty of such conduct, but no sooner was her child christened or herself churched than she began to follow her former occupation, although she was denounced by the Church or anyone speaking to her. When going to cure any person or animal she always fainted and went to consult the king or queen of the fairies and through her interference, she often obtained her request, although the parties had already been doomed to fairyland. On one occasion a young man went to consult her about his wife. He told her he thought she was overlooked or an evil eye bewitched her; so she fainted as usual and told him that his wife was already with the fairies and she would have great trouble to restore her to him. But by complying with her directions and paying the usual fee, his wife would be as well as ever in a few days. She told him the description of the person that bewitched her, but the best of it all was he had no wife and never was married!

The inhabitants of Knock were not very rich, nor were they very poor. There were some of them well-to-do, that is living comfortably on their little farms. For the most of them managed to grow enough potatoes for their families, which were their chief support. They grew enough oats to pay the rent and occasionally spared some to make a few hundred of oat-meal for the summer season when potatoes were getting short or old. In the summertime it was a very good diet to have stirabout and milk for breakfast; potatoes and milk and sometimes a few eggs and butter for dinner. But this was for the middle class and small farmers. A labouring man thought himself well off if he could have a noggin of buttermilk with some potatoes for his dinner and perhaps was well satisfied if he had a plateful of flummery for supper.

Now you can form an opinion of the diet we had at Knock. But first I must explain what a noggin is. It is not a naggin or quart of a pint, it is a quart measure made of wooden staves like a tub or pigin hooped with wood also, which every house in the parish took care to be supplied with, one for each of their family and one or two for strangers if they happened to drop in.

As for the butcher's meat it was a thing unknown to the poor class of the parish, and bacon was seldom to be had unless it was at the table of the well-to-do farmers, and they very sparingly supplied it to the labourer unless at Christmas and Easter Sunday. Tea was very rare, the country people never used it unless it was Christmas Eve or Christmas morning.

On the 10th November every householder tried to have a fat goose killed in honour of St. Martin. Many other customs and traditions were observed at Knock. After 1st November no blackberries were used on any account, for the Puckey travelled the country at night and it was dangerous to taste blackberries afterwards.

The *púca* and a great many other superstitions had long since disappeared from the parish, but the memory of the apparition, when Our Lady the Mother of God appeared in Knock, lived on as a light in the life of the people. On 21 August 1879, Our Lady, St Joseph and St John the Evangelist appeared at the south gable of the village church. Beside them was an altar on which stood a lamb facing the West, and behind the lamb a large cross. Angels hovered round the lamb and the whole scene was bathed in a heavenly light. There were fifteen official witnesses to the apparition, including men, women and children of various ages. Standing and kneeling in the pouring rain they watched the apparition for two hours, reciting the rosary all the while.

When I came to Knock Shrine I made a special study of apparitions and the attitude of the Church towards them. Up to that time I did not have a clear understanding of the canonical process which was carried out when an apparition occurs. In such cases canon law requires that the bishop must investigate the matter thoroughly to prevent any fraud or deception.

Six weeks after the apparition in Knock Dr John McHale set up a special commission to examine the witnesses and to explore all possible natural causes for the phenomenon. This commission examined fifteen witnesses and found their evidence "trustworthy and satisfactory"; it carried out exhaustive research into any possible natural causes and found none. Some months later, in March 1880, the commission reported to Dr McHale. At almost the same time an organised pilgrimage from Limerick, en route to Knock Shrine, called on Dr McHale also. The delegation included journalists travelling with the pilgrims and the newspapers carried a full account of this historic meeting:

"He blessed them and their families and friends and said, 'It is a great blessing for the poor people in the West that the Blessed Virgin, Mother of God, has appeared amongst them in their wretchedness and misery and suffering.'"

The archbishop's statement signalled his approval of the apparition. Having announced his decision, the account was subsequently carried in all the English and Irish newspapers and in the world press. As far as the Church is concerned Dr McHale's verdict was final in regard to the apparition and the recognition of Knock Shrine as a centre of Marian devotion. The recognition of any shrine, whether Lourdes or Fatima, Knock or La Salette, is based on a principle stated by the Congregation of Rites in 1877, when it was asked whether the Church recognised the apparitions at Lourdes and La Salette. The congregation replied: "Such apparitions are neither approved nor reproved or condemned by the Holy See: they are simply authorised as pious beliefs on purely human faith, according to the evidence which has been confirmed by suitable testimony." The canonical process in regard to apparitions was carried out at Knock in the greatest detail and Archbishop McHale's acceptance of the commission's report was the last word on the matter, just as Bishop Laurence's statement, read in the churches of his diocese, was the final step at Lourdes.

I was thrown in at the deep end at Knock. I started work in the parish in September, a very busy month for pilgrimages at the shrine. The going was tough for the rest of the pilgrimage season;

indeed, at the end of it I found that I had lost seven pounds in weight, though I was not worried as I had some to spare. Hard though it may have been, from the beginning I found work at the shrine very rewarding and fulfilling. This was especially true of time spent in the confessional and work for the sick and handicapped. Knock Shrine is a place where people bring all kinds of problems, spiritual, physical and temporal, and it gives the priest unlimited opportunities for exercising pastoral care and concern. You have the privilege of seeing God's healing hand touch the soul in a marvellous way in the tribunal of God's mercy, the sacrament of penance. You come to realise that there is no more intimate moment in God's relationship with man than when the penitent kneels before the priest in the confessional to be given pardon and forgiveness. I have always said that Knock's greatest miracles are miracles of grace and repentance in the soul. There is no other place on earth that I know where a priest comes into closer contact with invalids and the sick. All may not obtain miracles to heal the body, but there are always miracles of courage and strength to heal the soul. One learns very quickly that suffering does not mean unhappiness: the sick and the handicapped can be the happiest people that you will ever meet. They have learned to place themselves completely in God's hands, and only when one is fully resigned to God's will does peace and contentment reign in one's soul. "All for Thee, I am all thine; My Queen, My Mother, All I have is thine." When that motto is not merely on one's lips but in one's heart then nothing can upset the rhythm and tenor of life.

After a few months working at the shrine I came to the conclusion that in Knock one's faith and spiritual life cannot remain static. If one does not ascend to greater heights, then one may descend into mediocrity. If the atmosphere of prayer, penance and deep devotion at Knock Shrine does not inspire one, then there is nothing I know that can do so. I remember passing by a group of men who had just come on pilgrimage. As hundreds of pilgrims moved slowly round the Church of the Apparition the whole area resounded with the words, "Holy Mary, Mother of God". There were young and old, teenagers and children reciting the rosary; even the smallest child was saying his decades. One middle-aged man turned to his companions.

"Do you know," he said, "this is my first time in Knock, but I feel that Our Lady is here somewhere." He had sensed the extraordinary atmosphere of Knock Shrine. It is this atmosphere which grips the pilgrims so that even people who have been away from the practice of their religion for many years find themselves kneeling before a priest in the confessional, and having made their peace with God they come away with tears of joy in their eyes. The prayers, sacrifices and devotion of pilgrims down the years have made Knock Shrine a hallowed spot.

For all that it was holy, the grounds around the shrine were not without their black spots. One of the great environmental problems in Knock village down the years was the drab appearance, ugliness and unsightliness of the stalls which sprang up all about. The history of the stalls goes back to the apparition itself. When news of the apparition was spread abroad, not merely in Ireland but in other lands, thousands of pilgrims flocked to the village. The best transport system was the railroad – roads were very primitive and in bad condition – and pilgrims had to walk from the railway station to Knock or be transported by horse-drawn or donkey-drawn vehicles. You had carts, side-cars, traps and other vehicles pressed into service. In the press reports of pilgrimages of that time, crowds of up to 20,000 were mentioned on special feast-days of Our Lady.

All these pilgrims, the old, the feeble, the sick, had to be catered for at Knock and in those times a pilgrimage might take several days. Almost immediately stalls or shelters were built along the streets of the village and served as grocery shops. Outside each of the shops they built a round fireplace with a spit on top for boiling water and for cooking; the pilgrims bought their provisions in the stall and did their cooking on the fire. The stalls were constructed with boxes, galvanised iron sheets, asbestos and old doors; they were decorated with paints of all colours and looked garish, cheap and in bad taste. They suited people at that time as they were able to start a profitable business on a few pounds-worth of old timber and rubbish, but unfortunately the quality and standard of the stalls did not change much down the years.

With the introduction of motor-cars, bicycles, charabancs and buses the pattern of pilgrimages began to change. Pilgrims could now complete the pilgrimage in one day and there was less demand for food and groceries. As the demand for food decreased the stall-holders turned to the religious-goods trade. They began to sell beads, scapulars, prayer books, crucifixes and, in modern times, souvenirs. With the introduction of plastic goods the quality of religious objects and souvenirs reached an all-time low, but as the more profitable sale of religious goods increased so did the number of stalls. The landowners leased sites along the streets, reserving the best positions for themselves, and charged a rent of between £50 and £100 a year.

As the number of stalls multiplied the village became very ugly and unsightly. There was litter and mud everywhere. Newspaper correspondents reporting on pilgrimages described the village as a shanty-town. This situation continued until the 1970s when pilgrims began to tire of the stalls and as a result business declined. Some of the traders quit as there was little profit to be made, especially if the stall happened to be on a site too remote from the shrine.

From my experience as a priest in neighbouring parishes I had known of all the difficulties and problems at Knock. I had heard the stories from the priests stationed there and as well as the unsightliness of the village I knew that there had been difficulties over a right-of-way just in front of the shrine and that a law-suit had been taken against the Church authorities. Although judgement had been given in favour of the Church the situation was still very troublesome and awkward.

I did not have to wait long to come face to face with the problem. The week after my arrival I was coming from Bally-haunis in my car when I saw a pedestrian thumbing on the side of the road. I stopped and gave him a lift. He was a man in his sixties, medium sized, fairly stout. I took particular notice of his hat, a little green hat with a feather on the side of it. He told me that he was travelling to Knock. He knew me and asked me how I liked my new parish. "I like it very well," I said.

"Would you like it if people were fighting with you?" he asked.

"I am good at that too," I told him jokingly.

"Do you know who I am?" he asked me finally.

"I do not, but I would say from your conversation that you are Harry Byrne."

"The very man," said he.

Mr Byrne owned the property on the site proposed for the new church. Now, sitting beside me in the car, he asked me why the Church would not settle their differences with him. I told him that I did not know much about the problem but that I had heard it was due to his unreasonable demands. "What demands?" he said. I explained that I understood he would not make any settlement unless it included the old school site situated across the road from the shrine, which would be given to him in part exchange for his old property on the site which the Church wanted to develop. The Church authorities had decided that the old school could not be brought into any settlement for two reasons: the site was too near the shrine and any commercial venture there would be most inappropriate; it would take from the dignity of the shrine and destroy the peace and quiet necessary for prayer and devotion. The Church authorities did not doubt Harry Byrne's discretion in the use of the site, but if he disposed of it it could fall into the hands of unscrupulous speculators and the religious and devotional atmosphere of the shrine might then be destroyed. It might even become such an embarrassment that it could be used as an instrument of blackmail to extort an enormous sum to redeem the situation. It was decided that complete control would have to be retained over the site, no matter what the cost. In no circumstances could it be sold or exchanged in any deal.

I offered to mediate in the matter with the permission of the administrator and the archbishop. I got permission and had many meetings with Harry Byrne, his niece and her husband. I knew how difficult it would be, and on my way to his home I always went to the shrine to pray for help and guidance. The negotiations followed the pattern of similar efforts in the past. Whenever a settlement was in sight one or other party hesitated and all was lost. At one stage all of Harry Byrne's property was offered for £50,000 with no conditions attached. Unfortunately the offer was not taken up, and that was that: the negotiations were broken off, and when a new attempt was made the price was higher and the conditions more stringent. Finally I got a solicitor's letter telling me bluntly not to attempt any further negotiations unless the Church authorities were willing to concede the old school site, the bone of contention. That sounded the death-knell for the negotiations and I made no further effort as a curate to resolve the situation.

As a curate I had no responsibility for the condition of the village or stalls, and I had acted only as a mediator in the negotiations on the site for a new church, but on becoming parish priest in 1967 I was determined to do something to improve the situation. I contacted the Mayo County Council and arranged a meeting with the county engineer. I suggested that the walls and ditches in the village should be rebuilt or repaired – they were in a broken-down, dilapidated condition and looked very ugly and neglected – but the county engineer felt that nothing should be done until a comprehensive plan was prepared for the village as a whole. That seemed an excellent idea to me.

The firm of Boyle & Delaney, Dublin, was appointed in 1969 and were soon surveying the village and formulating ideas. They decided that Knock would be improved by building a new road to take traffic around rather than into the village, and that the stalls should be relocated on a prepared site. When they had published their plans three meetings of the Mayo County Council were held in Knock to consider them. At the first meeting the consultants presented a plan showing the proposed by-pass running on the east side of the village. This was not acceptable to the local people, so it was decided that another plan should be drawn up showing a by-pass on both sides of the village. It was felt that this would help the local people to decide what they really wanted, but by the next meeting they had changed their minds: now they did not want the road on the west side as it would cut through their lands. The stall-holders for their part were unwilling to move off the public road to a site where they could rent shops erected by the county council.

Our target date for finishing the job in the village was 1978, as the centenary of the apparition would be celebrated in 1979. In the meantime several meetings of stall-owners were held but these were disrupted by people who did not want change and always ended in pandemonium. Some stall-holders were making a good living as things stood and were quite happy to keep it that way. As well as that, every so often a big splash would appear in the newspapers reporting a £1m face-lift for Knock. These announcements were completely without foundation but gave the stall-holders the impression that there might eventually be big compensation for moving, if they held out long enough. Overnight, stalls that had been closed for years opened up again to qualify for compensation. The county manager, Mr Michael O'Malley, called several meetings and tried to reason with stall-holders, but without success.

The problem, it seemed to me, was that the council was negotiating with both landlords and tenants – those who leased sites for stalls – at the same time. I pointed out that it would be impossible to talk to both groups together when the interests of each party were directly opposed. After a lot of futile effort the county council got the message and decided to deal solely with landlords and let them in turn deal with their tenants. This method proved to be successful, though only after years of negotiation and hard bargaining. The landlords had a lot of difficulty persuading their tenants to vacate the sites; in the case of one landlord the problem went to the High Court. The landlord was successful but was burdened with three-quarters of the legal costs. The case was then appealed to the Supreme Court, but a month before the hearing the tenants decided that enough was enough and voluntarily removed the stalls.

Michael O'Malley, who had been appointed county manager to Mayo in 1967, was an administrator of the highest calibre; able, personable, trustworthy and with a persuasive manner, he undertook to negotiate with each landlord individually and I agreed to help him. I had a difficult role to play in this project. I knew that the people did not like change as they were genuinely afraid of what it might bring; they knew that I was a strong advocate of change and were fearful of what I might do. I was convinced that our progress would be to the advantage of all, including the stall-holders, and my job was to encourage and persuade them to this view. I had to persuade them that there would be better business in better buildings. To do so I had to win their confidence and I found that difficult but, thank God, I succeeded. In particular I had to prove my sincerity and concern for their welfare by getting them as much compensation as possible from the government.

We started with a person who was responsible for many private stalls and had a great many tenant stall-holders as well. After a number of visits we finally settled with him for approximately the sum of money it would cost to construct buildings to replace the stalls. That was the breakthrough we needed. Work began on the construction of the new buildings and they looked very impressive. Gradually all the others saw the wisdom of what had been done, and in two years the problem of the stalls was solved. The tenants were accommodated nearer to the shrine than formerly and adjacent to the pathway leading from the principal bus-park. After a slow start they are doing as well now as they did previously, if not better. At least, I do not hear many complaints; all is well that ends well!

It was difficult to persuade the state to provide the necessary funds to meet the costs of renovating roads and footpaths through the village, but with much patience and perseverance in lobbying ministers we succeeded. I was very pleased as I had previously thought that that difficulty would never be overcome. It was late in the day when this happened and there was now a great rush to finish the project for the centenary celebrations in 1979.

Most Rev. Dr Joseph Cunnane had been appointed Archbishop of Tuam by Pope Paul VI in February 1969, and was ordained a bishop the following month. He succeeded Most Rev. Dr Joseph Walsh, who had retired. While the question of a new church for Knock had been discussed with Dr Walsh, no action had been taken. However, the new man was a native of Coogue in the parish of Knock and Knock Shrine and its problems were well known to him. He had always shown a great interest in the parish; as a young priest he had done duty for Very Rev. John Canon Grealy in his last years as parish priest of Knock, and his appointment was a great boost for Knock and Our Lady's Shrine.

His first Confirmation in the archdiocese was held in Knock. We held a special reception for him: he was met on his entrance to the parish at Ballyhowley Bridge by a special welcoming delegation and a cavalcade of cars took him to Knock church where an address of welcome was presented by me as parish priest. It was a happy, joyous occasion for the priests and people of Knock parish, and a most auspicious day for the shrine and its surrounds. I remember his words on the first occasion that we discussed the shrine. "It is quite obvious to me," he said, "that if we are to continue to encourage pilgrimages, we must provide the necessary facilities at the shrine. It is an absolute priority to provide shelter for pilgrims and especially the sick and invalids in inclement weather."

I myself had realised, after only a few days at Knock, that the grounds and amenities were entirely inadequate. Buildings were needed where the hundreds of invalids who came on Sundays and Thursdays could be sheltered and given the necessary amenities and medical care. I always felt uncomfortable when I saw them exposed to wind and rain during the open-air Mass; it was particularly heart-rending to witness people on stretchers or in wheelchairs exposed to the vagaries of the Irish weather. I discussed the problem with Archbishop Cunnane and we both agreed that if we were to continue to cater for pilgrimages we would have to provide proper shelter and facilities for both pilgrims and invalids.

However, we had not been able to acquire the land we needed to site the necessary buildings and create processional grounds in the vicinity of the shrine. The best site for a new church or basilica was on Harry Byrne's property; that site would then determine the location of other buildings. It was also quite clear that we had to eliminate the right-of-way in front of the shrine, and to do so it would be necessary to purchase the complete holding, public-house and other buildings of Harry Byrne. Many efforts had been made by myself and other administrators of the shrine to negotiate the purchase and they had all failed. With every failure the problem became more and more difficult to resolve.

There was just one other possibility of developing the shrine grounds, and I decided to try it. Harry Byrne's property was to the east and would be ideal for the church and other development but the Church also had property to the south and that could act as our second choice. With this in mind I succeeded in buying extra land to the south which gave sufficient room for the proposed development. On my suggestion the archbishop made a decision to site the church to the south, on Calvary Hill overlooking the shrine. There was only a narrow strip of ground connecting this site with the shrine so I tried to purchase some of the adjacent property, but this attempt foundered.

Nonetheless we went ahead with our plans to build a large church on the hill to the south. We put our heads together, discussing what kind of a church was needed, how big it should be, and looking at all the financial and technical aspects. The budget would have to be moderate and the church would have to be well planned, but most of all we wanted a plain and simple building. In 1970 building churches, especially large churches, was not popular with the media and the liberal factions in our country, though I must say that our purpose was fully appreciated by the public. To emphasise the necessity of such a church for the protection and shelter of pilgrims, and especially the sick and the old, we called the proposed building the Church Shelter.

One day an architect, Mr Louis Brennan, called on me on his way to Castlebar to meet the county engineer in connection with the plan for the development of Knock village. I told him of my problem about the planning of the new church and he asked me to put on tape my thoughts and ideas on what was needed. Later, armed with a tape-recorder, I spoke for four hours concerning the liturgy of pilgrimage, the number of pilgrims, sick and handicapped to be accommodated; I dealt with all aspects of pilgrimages such as the position and size of car-parks, approach roads and plans for easy access to the shrine without entering the village. I tried to give an accurate picture of the various ceremonies that would likely be held in the new church. I discussed processions, devotions, Mass, the blessing and anointing of the sick. I mentioned vigils, retreats, prayer meetings and other functions. This brief was very helpful to the architect in planning the kind of church that was necessary.

It was clear that there was no way we could build a church that could accommodate the huge attendance that would be present on special occasions, when the number could be as high as thirty, forty, or fifty thousand. We decided instead to cater for the average congregation that was likely to attend on an ordinary Sunday or weekday. Our aim was to cater for 10,000, the majority standing and a smaller number seated. With the erection of an ambulatory around the church, where people could hear and see Mass, an extra 5,000 could be accommodated. We wanted also to provide shelter for pilgrims and especially for the sick, to take them in out of the rain on a wet day and provide shade and protection from the sun when it was hot. The ambulatory would also be useful for processions on wet days when they could not be held outdoors. The new church could be used for the later Masses on Sundays also, when the Church of the Apparition was not big enough to accommodate all the faithful.

Mr Louis Brennan went back to his office and after studying the facts and figures which I had given him offered to do a project analysis for us. An important part of his brief was to keep the cost of the building to a minimum: in fact the most daunting part of the operation was the raising of sufficient funds for such a huge undertaking. When I had discussed the plan with Louis Brennan I told him that I had visited a church in the Catskill mountains in New York State, the Church of the Martyrs, built in honour of Indian converts and children who had been martyred for the faith. The building was completely circular and had numerous doors on the perimeter wall, the altar was raised to a height of ten feet and was situated in the centre of the church while the seats were arranged all round in amphitheatre style.

The circular design had helped to keep the cost down as a circular building can accommodate people at a lower rate per head than any other shape. I told him that the Church of the Martyrs was run by the Jesuits and he offered to contact them for plans and specifications.

In a matter of months he had produced the project analysis which was a wonderful help and guide in producing the final plan for the Church of Our Lady Queen of Ireland. It gave us a general idea of what we were seeking and what was feasible, both economically and structurally. Subsequently many general features were changed and the design of many others improved, but Louis Brennan's work deserved all our congratulations. However, the archbishop wished to consult the Diocesan Chapter before making any final decision and some members of the Chapter, including Dr J.G. McGarry, made the mistake of looking at the analysis as the final draft plan of the new church and thought that the building "might look a bit drab". This meeting of the Chapter was held in the first days of August 1970, and the archbishop subsequently informed the architects that "in those circumstances he could not confirm their appointment".

The Chapter then discussed the possibility of organising a design competition amongst architects and Dr J.G. McGarry and I were deputed to contact the Architects Association for advice on the matter. We met with representatives in Dublin and discovered there would be many snags in such a move. Another meeting of the Diocesan Chapter was held, but the result was inconclusive; indeed some members were proposing their own choice of architect which made matters even more difficult. The Chapter was still worried that the church might look drab, so I was asked to write to the architects to that effect, which I did. Finally at a meeting on 25 February 1971 between the architects on one side and the archbishop, Dr McGarry, John Cunnane, Fr Michael Walsh and myself on the other, the architects, with Dáithí P. Hanley as consultant, put forward new proposals and alterations in the project analysis. The new proposals were acceptable to the meeting and everybody seemed happy, so Mr Louis J. Brennan and Associates together with Dáithí P. Hanley were appointed as architects to draw up plans for the new church. They began work and over the following year held many meetings with the Knock team, arriving at a final plan in 1972.

The site for the new church was still to be the Knock Shrine

Calvary, the hill to the south overlooking the shrine. When the architects and engineers moved in and began to survey the site the news spread rapidly through the village and came to the ears of Harry Byrne, who suddenly realised that his land would no longer be essential for shrine development. There was a danger that he would now lose the sale of the property and it was certain, too, that its market-value would fall considerably. In his dilemma, Harry Byrne sent me word that he would like to negotiate on the sale of his farm and buildings. As a curate I had bargained with him previously on behalf of the archbishop and the administrator, but when I had almost had the deal completed it became stuck once more on the question of the old school site. I did not wish to get into such a situation again, so I sent him a reply suggesting that our solicitors could now negotiate the deal and when all the details were fixed we would meet and sign the agreement. The solicitors set about arranging all the details and conditions in regard to the property, and the only clause not settled concerned the actual price.

We decided to meet in his solicitor's office on 7 February 1972, at twelve noon. In the meantime I had a discussion with my archbishop to arrange the parameters of the agreement. We met at the appointed time. Harry Byrne, his niece and Mr John O'Dwyer, solicitor, were on one side; Thomas Dillon Leech, Fr Michael Walsh, the archbishop's secretary, and I on the other. The discussions began and, unfortunately, many difficulties arose in regard to matters already agreed on by our respective solicitors. We had to start from scratch and the bargaining continued all day and up until midnight. By then everything had been agreed but the price. There was a difference of £5,000 between us and Mr Byrne's solicitor suggested that we divide it. I agreed, but Harry Byrne could not decide without consulting relatives in London. They rejected the compromise.

When the solicitors reported this to me I indicated that I would give the amount sought provided that the documents were drawn up and duly signed that night – otherwise there would be a danger of the deal being called off next morning and we would have to start all over again. The solicitors set their typists to work on the documents. They were completed at about 2 a.m. and signed by both parties.

Some months later Harry Byrne died suddenly. His heiress and executor was reluctant to take out letters of administration and until she did the contract with Harry Byrne could not be completed in law. We offered her St Joseph's dwelling-house to encourage her to take the necessary steps to carry out the contract. At last she decided to do so and gave us possession of the land on 9 July 1973. Work on the church was started in October on the site where we had wanted to build it from the start.

From the moment we decided to build a new church, big enough to house invalids and pilgrims, we were determined to avoid any mistakes or miscalculations. First of all, if we were to succeed in our plans, we would have to get the largest and best possible building at the minimum cost. Our Lord's admonition, as given in the Gospel of St Luke (14: 28-30) was always in my mind: "For which of you having a mind to build a tower, doth not first sit down and reckon the charges that are necessary, whether we have the wherewithal to finish it, lest, after he had laid the foundation, and is not able to finish it, all that see it begin to mock him, saying; 'This man began to build and was not able to finish it.'"

People tell me that I was never a man to shy away from an important decision because of public opinion. Nevertheless, we called the new church a "church shelter" because at the time it was not popular in Ireland to be seen building a church. Critics were fond of pointing out that Our Lord had spoken to people in the fields and in the countryside, and were quite happy to ignore the difference in the weather as between Palestine and Ireland. In any case Our Lord also addressed his people in synagogues up and down the country. But at times it may be more sensible to duck to avoid unnecessary "flak". Later on we did call it the Church of Our Lady Queen of Ireland, and later still, with the grace of God and the blessing of the Church, the Basilica of Our Lady Queen of Ireland. This title was publicly announced by the Holy Father after he said Mass at the shrine.

Our aim was to build a church, beautiful in its design and utility and with no ornamentation whatsoever. I think that we achieved our goal; certainly all pilgrims speak of the church as very beautiful . With ordinary materials – steel, cement, timber and glass – a church of great beauty was created. Our long-term objective was to decorate and embellish it when God might send the wherewithal, and in the years since the church was first opened we have made very modest progress. A little bit of paint has worked miracles in its appearance and decor. Praised be Jesus Christ!

There are many features in the design of the church which adds much beauty at very little cost. I always felt that good landscaping would give much to its external appearance. Together with some others I paid great attention to every detail of the landscaping and the laying of lawns, and the soft beauty of the landscaping takes the stranger's eye off the very ordinary concrete and steel structure.

An ambulatory was added later for processions and to give extra shelter, especially in bad weather. The roof of the ambulatory sat on cement pillars which ran all around the church and it was decided that they should be faced with masonry to make them more distinctive. For the pillars in front of the basilica we were fortunate to procure some beautiful granite from a quarry in Belmullet; we then had thirty-two pillars left, so we decided that we should get some stone from a quarry in each of the thirty-two counties. This we did. They gave the basilica a national dimension and we had the name of each county inscribed on a plaque above the pillar.

If I would boast about anything in the basilica I would boast about its centre-piece, the altar. The table of the altar is of grey Wicklow granite, with exquisite design beautifully executed. There is another feature of the altar that I like very much. The surround is done in masonry as are the pillars in the ambulatory: introducing the outdoor feature into the church gives the whole edifice a great sense of unity. The church masonry consists of a beautiful contrast in pattern between red and grey granite.*

We felt that the interior of the church needed some feature that would give it an ecclesiastical appearance, and decided that this might be done by installing a replica of a mediaeval church window in each of the four radiating walls between the five chapels of the basilica. Again we gave the Church of Our Lady Queen of Ireland a national dimension by taking the replica of a mediaeval church window from each of the four provinces. To represent Munster is a full-size replica of the famous east window of Holy Cross Abbey, Co. Tipperary; this window was constructed sometime between 1450 and 1475. To represent Connaught is a replica of the great east window from the Augustian Priory of St Mary in Clontuskery, near Ballinasloe, which dates from the

---

This masonry work was carried out by the monsignor's brother Pat, and Pat's son Jimmy

twelfth century. Ulster is represented in the original fifteenth-century window from the Church of St Mary's Abbey on Devenish Island. Leinster gave a window from Kilkenny's Black Abbey, founded in 1225, and one of the few churches in Ireland in which the celebration of Mass was never interrupted during all its troubled history.

Another beautiful feature of the basilica is a tapestry designed by Ray Carroll and handwoven by Donegal Carpets. It portrays the apparition as described by the witnesses, framed by beautiful vertical hardwood panelling which is an extension of the panelling style of the sanctuary.

The little Blessed Sacrament chapel is situated on the ground floor of the tower and contains a tabernacle large enough to hold up to sixty ciboria for use in distributing Holy Communion to tens of thousands of people. The two sides of the tabernacle are veiled and the central doors beautifully decorated with a representation of the altar, the lamb and the cross as portrayed in the apparition, carried out in a beautiful design of brass and coloured enamel. Dáithí P. Hanley, who designed the gates leading to the Blessed Sacrament Chapel, explains that their design represents the Veil of the Old Temple of Jerusalem.

As this was the new church of Our Lady we felt it would be nice to have Mary's rosary represented on the outer walls, and we did this by putting in a number of small circular glass openings or rosettes near the top of the main walls of the building. The Our Father and Hail Mary are represented by larger rosettes, the rosary cross is made up of rectangular shapes. All are pointing upwards and in line with the lighting ducts so that the daylight comes pouring through the coloured glass. There is one rosary on the outer walls of each of the five chapels, and when the sun shines on a fine day they light up and sparkle and are very beautiful.

A peculiar feature of the front wall of the tower is that it contains the outdoor altar which was meant to cater for pilgrims in fine weather. Over the curved copper roof of this sanctuary is a golden crown. Its design is based in part on a crown from the Petrie collection in the National Museum which is believed to be of Irish origin and corresponds to crowns mentioned in Irish legends, going back to King Cormac, grandson of Conn of the Hundred Battles. Our Lady was crowned when she appeared in the apparition, and so it is only right that she should have an Irish crown in her church in Knock.

There are three features which are much admired by all the pilgrims. We take pride in the foundation stone of the basilica which was blessed by Pope Paul VI on the feast of St Jarlath, 6 June 1974. Proudly displayed on the front wall of the basilica is the Papal coat of arms. Inside the church there are two beautiful mosaics representing St Peter and St Paul; these were given as a gift by the Holy Father during his historic trip to Ireland in September-October 1979. Every time we look at these mosaics and the Papal coat of arms, we remember that wonderful day when our Holy Father, Pope John Paul II, visited Knock Shrine.

THE POPE'S VISIT TO KNOCK

MANY PILGRIMS ASK who brought the Pope to Knock for the centenary celebration. How was the visit arranged? Who invited him?

Ever since Pope Paul VI visited Fatima in 1967 there was talk in Knock of inviting the Holy Father to the Knock Shrine centenary celebrations. If Pope Paul VI visited Fatima for the fiftieth anniversary of the Fatima apparition, then why not Knock Shrine for its centenary? When the question was raised people would say: "Why not? Why shouldn't the Holy Father visit Ireland?"

I was convinced that the Holy Father would one day come to Knock and Ireland. The apparition at Knock took place in a year of misery, hardship and hunger for the poor Catholics of Ireland, and Our Lady came to tell them that they should not lose heart and that she was praying for them before the throne of God. It was a heavenly vision that reminded Mary's Irish children that all the saints were praying for them, including St Joseph and St John. Irish Catholics had come through a gruelling time during the Penal Days, when the Mass was outlawed and there was a price on the priest's head, and the altar, the lamb and the cross reminded them that the Mass had served them well in the days of persecution. Ireland was ever staunch in the faith and ever loyal to the Vicar of Christ in Rome.

I attended a meeting of the Knock Shrine Society Council in 1976 and acted as chairman. I was astounded when I looked at the agenda. There before me were four astonishing items:

1. Invitation of the Holy Father for the centenary celebrations.
2. Petition to the Holy Father to present a Golden Rose.
3. Elevation of the Church of Our Lady Queen of Ireland to the status of basilica.
4. Special indulgence for the centenary year.

It was an historic agenda; indeed you might call it prophetic. I had no idea that the first three would ever be realised – at that stage I could only hope that an apostolic delegate would be appointed to represent the Holy Father at the celebrations.

However, I often discussed the possibility with my archbishop,

Dr Joseph Cunnane, and we were both convinced that the Pope should at least be invited.

A number of Irish bishops were due to make their quinquennial visit to Rome in October 1977. A "quinquennial visit" is a visit every five years, when the bishop makes a report to Rome on the spiritual state of his diocese. The archbishop asked me to join him on the journey so that we could explore the possibility of a Papal visit for the Knock Shrine centenary. At the Vatican the bishops went in a group for their audience with Pope Paul VI. They talked about Ireland and of his trip to Ireland when he was a secretary to a foreign nunciature. During a lull in the conversation one of the bishops said: "Your Holiness, they are building a new road into Knock hoping that your Holiness will join them in celebrating the centenary of Our Lady's Shrine."

"Why not?" he said, and asked his secretary to write it down just in case his successor might need it. He was very old and feeble and we had little hope that he would honour the shrine by appointing a legate to represent him. During the following year there were constant reports from pilgrims to Rome that he was growing weaker day by day.

Pope Paul VI died in August 1978. His successor, Pope John Paul I, was appointed in September. He was an Italian, Cardinal Albino Luciani. On his appointment we were hopeful that he would honour Ireland and Knock Shrine with a visit, and we grew more optimistic when we heard that Monsignor John Magee was his private secretary. But we had hardly had time to estimate our chances of a visit when, one morning, I heard on radio the brief announcement that the new Pope had died. It was such a shock. God called him just one month after his election to the highest office in the church, successor of St Peter and Vicar of Christ on earth. After the obsequies had taken place in St Peter's and the trauma of his sudden death had been overcome, speculation at the appointment of a new Pope started.

"Man proposes and God disposes" is an old saying. On Sunday, 15 October, the conclave began; the cardinals of the world gathered to choose a successor to Pope John Paul I. At the end of the second day of their deliberations at 6.18 p.m. the white smoke ascended from the chimney of the Sistine Chapel into the clear Roman sky. There was feverish excitement as everybody tried to get as near as possible to the central balcony overlooking St Peter's Square. There was applause and expectation and tension as the lights went on in the great hall. The window above the balcony opened slowly and Cardinal Pericle Felici stepped forward. "I announce to you a great joy. *Habemus Papam*: We have a Pope." The crowd roared with relief and approval, then lapsed into expectant silence. Now came the first hint of something sensational – the name Carolum Wojtyla. The strange unpronounceable name took the crowd's breath away and changed the face of the Papacy for the first time in 455 years. "Carolum Wojtyla? Who is he?" the crowd murmured. They looked at the photographs and the names of the cardinals in the *Osservatore Romano*. "Here he is. He is Polish." The cardinals had chosen the first Polish Pope in the history of the church, the first from Eastern Europe and certainly the first from a nation under communist rule. Cardinal Karol Wojtyla of Krakow, Pope John Paul II.

There was rejoicing in Knock when we heard that the new Pope was Polish. We knew that there had always been a great affinity between Poland and Ireland: both were old and staunch Catholic countries and both suffered for the faith; both had been weighed down for centuries by a heavy yoke of foreign domination and oppression. I knew that Pope John Paul II would respond well to the argument that I had been using in support of a Papal Visit to Ireland. Whenever I was asked the question, "Will the Holy Father come to Knock for the centenary?" I always replied, "Why not? After all, Ireland is one of the oldest Catholic countries in Europe. Ireland clung to the faith in spite of 'dungeon, fire and sword'. Ireland has always been loyal and true to the Pope, Christ's representative on earth."

Early in 1978 I had discussed with my archbishop the protocol involved in issuing an invitation to the Holy Father. The archbishop wrote to the Papal Nuncio, Most Rev. Dr Alibrandi, who replied that the invitation would have to come from the episcopal conference in Maynooth. I remember calling on the archbishop the morning he was leaving Tuam to attend the conference. He was confident that he would have its unanimous approval to invite the Holy Father. The decision was indeed unanimous, and the archbishop was commissioned to draft the invitation and send it to Rome. He gave me a copy which I still treasure. The most important part read:

"By unanimous decision of our Episcopal Conference, we humbly and most respectfully invite Your Holiness to visit Ireland during the year 1979, and lead us in celebrating the Centenary of the Shrine of Our Lady, Queen of Ireland, at Knock."

The invitation was dispatched to Rome in early December and we had high hopes of a good response. Our confidence grew further when we heard that an Irish bishop visited Rome for the whole month of January 1979 – rumour had it that he was briefing the Holy Father on conditions in Ireland and helping to pick the themes for his homilies at the different venues he was to visit. In March and April our morale was still strong but we were disappointed that no definite indication had yet been given by Rome. But early in May Dr Cunnane got some hint that the dates would be 29 and 30 September and 1 October. We got the Sisters in St Mary's Hostel to cancel all bookings for these dates so that the Papal entourage could be accommodated for meals, or even for an overnight stay.

Alas, in May the outlook turned more gloomy. Early in May I visited London to attend a press conference hosted by the Irish Heritage Musical Society which was launching a new recording on the pilgrimage to Knock Shrine. I was introduced to the apostolic delegate to Great Britain, Most Rev. Dr Bruno Heim. I chatted with him and then passed on to meet some journalists. One of the journalists asked me about the possibility of a Papal visit to Knock and I replied that I was very optimistic. Immediately the apostolate delegate, who was some distance away, turned round and said loudly: "It is impossible! The Holy Father cannot be going everywhere!"

Early in June I was invited by Bord Fáilte to visit New York and attend a press conference there. Bord Fáilte wanted to announce the ending of a long and paralysing Post Office strike and also the easing of a petrol shortage due to conflict in the Middle East. On my way to Shannon I called the archbishop who told me that he expected good news in about a week and that he would contact me in New York. In the USA I got in touch with three cardinals. I met Cardinal Cooke of New York, where I offered Mass in St Patrick's Cathedral each morning, but he could not give me any indication of the Pope's intentions. I had a half-hour's conversation with Cardinal Krole of Philadelphia and asked him what where the chances but he merely said that the Holy Father was very tired, in fact exhausted after his visit to Poland. That was not encouraging. I visited Cardinal Madeiros in Boston and had a long conversation with him; he was an old friend who had led pilgrimages to Knock Shrine in 1978. But when my visit to the USA had finished I returned to Ireland towards the end of June feeling somewhat disappointed.

June passed and with it our hopes of a Papal visit. As July came our hopes receded further: there would be no time now to prepare for the visit. Then, in the middle of July, the archbishop told me that the Papal visit would be announced in a week. Sure enough, on 21 July as I was travelling by car from Claremorris I heard His Eminence Cardinal Ó Fiaich making the announcement at a press conference:

"The Holy Father visits Ireland this year as a pilgrim to the Shrine of Our Lady of Knock. It is hoped that the time available to His Holiness will also permit him to visit a number of other Irish centres, so that the great number of Irish people who will undoubtedly wish to join the Holy Father in prayer will be facilitated. We know, for instance, of his special love for the young and of his concern for an increase in religious vocations."

It seems fairly certain now that the doubt and hesitation of previous months was caused by the political situation, especially in Northern Ireland. It seems that it was a difficult decision owing to the question of security, in particular the security problem that would be created by a visit to Armagh or, on the other hand, the embarrassment that would be created by not being able to visit Ireland's spiritual capital. That difficulty was eventually resolved by the Pope visiting Drogheda in the Archdiocese of Armagh, and it was at Drogheda that the Holy Father appealed on bended knees for peace and reconciliation in our land.

All through the year the mood of the people had alternated between high hopes and bitter disappointment; now there was jubilation and great joy throughout the country, the happiness and pride of the people everywhere evident. The celebration of the news was not confined to Catholics but to all religious denominations without distinction. There were some irreverent and disrespectful noises from familiar sources in the North – these were not unexpected. In the rest of the country the newspapers and magazines carried the story under banner headlines and television and radio had almost daily programmes dealing with all aspects of the forthcoming visit. All parts of the country vied with one another in staking a claim to the Holy Father but only one venue was certain – Knock Shrine. Knock was besieged by journalists and radio and television crews from all over the world. I had the responsibility of acting as PRO and it occupied a lot of my time each day, but I was well organised and got wonderful help from the typists and secretaries in the shrine office. The spirit of enthusiasm and dedication amongst my staff, both priests and lay people, was exhilarating and it was only a sample of the spirit which existed throughout the country. I heard it said that if only the enthusiasm and co-operation which was displayed at that time could be continued, then we would have a prosperous and happy country.

In the wake of the "tidings of great joy" to all the Irish people the hierarchy set up an organisation to prepare for the Papal visit. There was a special national committee established in Dublin to co-ordinate the preparations at all the venues; it consisted of Most Rev. Dr Edward Daly of Derry, an official from the Department of Posts and Telegraphs, and Mr Jim Cantwell, Director of the Catholic Press Office. Each venue formed its own individual committee to prepare for the Pope's arrival and the Papal Mass which was to be the highlight of the celebration. The biggest problem was the erection of a suitable Papal altar. The Irish weather can at the best of time be very fickle and unpredictable so the Holy Father, the other concelebrants and the choir had to be protected from the possibility of rain. The altar itself would have to be made safe and secure and that meant the use of steel which proved very costly. In our case we gave the construction of the altar to a contractor who guaranteed to have it ready before the day of the visit. All other construction work, such as press galleries, television platforms and radio studios were to be left to local teams. At the request of the archbishop and myself RTE very kindly showed us a videotape of the Papal visits to Poland and Mexico. In Poland they used an altar surmounted by a very high cross and immediately the thought struck me that it would be a great idea to construct a similar cross for our altar and keep it as a memento of the Papal visit. I suggested this to the contractor and he was delighted with the idea. He erected the cross on the site and built the altar around it.

In Knock we formed various sub-committees and gave each a specific job to do. They included the catering committee; the committee in charge of the sick and handicapped; liturgical committee; committee in charge of traffic-control; committee to keep order in grounds; communications committee; security committee and others. This committee system had many deficiencies and, in my view, did not function as efficiently as expected. It involved too many long hours of debates that were wearisome and exhausting, and this precious time might have been more wisely spent working on the ground. In the end we found that we had a lot of talk and little action. The various members wasted much time in airing their pet theories on all aspects of the operation and there was such repetition in the speeches made at each committee session. This pattern continued for meeting after meeting and there was little or no progress. Many decisions that were made proved impractical and were never implemented.

I remember the subject of traffic-control being debated day after day for weeks, and all the time the decision agreed today would be changed tomorrow. After the marathon debate it was decided, on the principle of "first come first served", that the first cars to arrive would be parked within a reasonable distance of Knock; the late arrivals would be catered for in parks more distant from the village as the parks nearer town were gradually being filled. Alas, all that was changed on the morning of the big day. The first cars were parked in Claremorris and in parks on the far side of the town, with the result that all the car-parks in the vicinity of Knock remained empty. This had disastrous consequences later in the day when, at the conclusion of the ceremonies, thousands and thousands of people got on the road to walk the seven miles to Claremorris, so that no vehicles at all could move until this great mass of people had reached its destination. There were special buses carrying foreign prelates and bishops back to Dublin and it took them five hours to reach Claremorris owing to the vast crowds on the road. It was an unfortunate decision and I have never discovered who made it. If I had to plan the operation again, I would choose one good sound person to replace each committee – such a person would do a better job and save time and energy. But of course it is always easy to be wise after the event.

Generally speaking, however, all our plans worked well. There were tense moments. We had a bomb-scare, when somebody sent a bogus telephone message that there was a bomb hidden in a wheelchair. The wheelchairs at the shrine had to be searched with a lot of inconvenience and hardship to the invalids. What warped twisted mind thought up that hoax? Another crisis arose when the security personnel forgot to open toilet buildings and cabins. They had been closed and locked during the night for security reasons, and now all the locks had to be broken in the early hours of the morning. It was an expensive error but not disastrous. Nonetheless the Gardaí, security men and army did a magnificent job and the public relations work carried out by them and the shrine authorities was excellent. Security was very tight owing to the disturbed state of the country – Lord Mountbatten had been assassinated in August and there were fears of retaliation owing to the close relationship of Mountbatten to the royal family. There was a very tight security area at the back of the Papal altar and all around the basilica and shrine buildings. This area was reserved for bishops, priests, journalists and media personnel, and that rule was stringently applied. Notwithstanding all the fuss about the location of the press centre in Knock – a lot of unpleasantness and annoyance had been caused when a decision was made in Dublin to site the press centre in Claremorris – the journalists and media personnel assured us that we had the best press centre in Ireland. And in the end of all the Papal reception and the ceremonies themselves were carried out without a hitch and with great dignity.

On the morning of Saturday, 29 September, the sun shone gloriously on Dublin Airport as if to give a worthy welcome to Pope John Paul II on his first visit to Ireland. The great green bird, an Aer Lingus Boeing 747, circled the airport and then alighted gracefully on the tarmac. Every nook and cranny at the airport was filled with people and the place was alive with a thrilling air of expectancy. The plane at last came to a halt and after some moments the ramps were put in place and the doors opened. There was a huge roar from the crowd as the white figure appeared. Slowly he descended, with the white cape blowing over his head, shoulders and face. He reached the ground and then going on bended knees he stretched out at full length and kissed the ancient sod of Ireland. At that moment I wondered had St Patrick himself kissed the Irish soil before he lit the paschal fire on the Hill of Slane. The Holy Father remembered Patrick's coming when he said in his homily in Dublin: "Like St Patrick I too have heard the voice of the Irish calling me, so I have come to you, to all of you in Ireland."

As he moved away from the plane there came into view the serried ranks of all kinds of uniforms, from the purple of the bishops to the more sombre uniforms of priests, military personnel and Gardaí. I watched him as he moved along among the various ranks of VIPs, clasping their hands, chatting, smiling and looking like a real *sagart arún*. Finally, as he moved amongst the lay people he saw a little child and took him in his arms, as Christ himself would have done. During those intense moments of deep love and emotion the Holy Father won the hearts of millions of people who watched him on television all over the globe. That first encounter in Dublin set the pattern for every other venue.

The Holy Father had three hectic days ahead of him – he must be a man of tremendous physical strength and sound constitution. From the airport he went to the nunciature and from there to the Phoenix Park where he was greeted by over a million people. The proceedings were televised to a viewing public of more than 500 million. As I watched on television the thing that amazed me was his command of English. Every word came out loud and clear and was easily understood by all – he almost had an Irish brogue! As at all venues he lingered among the crowd, finding it hard to drag himself away. He loved people! His heart went out to the sick and the handicapped. As he moved amongst the throng you could see Christ in this man. In his homily he reviewed the history of Irish Catholicism down through the centuries. Like an expert historian he moved from Paladius to St Patrick to the Irish monks of the fifth and seventh centuries, to the evangelisation of Europe in the Dark Ages and on to Irish missionary activity in modern times. It was obvious that he loved Ireland and the Irish people, while people of all denominations and creeds in the audience fell in love with this man of God.

Again on to his helicopter and he was heading for Drogheda and the premier archdiocese of Armagh. Here he would deliver his most important sermon, imploring on bended knees the rejection of violence and a return to the ways of peace:

"Now I wish to speak to all men and women engaged in violence. I appeal to you in language of passionate pleading. On my knees I beg you to turn away from the paths of violence and to return to the ways of peace."

This was one of the objectives of his visit that was dearest to his heart, the opportunity to make his appeal to the Irish people at close quarters. It is now one of the greatest disappointments of the Papal visit that this appeal has so far remained unheeded, but please God it is still ringing in the ears of the people concerned and maybe, some day, it will bear fruit.

For weeks beforehand we had a lot of people, clerical and lay, working at the shrine and as Knock's day came nearer they became very tense. That was not surprising as the visit of the Holy Father was such an historic event. I felt that everyone was watching me to see how I would stand up to the great tension and emotion that permeated all of Knock. In my own mind, at least, I seemed to be quite cool and had no nerves whatsoever.

The eve of the great day arrived and brought with it an air of expectancy, exhilaration and joy. People milled around or walked up and down the streets of the village; everybody seemed to be restless, waiting. It was a fine mild evening and the crowds increased as the night wore on and darkness fell. The lights of the village were beaming and the streets of Knock looked like O'Connell Street on the night before an All-Ireland final, only more so. Already people were taking their places in the various corrals assigned to them. They came laden with sleeping-bags, chairs, cushions and food for at least twenty-four hours, and settled down to their vigil.

An RTE crew told me that they found an old man on Calvary Hill overlooking the shrine, kneeling on the grass reciting the rosary at ten o'clock that night. It was a vigil of prayer, penance and endurance. Of course, it is everybody's experience that when the excitement reaches its high-point one no longer feels the pain or the hardship.

I had engaged the services of a London company to make a special film of the Papal visit – I could not get a crew any nearer than London as every camera in Ireland was engaged on the RTE coverage. They began filming in the early hours of the morning, before the break of dawn, and one of the first buses that they met was full of Scottish pilgrims led by their own chaplain. On being questioned the chaplain said, "We Scottish people love the Holy Father, too. Don't we?" and there was a great chorus of "Yeah! We do!" A pilgrim seated on Calvary Hill was asked what she thought of the Papal visit and she said: "Ireland has had her good days and her bad days, days of joy and days of sorrow, but this is Ireland's greatest day."

Roads and by-roads were soon packed tight with people walking towards Knock. They had been coming all through the night and morning and by noon some 450,000 had arrived. As I walked towards the shrine the surrounding hills were covered with pilgrims, waving their flags, singing hymns and happily awaiting the arrival of the Holy Father.

The Pope's Visit to Knock

Around 2 p.m., when it came near to the expected time of his arrival, 450,000 pairs of eyes scanned the skies to see some sign of a helicopter. At last one appeared and there was a great surge of excitement in the crowd, but it turned out to be a police-escort. A few more arrived, and then one came and circled so low that the white soutane could be seen as he waved from the window. The Holy Father had arrived. The helicopter hovered over the crowd and finally came to land on the helipad at the back of the church. Soon the door opened and the white figure of the Holy Father emerged to be greeted by Most Rev. Dr Joseph Cunnane, Archbishop of Tuam.

My great moment had come. I had crossed the shrine grounds with the archbishop before the arrival of the helicopter and, as the old saying goes, I had not known whether I was walking on my head or my feet. I have often looked back at that moment and wondered how I felt but I could never really put it in words. Maybe I was so numb with excitement that my mind was blank, though my heart was full of joy and exhilaration. I was wondering what the Holy Father would say to me and what I would say to him. When the archbishop introduced me, the Holy Father greeted me warmly and said: "Monsignor Horan, parish priest of Knock."

"Your Holiness," I said, "*Céad míle fáilte romhat.* Welcome to Knock Shrine!"

The procession began. The Holy Father, his entourage, the Archbishop of Tuam, myself and some security personnel went up the ramp and on to the roof of the ambulatory. The hills around resounded with the cheers of pilgrims. The atmosphere was one of exhilaration, emotion and love. Every few yards the Holy Father stood and stretched out his arms and hands as if he wanted to embrace this crowd with one magnificent gesture. Here and there amongst them a child would be raised aloft in its mother's arms, hoping to catch the eye of the Holy Father. When he did notice a child he stood and made a gesture of love and affection. Just before he entered the sacristy, which is on the second floor of the basilica, he spied a little child in its mother's arms. He stood there wide-eyed with hands outstretched and made facial expressions to the little one. That gripping moment reminded of the Master himself, Jesus Christ among the children, when he took them in his arms. Then, in the silence of that intense moment, a voice from the crowd shouted "Viva il Papa!" I was filled with emotion; tears came to my eyes as they came to the eyes of many others, even the toughest of characters. There were few dry eyes in Knock that day and, afterwards, looking at the Holy Father in the film, I felt he, too, was almost in tears when he sensed the love, affection and loyalty of the huge gathering. As he moved a few steps further on he saw a multitude of vested priests; at the sight of so many ministers of Christ the Holy Father seemed to be deeply moved. When he approached the door of the sacristy a tumultuous applause greeted him and Papal flags were raised high in the air. He entered the sacristy and went immediately to the vesting bench to put on his vestments for Mass.

At that stage the Holy Father looked tired because he had been on the move since seven o'clock that morning. In Dublin he had visited hospitals and met ethnic groups before he started on his journey to the West. He made an unscheduled visit to Clonmacnois which took a much longer time than had been anticipated. He was fascinated by the ruins of the ancient monastery which stood as a monument to the great Irish missionaries and monks who spread the faith in Europe during the Dark Ages. The Holy Father's love for people is so great the he always finds it difficult to separate himself from them, but urged on by the members of the Papal entourage he had to leave and turn his face west to the City of the Tribes – Galway. There he had a rendezvous with the youth of Ireland, the mainstay of the future Irish church. His meeting with them was one of the highlights of his visit to Ireland. Gone now were all the myths and media stories of the young people of Ireland having lost their faith – the young people in Galway were representative of the youth of all Ireland and they took the Holy Father to their hearts. The Holy Father's heart went out to them also as they waved their banners and shouted their greetings and hosannas. His homily was punctuated with long pauses as he waited for the applause of the vast assembly to die down. It is nearly impossible to describe the atmosphere in Ballybrit on that day, of the spiritual encounter between the young and the Holy Father. He was unavoidably delayed by the exuberance and the enthusiasm he met in Galway and as a result was late in getting to Knock, but who could blame him for lingering to savour this wonderful reception?

Now standing at the bench in the sacristy at Knock, after he had put on his vestments he raised his hands and said wearily,

"Two big ceremonies on that one day!"

The Holy Father did not know that there was a kind of spiritual conspiracy among his entourage to see to it that he had his vestments on before meeting the thousands of invalids and sick who waited for him in the Church of Our Lady Queen of Ireland. The plan was to have him in vestments so that his movements and contact with the sick would be restricted to a minimum.

I will never forget the encounter. I was standing on the altar watching him walk among the sick with vestments flowing and the Papal staff in his left hand. Everywhere hands stretched out to greet him and now and then he grasped one warmly. Mothers raised sick children aloft or held them outstretched so that the Holy Father might touch them. All were overawed by the sight of the Vicar of Christ amongst them, for the first time in Irish history. They all had a feeling that somehow power went out of him as Christ's representative and even at the touch of his hand the sick might be healed. Notwithstanding the formality of being vested and mitred, he still lingered amongst the sick, the old and the handicapped. Like Christ, he had "compassion on the multitude". Reluctantly he moved on, step by step, until at least he ascended the altar to address them. With outstretched arms and in tones of love he began:

"Today I am happy to be with the sick and the handicapped. I have to give witness to Christ's love for you, and to tell you that the Church and the Pope loves you too. By your suffering you help Jesus in his work of salvation. Your call to suffering requires strong faith and patience. But remember that Our Blessed Mother, Mary, is close to you just as she was close to Jesus at the foot of the cross, and she will never leave you alone."

He then addressed the handmaids and stewards who had done such magnificent work down the years in attending to the needs of the sick.

"As pastor I feel in my heart a special joy in addressing a few words also to the handmaids and stewards of the Knock Shrine Society and to the directors of pilgrimages to *Cnoc Mhuire*, the Mountain of Mary. In a special way you are the servants of the Mother of Jesus. You help to approach her, to receive her message of love and dedication. You are also the servants of your brothers and sisters, in helping and guiding the many pilgrims and especially the sick and the handicapped. I pray for you, I thank you, and I invoke upon you abundant graces of goodness and holiness of life. Receive the blessing which I cordially extend to you and to all your loved ones."

Once again the Holy Father descended the altar and moved through the invalids, then out through the south entrance of the basilica. As he moved along he blessed foundation stones for new churches that had been sent from all parts of Ireland. When he came in sight of the crowd again 450,000 people raised their voices in one great ovation. The applause continued as he moved along the new Papal altar surmounted by the ancient high Cross of Ahenny. He ascended the altar and went to his chair for the beginning of the Mass. All the while the choir sang the entrance hymn, "Priestly People". The Holy Father was prevented from starting the Mass for a few minutes until the applause abated. A great calm descended on the immense gathering but not for long, because the first words spoken by the Holy Father in public at Knock were, *"In ainm an Athar agus an Mhic agus an Spiorad Naoimh."* Then an ovation was given to him that resounded through the hills and valleys of Knock.

The choir, assembled from choirs throughout the archdiocese under the baton of Charles Canon Scahill, sang beautifully. The Holy Father's voice rose above them reciting the beautiful prayers of the Mass of Our Lady of Knock. I felt the tension mounting within me because my turn had come: I was chosen to read the First Epistle which was taken from the *Book of Ecclesiasticus* and speaks the praises of Mary, Seat of Wisdom. I moved towards the ambo and bowed reverently towards the Holy Father.

In his homily the Pope said:

"We entrust to your motherly care the land of Ireland where you have been and are so much loved. Help this land to stay true to you and to your Son always. May prosperity never cause Irish men and women to forget God or abandon their faith. Save them from greed, from evil, from seeking selfish or sectional interests. Queen of Ireland, Mary Mother of the heavenly and earthly church, *Máthair Dé*, keep Ireland true to her spiritual tradition and Christian heritage.

A Mhuire na nGrás
A Mháthair Mhic Dé
Go gcuire tú
Ar mo leas mé."

For many years it had become a tradition at Knock to have the anointing of the sick after the homily. Ten sick people, aged from seven to 91, had been chosen for the anointing ceremony, among them my own mother. The Holy Father moved from one sick person to another, anointing them on the forehead and on the palms of the hands. My mother suffered from bad circulation in her legs; there was a great danger of gangrene setting in and the prospect of an operation was rather frightening for me and the members of my family. She had spent some time in the Regional Hospital, Galway, but nothing could be done for her – doctors threw up their hands in despair when they discovered she was over ninety years of age. But shortly after the Papal visit the colouring of her toes became normal and the threat of gangrene disappeared. She claimed that she had been cured by the Holy Father. *Moladh go deo le Dia.* Some years later, on 20 June 1985, she had a very peaceful and happy death.

We now came to what I thought was one of the most moving experiences of the Papal Mass – the offertory procession. Every object carried in that long procession told its own story. First of all we had the flags of the four provinces which represented the dedication of Ireland to Christ Our Saviour at Ireland's national shrine of Our Lady. A young invalid boy carried the cross entwined with a rose to signify that suffering can be mingled with joy. St Jarlath was patron saint of the Archdiocese of Tuam: tradition recalls that while passing through Tuam the wheel of his chariot broke; he regarded the incident as God's will and built his church in the vicinity. Thus a broken wheel was carried in the procession to signify St Jarlath's foundation at Tuam. Children carried flowers in recognition of the fact that 1979 was the Year of the Child. There was a representation of the Galway rosary, which was smuggled into Ireland in the Penal Days and epitomised the love and the loyalty of the Irish people to Mary and the rosary even in the bitter days of trial and anguish. Knock Shrine was not forgetful of other Irish shrines which the prayer and the feet of pilgrims had sanctified down through the centuries. We had a stone from Croagh Patrick and water from St Patrick's well, Knock, where he had baptised the ancestors of some of those present.

As the Mass moved towards the consecration a great calm stillness fell on the shrine grounds and the surrounding hills. The enthusiasm and exuberance that had pervaded the crowd was now tempered by the dignity of the consecration of the Mass. As the Holy Father raised the host and chalice almost half a million people bowed in adoration and reverence. The Mass proceeded to the communion, when 1,000 priests distributed holy communion to the multitude.

There was a great surprise in store for us at the end of Mass. The Holy Father proclaimed: "It gives me great pleasure to announce that, to honour Our Blessed Lady on this her centenary year at Knock, the new church recently built in her honour will from this day forward be known under the title of the Basilica of Our Lady Queen of Ireland."

It must be unique in the history of any basilica that the actual announcement should be made by the Holy Father in person. Another unique privilege was conferred on the shrine when the Holy Father presented the Golden Rose with these words:

"I am happy to offer as my personal tribute and gift to the Shrine of Knock a rose in gold which will remain as my testimony of gratitude to Mary, Mother of the heavenly and earthly Church."

He also presented a special candle to the shrine which, like the paschal candle, is symbolic of the light of Christ. Perhaps this candle has a special significance for Knock, where the paschal mystery of the lamb and the cross were a special feature of the apparition at which the lamb was standing and there was no figure on the cross, which in old Irish symbolism meant Christ risen. May the "light of Christ" always shine brightly at Knock to illuminate all pilgrims and invalids.

Now it came to that part of the Mass which is often called the dismissal. Unfortunately, in this case it meant goodbye, for the Holy Father was now going to leave us. So many times we had been thrilled by the voice of the Holy Father on radio and television giving his blessing, *Urbi et Orbi*, in St Peter's Square; now St Peter's Square was in Knock as the Holy Father gave his final blessing to the crowd.

As the day wore on and the light had begun to fade, there was growing anxiety amongst the Papal entourage about the Holy Father's journey back to Dublin because the helicopters were not equipped to fly in the dark. A decision was made, most probably by Archbishop Marcinkus, that the Holy Father could not move around among the crowd in the Popemobile as he had done at other venues. The Mass was now finished. The Pope descended the altar slowly and approached the Popemobile. There was a great round of applause and flag waving from the crowd, who did not know of the decision not to go amongst them.

Yet the great moment had arrived; the Pope had reached the goal of his journey. He alighted from the Popemobile and climbed the steps to the hallowed place where Our Lady, St Joseph and St John had appeared to the Mayo children one hundred years before. He knelt, head bowed, and prayed. The shrine and the surrounding hills echoed to the lovely tones of Mozart's *Ave Maria*. The Holy Father lit a candle at the shrine as a sign of Ireland's love and loyalty to Mary and her rosary. May that light continue to shine during the coming centuries in the hearts and homes of Irish people.

Having prayed on bended knees he went to the sacristy to take a cup of tea and some apple tart. Unfortunately, everything at this time was rushed and after only ten minutes the Holy Father had to leave for the waiting helicopter. By this time darkness was descending fast. I heard afterwards that the helicopter could not land as arranged in the vicinity of the nunciature in Cabra but had to make an unscheduled landing at Dublin Airport. As he made to leave the crowd joined with the choir in singing some popular songs, amongst them old favourites like "We Won't Go Home Until Morning" and others. The helicopter rose slowly from the ground and great sadness and stillness descended on Knock. A multitude of faces looked up to heaven as the helicopter sped away and asked, "Would he e'er come back again?" Many wondered if it had all been a dream.

Afterwards I was asked what my feelings were as the helicopter rose into the air. I said: "He was three hours with us. I wish he could be three years because he is a wonderful person He was very fond of saying: 'I love you'; 'Young people of Ireland I love you'. Millions and millions of people will come here to Knock Shrine because our Holy Father came as a pilgrim. Knock will never be the same again."

I do think that the Holy Father will return again to Ireland and Knock Shrine. I know that he was sad because he could not go amongst the pilgrims on that historic day, but he will come again. "All things are possible to him who believes."

The arrangements for the Pope's visit to Ireland were so satisfactory that the same format was adopted for his later visits to England and America. Ever since the first announcement by Cardinal Tomás Ó Fiaich, the work of preparation at Knock had gone on feverishly, almost day and night, for two months. All the various committees had worked with great urgency and had made all the preparations for the actual visit. I had had no worries whatsoever except one, and that was security. The safety of the Holy Father was a constant worry that nagged me for many days prior to the visit. A few things happened that gave some foundation to that fear. Some electricity wires had been cut and public address links had been severed. Afterwards I found out, from a very reliable source, that I myself was under constant surveillance by the security forces for some time before the visit – it appears that they had received some information that put them on the alert and made them fear for my safety. Security in Knock was so strict for the occasion that all the public buildings were thoroughly searched three days beforehand and then sealed. They were not opened until the day of the Pope's arrival.

I was very conscious of the fact that I had had a hand in organising the invitation to the Holy Father and if anything were to happen to him I would have to bear a great burden of responsibility. I was so relieved when I watched his plane lifting off from Shannon and saw that he was safely on his way to America. That relief, however, was soon replaced by sadness. Pope John Paul II's visit to us had been such a happy occasion which created so much good will and co-operation between people of all denominations and creeds in our country. If only time would stand still so that we could go on savouring the joy of that visit!

Yet the success of Pope John Paul II's pilgrimage to Knock was a credit to all the people involved in organising the day, and the whole operation had been carried out with reverence and dignity. And so it should be. Not only was the Holy Father received on that wonderful day at Knock, but Christ himself became our guest in the Mass and Holy Communion.

A Helping Hand

SOMEHOW IN LIFE you set your own pattern or standard. I had done much social work in Cloonfad and my reputation had travelled before me to Knock: if you have the reputation of doing social work in one parish, you are expected to do it in the next.

When I had arrived in Knock in 1963, the parishioners looked to me to help out in their various enterprises. As in other parts of the West there was no shortage of projects to get stuck into. I found that all the by-roads were in a frightful condition – in winter you could get lost in the potholes and in summer suffocated with the dust. If for no other reason than my own convenience I made representations to the council engineers and to the local councillors of all parties. I had much success. For years Knock people had been voting for county council candidates in other areas on the strength of promises that were so much "hot air". I advised them to pick their own candidate and vote for him. This they did and the tactic was most successful. No longer was the parish of Knock the Cinderella of East Mayo parishes; now it got its fair share of the local-government cake. In the space of ten years the by-roads were tarred – no more gutter and muck in winter and no more dust in the summer.

It was not a bad start, and during the course of my time in Knock I found myself making representations to politicians of all parties on issues and ideas and projects that were needed in the area. My politics always depended on what TDs and county councillors were willing to do for the West and for their local electoral areas. I never took the political tradition of my family into account but always voted for candidates who were capable and willing to work for the development of the area. People who vote according to family tradition vote with their feet and not with their heads. Parties and candidates must be judged on their track record and nothing should be taken for granted: conditions and circumstances are changing all the time and the issues in each election are different. In a general election one is faced with both national and local issues, and while the national issues may be over-riding, there are times when local concerns can predominate and should be given much consideration.

If the West is neglected then all TDs of every colour should stick together and see to it that the western province gets fair play, otherwise the different parties will woo areas of dense population by sending the goodies their way. I am not a politician and never was, but if fighting for the rights of the people of Connaught makes me a politician then I am one and proud of it. I regret to say that party politics are the ruination of the West of Ireland. No matter how good the western politicians may be they are not numerous enough to sway party decisions. When decisions come before the Dáil these same politicians are under a triple whip and must vote for issues that may not be for the benefit of our province. I think that all TDs and senators, from all parties in Connaught, should stand together and fight for equal opportunities for this province. A united and determined Connaught can always demand fair play from any government and get it, and it is sad to see Connaught's politicians having to fight for the crumbs that fall from the national table. Every western politician should be glad when a project comes to any place across the Shannon. This, unfortunately, is not always the case.

In my twenty years in Knock I worked very closely with the farmers. All through my early years in the parish I attended all the National Farmers Association meetings and I worked hard on the lime and fertiliser scheme that was introduced, encouraging farmers to use the scheme to raise the productivity of their farms. Many farms were impoverished for want of certain trace-elements in the soil and travelling through the parish the low standard of upkeep on the smallholdings was clear to see. It was not that the farmers did not use fertilisers on their land – they did, but they were using expensive manures that were not needed or were ineffective because of the absence of chemicals like lime which act as a catalyst for other trace-elements in the soil. It was most important to have the land tested and know for certain the missing elements, and I encouraged all farmers to take advantage of all possible scientific advice that could be had from the local agricultural instructors, otherwise they would just be wasting their time and money. The farms in the West are so small it is important to make use of every possible acre. I used my influence to get the farmers to avail of grants for land reclamation, work which could be done in the winter season when they were not too busy. About thirty per cent of the local farmers became interested in the lime/fertiliser and land reclamation scheme and it made a tremendous difference to the appearance of the farms and to their output: in some cases it almost doubled output as the farm could cater for twice the number of livestock.

I also encouraged farmers to improve the breeding of their stock and particularly the quality of the milch cows. We organised the purchase of Freisian heifer calves from dairy farmers in the South and the result was most successful. I am proud to see so many herds of beautiful Friesian milch cows on farms all over the parish and even in the surrounding parishes now – the good news of success and progress quickly spread beyond Knock. The Irish farmer may be conservative but he appreciates a good thing when he sees it.

I was asked by many farmers and local householders to hire turf-cutting machines: the cutting and saving of turf had to be carried out at a time when farmers were busy with sowing and harvesting, and turf-cutting machines would be faster and more economic then slanes. They would also help farmers who had large tracts of bog and wanted to cut and harvest a large quantity of turf for sale. I had been doing all the secretarial work for the Irish Sugar Company in the area, and in response the company undertook to get the turf-cutting machine initially. A machine could not be hired unless a certain amount of work was guaranteed and to help the project I contracted for the cutting of my own supply of turf and enjoyed the work of saving it: I had good practice from the days of my youth in Partry, where I often worked in Durcan's bog in the vicinity of Killawalla. The venture was profitable and successful and continued for twenty years. It ended only a few years ago when a smaller and cheaper machine came on the market. Called the "sausage machine", as the sods of turf are turned out in the shape of a sausage, these machines were purchased by a local man and they put pressure on me to abandon the Sugar Company scheme: there was no option but to support local industry. I did so, but unfortunately the new machines were not a success and have been more or less abandoned. A local enterprise then acquired the larger machines and now carries out all work in the local bogs.

My involvement in afforestation in Cloonfad was well known throughout the West and naturally it was expected that I would continue the campaign in Knock. My interest in afforestation stemmed from a desire to create local employment and from a desire also to enhance and beautify the countryside. I loved trees, shrubs and flowers as my upbringing had kept me very close to Mother Nature, and nothing changes the appearance of a desolate countryside more dramatically than forestry. It has always been my conviction, too, that every acre of land in Ireland should be contributing to the economy of the country. In parts of the West there are thousands of acres of poor land which could be used for growing trees. I tried to interest the Forestry Department in Knock and at the same time I canvassed the farmers to sell their waste land to the Department, but I did not succeed in my campaign. I did not get the same co-operation from the department and there was a reluctance, too, on the part of farmers to dispose of land. Agricultural land was dear at the time and the price paid by the Forestry Department was meagre. I might have been more successful at afforestation at Knock if I had not had so many duties to perform – I had had more time at my disposal in Cloonfad. Nevertheless, I did succeed in persuading a few farmers to sell 150 acres to the Forestry Department and the trees which were planted are now making their presence felt. When one sees lovely patches of green in an otherwise drab landscape one realises what a difference afforestation can make. It also seems to provide shelter for adjacent farms and helps to increase their fertility.

I worked closely with the St Vincent de Paul Society in Knock. The society was very active in the parish and always on the alert for the chance to help a neighbour; they visited the sick and the old and helped all who were in need. With a grant from the Western Health Board a "meals on wheels" scheme was arranged to distribute meals a few times each day to old people living alone. The society also organised special reunions for the old and handicapped a few times a year. A reunion consisted of Mass with an anointing of the sick ceremony, which was followed by a tea-party and a concert of Irish music, songs and dance. It was always a great success and it gave people a chance to meet friends and neighbours that they might not otherwise meet. It showed them, too, that they were wanted and that people cared about them, which is a great boost to the morale of any person living alone. I felt an obligation to take care of the temporal as well as the spiritual welfare of my flock. I was concerned about the welfare of the old as well as the young, and I cared for the sick and the handicapped in the parish, apart from my work for invalids at the shrine. I arranged for the installation of the "free electricity" in the old people's homes and for any other benefit due to them under the social welfare system. I had to solve or make representations in regard to problems in the payment of old-age and unemployment benefits. I even had to bring to the notice of the Department of Social Welfare certain anomalies in the regulations or in the law.

I remember being called to attend a sick man, the father of a family of six young children aged from one to fourteen years. When he was sent to hospital in Galway his unemployment assistance was stopped immediately. As far as the regulations were concerned he could starve! "How can his family afford to travel to visit him in hospital?" I protested to the labour exchange, and was told that the man was sick, unfit for work, and therefore did not qualify for unemployment benefit. I was advised to apply for home assistance for the family and did so, but the amount given was only a pittance compared to his unemployment benefit. Here was a family being allowed to starve because the head of the family was ill! I wrote to the minister in charge of social welfare and I am pleased to relate that the law was later amended.

I came to Knock during a transition period between modern and old-style housing. As the number of thatched houses dwindled the art of thatching was gradually being lost and the number of skilled thatchers became fewer and more expensive to hire, so that the old people who still had thatched houses found it impossible to pay for their upkeep. Many houses became so run down that in the end their wet, sodden roofs collapsed. This was a crisis situation for the old and for poor families. I was always called upon in a crisis and immediately I applied to the Mayo County Council for an "essentials repairs grant" of £200. For that money I had to purchase timber for the doors and windows and for a new roof. In some cases the windows had to be enlarged, the thatch completely stripped and asbestos sheeting purchased for the roof.

I employed a wonderful man named Paddy Kenny, Meeltrane, to do the work, and organised some voluntary labour if the householder was not able to help owing to illness or old age. Paddy Kenny worked wonders, always completing the renovation within the limits of a tight budget. In one case we obtained a grant for a new house which just about purchased the necessary materials, but I arranged for voluntary helpers and tradesmen to come each day: we did an excellent job and I was so proud of the charity and skill of the workers. In another case the roof of a house had collapsed completely, so we covered it with a tent-like structure made of poles and plastic to keep the family dry while the repairs were being carried out. One new house was built and essential repairs on about twenty others were carried out in Knock, a project which all in all was most gratifying and fulfilling. It is amazing what can be done where there is good will and a good heart. I wish we had such dedicated workers nowadays, who would give of themselves unselfishly to lift our poor country out of the depths of recession, but unfortunately, selfishness, greed and laziness are tearing our country apart. Nonetheless, the Germans did it after the Second World War when their country was in a shambles, and what the Germans can do, we can do!

In the old days it was often said the the greatest disadvantage of living in a rural area was the lack of running water, sewage, light and power, and it was everybody's dream to live in a townhouse. But the introduction of schemes in the fifties and sixties to provide water, sewage and electricity in the rural areas changed all that dramatically. The "in thing" now is for business people and other to have a house standing on its own grounds in a rural setting. This change is due entirely to the availability of services in the country. Beautiful bungalows can now be seen stretching for miles along the approach roads leading into every town, architecturally in good taste and beautifully landscaped, and they are much admired by tourists and especially by Americans who have a long tradition of building beautiful homes in their own country. This development should be encouraged as it avoids overcrowding in the towns with all its attendant problems; it is also healthier and safer, physically and morally, for the upbringing of young families.

I organised the first rural group water scheme in Co. Mayo, in Coogue, Knock parish, in the late sixties and early seventies. The beneficiaries each contributed £40 towards the cost of the scheme and the Department of Local Government and the county council added another forty each; a further contribution could be obtained from the Department of Agriculture for the installation of facilities in the farmyard and outhouses. Before the scheme could be approved or started the local subscriptions had to be lodged in the bank, but if the participants wished they could get work on the project and earn back their contributions.

There was, of course, a public relations job to be done to convince householders of the enormous advantages of the scheme. For instance, some farmers in the village had to drive their cattle to a watering place twice each day: under the scheme they could have troughs that worked automatically in their pasture land. A thirsty cow found no difficulty in learning to cope with modern technology. It was easy to sell the group water scheme; the annual subscription was no more than £10 and all householders joined. A contract was given to a JCB owner for the opening and closing of the trenches and the piping was laid by local labour. We got full co-operation from everybody including the local farmers who gave us leave to lay pipes through their land. The water was pumped from the source or spring to a big tank situated on a hill overlooking the village and gravity-fed to each house in the area. One potential problem which I foresaw was the fact that the cost of bringing water to each individual house could differ according to its distance from the main pipeline, but the difference would not be great in most cases, so I asked the members to agree beforehand that the cost to each householder should be made the same and this arrangement made the operation of the scheme very simple and straightforward. There were times when a whole scheme was threatened by the awkwardness and stubbornness of some individuals, due usually to an old spleen between neighbours, but on this earth no good can be achieved without some trial or tribulation. One should never be discouraged by difficulties but should "keep right on to the end of the road". In the space of ten years I helped to organise group water schemes for all the villages in the parish. There is only one village in the area without water at the present time, the reason being that there is no suitable spring or source in the village, which is most unusual for Ireland.

I took an interest in the plight of travelling people also and adopted a family. I provided them with caravans and began to organise the building of a suitable house on a site adjacent to the church grounds. There had been some local opposition to my plans at first but that faded very quickly. One of the conditions that I laid down for the travellers was that they would not beg in Knock or harass pilgrims, and they kept their side of the bargain. I put them to work on an experimental basis. They were tinsmiths so I set up a workshop for the father beside our museum. I carpeted the floor and furnished it so that he could sit on the floor in traditional style and ply his trade, and I allowed visitors to call to see him as he worked. I got a market for the tins with a firm in Sligo, though eventually the demand for tin vessels diminished as plastic utensils flooded the market. In the end I had to give up producing tin-goods as the market price would not even pay for the tin itself. I then gave employment to the father and his son in landscaping and fencing the shrine grounds, a job which they did extremely well. I also got jobs for two of their teenage girls in the hostel run by the Daughters of Charity in Knock.

Everything went well for three years. The children were bright and got on well at school, the young ones learned to read and write and I organised private tuition for the older members of the family. The local teachers gave me wonderful help and worked with vigour and enthusiasm, and the local housewives called on the travellers and taught them how to keep the caravans in good trim. I was told that biscuits seemed to be their staple food – "food" which was expensive and unwholesome. I was proud of their progress and the success of my experiment. The only worry I had was that they still kept their horses on the roads in various parts in Mayo.

I now know that this precaution was meant for the day when they would take to the road again. At the end of their third year in Knock a cart suddenly appeared at the site that I had built for them. This was the signal that they were about to move. It was May, the beginning of summer. I pleaded with the father and advised him to stay for the sake of the children's education and their future. They were doing so well at school they were a credit to their parents; they were accepted completely by the local children and played games with them. But all my efforts were in vain. One fine day they vanished across the hill, people of the road once more.

Why did they leave? I honestly do not know. I have a few theories of my own, which may be correct and may not. It is customary for travellers to marry when they came to the age of seventeen or eighteen. One of the teenage girls got married shortly after they had arrived in Knock. At the time I had asked the parents to postpone the marriage for six months until she had received pre-marriage instruction and some private tuition from the local teacher, and I promised to provide a caravan for the young couple after the marriage in the spring of the following year. It was only a few months delay but, alas, my efforts were in vain. Later, I got the feeling that they left because they feared that the other teenage members of the family would not have the opportunity to marry – they knew that they were unlikely to marry among the settled community and there was also the danger that other travellers would not marry them in their settled state. There also seems to be a wanderlust in travellers, an urge to keep on the move. The mother of the family told me one day: "We were always travellers, we are travellers and we always will be travellers."

These few explanations are my own and I cannot be sure that they are correct. Perhaps they just got lonely for the long road, although many travellers came to visit them during the years they resided here. I was disappointed because all my efforts seemed to have been in vain. The unfortunate result of my experience seems to be that it coloured my views in regard to travellers and I seem to have no hope that they will ever settle down. I know that it goes against my real instinct, but I seem to have less sympathy for travellers nowadays. A few days after they had left the oldest and unmarried son had returned and asked me for a job. I was delighted and gave him work but he only stayed three days. I can only presume that he got lonely or was enticed away by the family. They say that the patriarchal system reigns supreme in travellers' families. If the father says go, he goeth. Still, it is better to have tried and failed.

The work of two decades came to a climax with the organising of Knock's reception for Pope John Paul II, a great day in the life of the village which will be remember for ever more. A month after the Papal visit, in October 1979, the archbishop, Dr Joseph Cunnane; Fr Tommie Shannon, Diocesan Secretary; Fr Dominick Grealy and myself took a belated golfing holiday in Fuengirola in the South of Spain. We must have brought the Irish weather with us as it poured from the heavens on the first two days and the golfcourse was completely sodden, but once the rain cleared away we enjoyed glorious sunshine. We played golf every day for eleven or twelve days and in the end felt like veritable professionals. However, I felt so exhausted after so much golf that I nearly needed another holiday to recover.

We had travelled from Dublin in the same plane as a number of Irish golfers, amongst them the famous radio and television star, Liam Nolan. I thought that I had left the media behind me until I was cornered one afternoon by Liam Nolan in the vicinity of the hotel swimming pool. On the spot the microphone was placed before me and I was asked to give my views on every subject under the Spanish sun. You have guessed it! I was asked the inevitable question about the Holy Father's visit to Knock Shrine and the effects it was likely to have on our dear country. Of course, I was very optimistic of the effects it would have on people of all countries and denominations and indeed during my Spanish holiday I met many people, Catholics and Protestants, who told me unashamedly that they had shed tears of emotion on watching the Papal visit on television.

Once the holiday was over it was back to the reality of parish work at Knock Shrine. To my surprise the parishioners and priests had planned a public reception during my absence, and presented me with a citation and a beautiful plaque. In the citation, beautifully read by retired teacher Thomas Ryan, one of the sentences that has stayed in my mind ever since is that "Notwithstanding all the work that Monsignor did for the shrine he never, at any time, neglected his parish or his parishioners." I felt then, as I do now, that there was no tribute that could mean as much to me as that. It is true that since the Papal visit in 1979 the work at the shrine and in the shrine offices became so enormous that I could not do as much visitation of the homes as I would have liked, and I left that very important pastoral work, for the most part, to my assistants. But I never neglected my parish and especially the sick and the less fortunate. I have now spent twenty-two years in Knock and have come of age as far as Knock people are concerned.

In the priesthood there is a wonderful fulfilment, especially in the confessional, where the priest can do such marvellous work with people. When you are involved in social affairs or social work you can look back and see that you helped so many people. A priest must take part in this work, he just cannot sit back and relax when somebody is in trouble, and all my life I have been involved in helping others out. But, of course, you must also have time to pray. Prayer is the power-house that enables you to carry out your social work and to do it for the right motive. It was impressed on us in Maynooth, by all our spiritual directors, that prayer was fundamental and that work without prayer would become very worldly. There is really no difference between social work for a priest and the lay person because the lay person will also have a spiritual input into his or her social work.

If there is any fault with our modern society today, it is due to the fact that there is too much social activity while the spiritual side of life is neglected. I think it is important to meditate and pray because from that well-spring you will go forth and do things for others with the proper motive. Only through prayer and meditation will you be able to work and continue to work in spite of set-backs and disappointments. The spiritual directors in Maynooth always told us that we could not give what we had not got. I think that is something that is stated in philosophy in a different way. Unless you have faith and spirituality yourself, you cannot impart that spirituality and faith to others. People's faith shines through them. I met them every day at Knock, and I could have knelt down and kissed their hands. When they began to talk to me, the very things that they had to say absolutely astounded me as their faith was coming through so strongly. I would say to myself, "Here I am, having got all this training and all these years of experience, and I still envy these people with their simple, strong and vibrant faith."

I think that one of the reasons why the experiment of the "worker priest" in the Church of France failed was because the priests who went out to do social work may have neglected the mainspring of all spiritual activity and all apostolic work, namely faith, spirituality and meditation. You need all these things in order to keep you right. But if you neglect them, dive into social work and keep at it, then in the end you get lost.

During my years in Knock I formed a wonderful relationship with all my parishioners, and I can say truthfully that I never refused help where help was requested. If they had a problem my door was always open, and if they did not avail of it it was not my fault. It has often been said that you cannot please all the people all the time, but I must confess that I always tried. Sad to say, sometimes it is only when people die that they get credit for their good work, but I will always appreciate the citation given me by the Knock people after the Papal visit:

"We the people of your flock, parishioners of Knock, make this presentation and address to you, our beloved pastor, to express publicly and convey to you our appreciation of, and gratitude for, your labours amongst us as our pastor.

"We are aware and proud of the recognition that has been accorded and the honours conferred upon you, nationwide and indeed worldwide, but tonight we turn off these highlights and concentrate on your sacred ministry in our parish of Knock, and who knows better than we the spiritual impact of that ministry. In spite of the many and heavy calls upon you from outside, we in the parish were never stinted of your help. You were with us in our joys and sorrows. Our material as well as our spiritual needs had your vigorous and effective help. The children, the old, the sick and the poor experienced your kindness and charity. All these ministrations were characterised by your own special brand of down-to-earth practicality and bluff, hearty good humour. Social life among us was enriched by your enthusiastic, talented and merry participation in all parish gatherings. May your *bosca ceoil* never go wheezy, your singing voice never lose its quality nor your ear its musical keenness. We look forward to more frequent renderings of your own verse compositions at our social gatherings.

"Service of God and the neighbour you have shown us as something happy and joyous. We pray to God through His Blessed Mother to reward you for your service to us as our parish priest, service to us in the spiritual and temporal spheres.

"May He preserve you in health and vigour with us for many years. To be aware of your greatness we have but to look about us in Knock today. But your crowning achievement was when you lead our Holy Father, Christ's Vicar on earth himself, to pray at our apparition gable. Memory of that will thrill every Knock person forever; an event second only to the apparition itself.

"We bless you and rejoice with you for all this, but again we emphasise that tonight we want to regard you as our parish priest. With all your fame and honours, such an approach to a less humble and spiritual man might be off-putting. We have no such disadvantage. Admiration and fame you have indeed gained, but from us, your parishioners, something more precious – love."

It was as much and more than I had merited, but the presentation reflected, too, the closeness that had been built between myself and my parishioners.

One of the closest ways of building contact in parish work between priest and people is on the occasion of the Stations. I know that some priests are of a shy and retiring nature and find it hard to mix with parishioners on such occasions but, having been brought up in a country village and having been used to mixing freely with people from my young days I always felt at home in a

Station house. I looked forward to the occasion and enjoyed myself immensely. I shared people's outlook, interests and aspirations. I could speak their language and was always glad that I had the privilege of being brought up in a village with simple lovable and good-natured people. Thank God, as I write, Stations in country places are still big, sociable and inspiring events. They create an atmosphere of friendship, co-operation and good neighbourliness in an area and encourage a rapport with the priests. From my experience at Stations since I was an altar-boy I find very little has changed down the years. The people, young and old, are just as friendly, hospitable and kind as they ever were. I loved the people of Knock and the people of every other parish in which I worked, just as I loved the people in my own native village. Problems there may have been, but they never seemed to generate the hatred, antipathy and violence that is so evident in life today. Long may the traditions and native culture of our land be preserved in the villages and homes of Ireland.

An Airport for Connaught

I HAVE ALWAYS been fascinated by the aeroplane. When Shannon Airport opened in the late forties and fifties I would visit the airport and stand on the balcony for hours, watching the aeroplanes taking off and landing. Later I often brought schoolchildren to the airport and they, too, stood in wonder.

Man had made all kinds of wonderful machines to carry people over land and sea, but the flying machine was the last form of transport to be invented. After many attempts with wings and other gadgets the Wright brothers of America at last transported man through the air, if only for a very short distance. It was a big breakthrough and subsequently the aeroplane played a part in the First World War and was decisive in the Second World War. What a pity that it takes war to sharpen man's inventive genius and make life easier for those who survive! Commercial air travel did not come into its own until after the Second World War. Aer Lingus planes must have been among the first to land on the grass-strip at Lourdes in 1947. Statistics tell us that 1,300 pilgrims flew into Lourdes in that year; by 1979 the figure had risen to 359,000. In the middle and late fifties I travelled with Aer Lingus to Lourdes, Rome and to other parts of the Continent, but at that time I had no intention of becoming involved in the building or operation of airports: I was quite happy just to use and enjoy them to see the world, and I was proud to see the Irish flag and shamrock displayed on an Irish air-fleet. I could not see into the future and know that one day I would be associated with a world-famous airport!

How did it happen? Where did I go wrong?

I read with interest in the local press about a development plan for Knock Shrine and its environs in the early fifties which included the provision of an airstrip for Knock. This may silence some critics who say that an airport was the brainchild of a certain parish priest in the 1980s, a full thirty years later. It is interesting to note that they were thinking of an airport for Knock even before Shannon had developed into a fully fledged international airport. As a matter of fact, I remember when a certain government sold Super-Constellation aircraft at give-away prices rather than start a transatlantic service. Even at an early age, white elephants were quite common! However, the resolve of the Knock flying enthusiasts was not strong enough in the 1950s, so the idea was put on the government's "long finger", as usually happens in the case of the West of Ireland.

Under the auspices of a Knock Development Association another attempt to procure an airstrip for Knock Shrine was made in 1960. In June of that year Delap and Waller of Lower Baggot Street, Dublin, prepared a feasibility study for the Knock Development Association which examined the viability of building an airstrip in the vicinity of Knock. A number of sites were surveyed and found unsuitable. Only one site was even considered by the consultants and they viewed it with great reservations, concluding that "In our opinion, site B is the only one with possibilities for even first stage (light aircraft) development, but for the reason given above, it cannot be considered ideal and is unsuitable for second stage development. We, therefore, recommend that a more suitable alternative site or sites be sought, if such exist." The consultants carried out a very extensive search of the area for a suitable site and found none.

I was transferred to Knock by the Most Rev. Dr Joseph Walsh in September 1963 as an assistant to the administrator, Rev. Fr John Fitzgerald. Soon I was approached by some members of the Knock Development Association who asked me to help out with the Knock Airport project. I made enquiries about the site that was recommended, with reservations, by the consultants. The owner of the site seemed to be quite enthusiastic about the development and encouraged me to press ahead.

Without hesitation I set to work and visited the Aeronautics Section of the Department of Transport to discuss the matter. I met with a Captain Reidy who was very polite but not encouraging. He informed me that Castlebar Airport was now in operation and had been grant-aided by the state. In his view, and I knew he was right, there was no way that the government would grant-aid a second project at Knock. I also visited Aer Lingus to explore the possibility of developing internal air-transport. I had always had sympathy with Cork and Kerry pilgrims, and most of all with invalids, who had to travel long distances to and from Knock. They had to rise at a very early hour on Sunday, journey to Knock, and return home in the early hours of Monday morning. If they could come by air it would be less than an hour's journey and they would have ample time at Knock Shrine to pray and have a meal. But I was politely told that Aer Lingus was not interested in internal transport. I asked why not. "We could fly passengers on Aer Lingus planes from Cork to Dublin much cheaper than they could be carried by CIE trains," I was told, but the government would not sanction it. After a few more frustrating expeditions of this kind I gave up, and my enthusiasm for the airport project died within me.

1979 was a most eventful year. When our Holy Father visited Knock for the centenary celebrations at the shrine he travelled by air, and I was disappointed that an airport was not there to receive him. On the day of his visit I saw 450,000 people perched on the hills overlooking Knock as they watched the Holy Father go to the shrine and kneel in fervent prayer. As I saw him there I knew that thousands and thousands would follow in his footsteps and kneel at the same hallowed spot.

The next day, Monday 1 October 1979, the Holy Father's aircraft took off from Shannon Airport. The Chief of Staff of the army and an engineer had lunch with me that day. The engineer told me afterwards that I talked about nothing else at the meal but an airport for Connaught.

In December I contacted Jim Ryan, one of the Ryan brothers who had pioneered the building of Castlebar Airport. I wanted to explore the possibility of extending Castlebar Airport as part of the infrastructure of the West of Ireland. I did this on the advice of people in the aviation industry who told me that small airports like Castlebar were of little benefit to the region. Like many small airports throughout the country, Castlebar was only suitable for a flying club and for the accommodation of light aircraft. An airport of that size only benefited people who could afford to have their own plane or hire one; to do either, one would need to be a person of considerable wealth.

On the suggestion of Jim Ryan, we gathered around us a number of people interested in industry, tourism and local government. The group comprised the county manager, a county development officer, a Bord Fáilte official and business representatives. A committee was formed and chaired by me. We first explored the possibility of extending Castlebar Airport but found that that was impossible as there was a railway on one side of the site and a public road on the other, and we could not get the interested parties to agree to the closure of either amenity. We had no option but to look for an alternative site, and while there were alternative sites we found it difficult to agree on any particular one. It was then decided that we should appoint consultants to carry out a feasibility study which would include the recommendation of a suitable site, and the committee agreed that it would accept the consultants' recommendations. We got in touch with the Department of Transport and asked them to recommend a suitable firm of consultants; the department suggested Aer Rianta or Transportation Analysis International. We chose TAI as they were international consultants and had already carried out a study on aviation for the Irish government.

The leading consultant for the firm in our study was Dr Ken Holden, who is now the head of the Central Remedial Clinic in Dublin. He made it quite clear, at our very first meeting, that he would do a thorough study of the project and would give an independent verdict. He would meet with us once a month and listen to our views, but need not be influenced by them. He was not of our faith and, at first, did not think that a shrine would be an asset to an airport, though he had reason to change his mind later after visiting Lourdes Airport and examining the statistics of its success. If, he told us, he considered at any stage that the project was not feasible, he would advise us accordingly and terminate the study there and then.

We had the first meeting with him in January 1980, and had one each month until May. At each of these meetings he told us that the work was going well and he was optimistic that he would be able to give a favourable report. During the six months from January to June he made an extensive study of conditions in the West of Ireland which covered agriculture, industry, tourism and business interests. He carried out an intensive appraisal of the catchment area, its population, social structure and occupations, and assessed the local interest in air travel. He spoke to industrialists, business people and indeed to anyone who could help in his analysis. He visited various countries where airports were run successfully by private companies for the benefit of particular regions; these were mostly found in small countries like Denmark. He also visited shrines such as Lourdes and Fatima to assess Knock Shrine's potential in regard to pilgrimage traffic. In early June the study was completed and published. On the whole he did a magnificent, thorough and expert job, as can be seen by the quality and detail of his study. He gave statistical tables of figures, maps, diagrams, drawings and graphs in support of his findings.

His conclusion was that an airport for Connaught would be useful, viable and economic, provided it were run in a sensible and businesslike manner. Having surveyed the whole region he decided that the best place to locate the airport would be within a five-mile radius of Charlestown. That location is almost in the centre of Connaught, but he moved it a little to the north to take it outside the Shannon catchment area.

At a meeting in February 1980 of the Connaught Regional Airport Committee it was agreed that contact should be made with public representatives in Galway to give them an opportunity to share in our deliberations. We decided to invite them to attend our next committee meeting and Mr Pat Donlon, manager of the FUE office in Galway, conveyed our invitation to the Galway Port Authority and others. We were willing to hold our next meeting in Galway to facilitate their attendance, or, if they preferred, they were welcome to come to our meeting in Knock. Unfortunately, the invitation was not taken up by the public representatives in Galway. We never got a reply.

At that time the committee had an open mind as to the location of the airport; in fact, my first thoughts on the matter were that Tuam would be a suitable area for a regional airport for Connaught. But the invitation to discuss these ideas was ignored by Galway. I do not know why; some suggest that they thought the idea of an airport in the West was just "pie in the sky", but that could hardly have been the reason as they later started a campaign for a regional airport in Galway itself. I always made it plain to our consultants that I did not mind where the airport was built provided that it was within an hour's journey of the shrine. I felt that Knock Shrine would be a great asset to the airport and a major factor in making it viable.

We decided not to approach either the politicians or the government until our study had been completed. We wanted to be well-armed with facts and figures before discussing the matter with the minister or departmental officials. The decision to build an airport was not lightly or hastily taken; every step was followed with great caution and circumspection and the magnitude of the project was fully understood. Everybody who got a copy of the consultants' report knew exactly what we had in mind.

After the publication of the feasibility study there was intense controversy in the local newspapers as to where exactly the airport should be built. Jim Ryan was selected by the committee to find a suitable site. The consultants had recommended a location within a five-mile-radius of Charlestown and now Mr Ryan began to pinpoint a number of possible sites. He found six or seven potential sites and, rather than show a preference for any particular one, he invited an expert from the Aviation Section of the Department of Transport to vet them. Captain Reidy of the department picked two sites as being suitable.

The site chosen was situated in the townland of Barnalyra, where the bog was not as deep as it was at the Swinford Road site. Barnalyra was also attractive because there were no farm dwellings or any other obstruction on the site, whereas there was at least one farm on the other site and it might have taken years to negotiate a deal with the owner.

Now that we had fixed on a site and the news had spread abroad, we were faced with a new problem. Speculators moved in to make enquiries and, if possible, buy the land from local people; they would then be in a position to hold the airport committee to ransom and demand a high price for the land. I had a phone call from a member of the committee advising me of the new situation and, in consultation with other members, we decided that it was imperative to buy or take an option on the required acreage. In early July, Jim Ryan, secretary of the committee, was commissioned to go to Dublin to procure Ordnance Survey maps for the whole area. He then made discreet enquiries as to the owners of the property, and brought them all together in an old school in Shammer. In the meantime he had assessed the value of the property on the basis of the price paid by the Forestry Department for similar land; some time previously the department had paid £70 per acre for land in the immediate area. We decided to pay £200 per acre.

There was general euphoria in this depressed area near Kilkelly when the idea of an airport was mooted. After our first meeting with the local people I was informed that the vast majority wanted to give the land for free, but I felt that we should not accept their kind offer. I should pay tribute, though, to the kindness and co-operation of the people in the area – they were simply magnificent. Imagine, twenty-seven owners gave their land, spontaneously, without even one dissenting voice. I hope that the airport will be so successful that in future years they will be proud of the gesture they made then.

There was just one problem which caused the committee some concern at a second meeting in the old school. Apart from the owners of the property a large number of people had turbary rights on the proposed sites. It was more difficult to deal with them than with the people who actually owned the land. It was suggested at the meeting that monetary compensation should be given for the turbary rights, but we felt that this would give rise to many difficulties. The committee decided instead to buy twenty acres of bog, drain it and build access roads. The bog would then be striped and each claimant allotted one acre in compensation for their loss of turbary rights at Barnalyra. This worked out very satisfactorily and again I compliment the people of the area on their co-operation.

Now that we had got agreement and had decided to pay £200 per acre for 520 acres, we faced the problem of getting the cash to pay for it. I knew something of the system of taking options on property so I decided to phone my solicitor, who was later appointed solicitor to the Connaught Regional Airport Company. I told him about the problem and asked how much one would have to pay to take out a five-year option on the land – I had decided on a five-year option because that was the time I thought it would take to get the project moving. The solicitor told me it could be any sum of money and that it need not necessarily bear any relation to the final amount to be paid to an owner, and in the end we fixed on a sum of £200 for each owner, whether he had five acres or twenty. If the option of buying the land was not taken up within five years the £200 would be forfeited; on the other hand, if the sale moved quickly, the land would be ours on payment of £200 per acre. We took up the option a few months later, in the summer of 1980.

In all its deliberations the Connaught Regional Airport Committee had been adamant that before presenting our case to the department we should be well armed with facts and figures. Now we dispatched copies of the feasibility study to the Department of Transport and to the Minister, Mr Albert Reynolds TD. The Minister of State at the department was Mr Pádraig Flynn TD, and it fell to his lot to deal with our case. The meeting to decide the fate of the proposed Connaught Regional Airport took place in the Department of Transport on Thursday, 25 September 1980. It was a good omen, I felt, that the apparition at Knock had also taken place on a Thursday. Whenever the going was difficult the Friends of Our Lady would say to me: "Don't worry, Monsignor, if Our Lady wants this airport you will have it."

It was a very high-powered departmental team headed by the Minister of State, Pádraig Flynn, that met us. It was a good, constructive meeting with many forthright and candid exchanges. It lasted for several hours and all aspects of the airport project were discussed. I was glad then that we had had so many meetings with our consultants as I had learned a lot about aeronautics and airports from them. The members of our deputation were well armed with the relevant facts. Two aspects in particular were fully explored and discussed: the meteorological report from Mr McWilliams, the meteorological officer at Dublin Airport, and the soil mechanics on the site. Mr McWilliams reported that the meteorological conditions on the site were better than Cork Airport and in some respects better than Dublin and Shannon. It had an advantage over Cork, Dublin and Shannon in that it was further inland and less likely to be affected by mist or fog, though it was pointed out that low cloud might be a problem in certain weather conditions. However, it was felt that an Instrument Landing System would solve that problem.

Neither was there a problem with the land on which the airport would be built, because when the bog was removed there was a gravel and stone base which was perfect for the construction of a runway. The Aer Rianta engineers had some doubts until trial-holes were dug, but they could then see clearly that the base was of stone and gravel and no material could be more perfect for a foundation.

To make assurances doubly sure, our architect and engineers engaged the services of Dr Edward Hanrahan, Professor of Soil Mechanics, University College, Dublin, who inspected the site in December 1980 and pronounced it perfectly sound. Later I marvelled to see 40-ton trucks travelling on the base after the removal of the bog. Jim Ryan, who acted as the liaison officer for the Regional Airport Committee on site, also kept a diary of weather conditions in the area for the years 1980-84. According to his records there were only five days in that period on which the airport would not have been operational owing to weather conditions. During that period Shannon and Dublin were closed many times owing to fog. There seemed to be no serious problem with fog on the plateau where the airport was sited; when there is fog on the plain all around, the airport site is still clear.

The result of our meeting with the Department of Transport was that, on behalf of the government, the minister gave "approval in principle" for a Connaught Regional Airport. Ten weeks later, on 6 December, a decision was made by the government that a new airport would be built on a site between Charlestown and Kilkelly. That same day we held a ceremony at Barnalyra and raised the Connaught flag over the site.

There was one problem outstanding: the discovery of springs in the area on which the runway was to be built. These had to be drained and the water piped into the general drainage system but everything was now set for the final push, the removal of the bog and the spreading of gravel. The gravel pits were so convenient that a lorry-load could be delivered on site in six minutes; this was one of the reasons why the airport could be built at such an economical price. The final decision was now made by the committee and the site was accepted as suitable by all, including the Aer Rianta engineers and the aeronautical consultants. The engineers and architects were busy preparing plans, procuring the necessary planning permission, seeking tenders and selecting a contractor. Notice of application for planning permission was published in October and outline planning permission was granted to the Airport Committee on 2 December 1980. In early January preparatory work began on the site and continued during the first months of 1981. A new road was built to replace the country road that ran along the pathway of the proposed runway; drainage on the site was completed and a parking place was built for the machinery which would build the runway.

On 2 May the first sod was turned by the Minister for Transport, Albert Reynolds. All politicians in the Connaught region were invited to the event, but most politicians from the Galway area, both Fianna Fáil and Fine Gael, were conspicuous by their absence. It was evident even then that the project was not popular in Galway. A plaque was unveiled at the site, and the minister delivered a lengthy speech to a crowd of about 5,000. There was a feeling of euphoria in the air and the ceremony had about it the atmosphere of an historic occasion. I believed firmly that it was one of the most important events to take place in Connaught for over a hundred years. The minister spoke and this is what he said:

"Your Grace, my Lord Bishops, Monsignor, Reverend Fathers,

distinguished guests, ladies and gentlemen, I think I can justly say that today is an historic day for the people of Knock itself, for the county of Mayo and for the whole of Connaught. Today we have taken a step forward on the road to building a new airport that will serve the whole of the West of Ireland.

"This airport will add a new significant element to the infrastructure of the Connaught region. It will be a major benefit to the business community. It will facilitate the development of tourism and will help Knock to establish itself as a pilgrimage centre.

"So far as business and industry are concerned, I know that Mayo people have often felt cut off from the rest of Ireland and that this isolation creates difficulty in attracting new industry to the region. I believe that this new airport will go a long way towards ending this sense of remoteness and I hope that in due course it will open up the whole of the region for development.

"Business people know that time is money and this knowledge is reflected in their willingness to pay a premium to avoid losing time on travel. Connaught Airport, which will give them a link with the major commercial centres, will be invaluable. The airport will also allow the rapid movement of freight, especially perishable goods such as shellfish, as well as high-value consumer products, and will give easy access to the area to firms engaged in exploration for oil, gas or minerals.

"For the tourist, the airport will make this part of Ireland more attractive and will open up whole new areas of unspoiled countryside for visitors. The airport is bound to improve considerably the competitiveness of the Western seaboard and I am confident that the improved access which the airport will provide will lead to a resurgence of tourism in Mayo and surrounding counties.

"The airport's biggest contribution will be in enabling Knock to achieve its full potential as a pilgrimage centre. It seems to me that, as the world becomes more materialistic, the minds of men and women seek more diligently for some spiritual anchor. In Knock, the people of Ireland have a source of devotion and inspiration which, I have no doubt, will in the next few years spread its appeal to Christians in the rest of Europe and even the world. The visit in 1979 of Pope John Paul II to this shrine gave us a preview of what the future holds for Knock.

"I am pleased and honoured as Minister for Transport to formally initiate this project. Its development is a credit to the enterprise and initiative of the local people, and I think I am not being unfair to anyone else's efforts when I say that, were it not for the drive and enthusiasm of Monsignor Horan, this great project would still be just a dream. I regard the government's decision to approve the Connaught International Airport project at a cost of £8.5 million at 1980 prices as proof, if further proof were needed, of the government's commitment to developing the West of Ireland.

"In addition, my department will make its technical and specialist advice available to the promoters, as will Aer Rianta and Aer Lingus where appropriate, and I look forward to the close cooperation of the promoters of the airport with these organisations.

"Between us, we will provide for Knock an airport built to international standards with a 6,000-foot runway and supporting facilities capable of handling aircraft up to the size of the Boeing 737s, which Aer Lingus and other international air companies operate. Thus the airport will be able to support scheduled services to Dublin and UK destinations, charter flights from Europe, taxi services to other parts of Ireland and abroad, and, hopefully, a scheduled service operating as part of a network to other airports in Ireland.

"I look forward with great optimism to what the future holds for the airport. Many of you will recall that doubts were raised by faint-hearted people about earlier developments in this country in the aviation sphere. There were some who expressed no confidence in Shannon Airport when the project was first mooted. But Shannon Airport later achieved a significant place in world aviation and has transformed the economy of the Mid-Western region. The vision and the enterprise that built Shannon Airport has not been lost and I have no doubt that this project which we are inaugurating here today will do as much for Mayo and for Connaught as Shannon Airport has done for the Mid-West. But this will not be achieved without considerable local effort; Knock will have to be marketed and people persuaded to come here. Hotels and accommodation will have to be provided, and I will be looking to private enterprise in County Mayo to accept the challenge and take the initiative in providing the services that visitors require.

"I know that you all have great plans for the shrine at Knock and for Mayo and for Connaught as a whole. I believe that the airport will bring these plans to life and enable your dreams to be realised. I wish the project every success."

I replied to the minister, saying:

"To make use of liturgical language: 'This is Connaught's great day. Let us rejoice and be glad in it.' It is the day in which we bless and dedicate this beautiful site and turn the first sod. It is a day that the young people present will remember and relate to their children's children in years to come.

"Up to the present, this site had been known for generations as the 'Black Triangle'. It was boggy and wet, so wet that a local cynic said that even the snipe had to wear wellingtons. In two years time, when the airport is completed, we will have to find a new name for something that will be bright and beautiful. Then it will really be living up to its name *Barnacúige* – Top of the Province. Still, from what I know of Barnalyra, Barnacúige, Barcúil and Kilgarriff people, they will not allow pride to run away with them and they will still have a kind word and a smile for the Tarpeys and the Harringtons in the lowlands. These people know their scripture: 'No man lights a candle and puts it under a bushel but on a hilltop that it may be seen by all men.'

"We are all honoured to have with us on this happy occasion Mr Albert Reynolds, Minister of Transport and Posts and Telegraphs. I am most grateful to him for performing this beautiful ceremony of turning the first sod and for unveiling a plaque to commemorate this historic event. I would like him to know that the people of our beloved Connaught appreciate the important part that he played in getting government approval for our regional airport. I congratulate him on a magnificent job, not merely in transport but also in telecommunications. He is one of our most popular ministers and even the media love him. They tell us that in a very short time we will have a telephone on every bush in every bog-road throughout the country. Mr Minister, *go n-eirí an t-ádh leat.*

"I know how delighted you all are that we have with us today that bright young thing, none other than the Minister of State in the Department of Transport, Mr Pádraig Flynn. We cannot say that he is one of Charlie's Angels but he is very close to the throne. I have heard on reliable authority – from none other than himself – that the Taoiseach placed special responsibility on him to get this project off the ground as quickly as possible. We all know, now, that he moved so fast that he met with a slight accident, but thank God, he is with us today, walking tall, walking straight, with a new airport under his belt. Thank God that we had the right man in the right place at the right time when we made our move for an airport. The Taoiseach has a keen eye for talent and this young man will go far. How well I remember our first meeting with him and his officials in the Department of Transport. He brought all of us country lads into a hotel and made quite sure that we had no bog on our boots. When we were all dolled up, I remember him saying to me: 'You shut up and let me do all the talking.' I thought this very strange because he was always a lad who had not much to say.

"I could not let this occasion pass without showing my deepest appreciation for the understanding, sympathy and enthusiasm that the Taoiseach, Charles J. Haughey, has shown for the project, from the very first occasion that it was mentioned to him. It was at a luncheon in the Knock Shrine presbytery and John Healy of *The Irish Times* has already stated that it must have been the most expensive lunch that the Taoiseach has ever had. He has given the people of Connaught their greatest break in more than a century. I am certain that the people of the province will not forget him for it. It's a pity that he is not with us today to celebrate a very big occasion. I hope to have the opportunity of showing him around the new airport in the very near future. He will find it to be a truly Irish airport, with the turf piled high on the fire, and the flagstones spick and span on the floor, and the swish of a windmill to be heard outside. *Go n-eirí go geall leis i rud ar bith atá ar intinn aige.*

"I could not let the occasion pass without expressing my gratitude to P.J. Morley, our local TD, who is always at hand to advise me, guide me and encourage me. No better man than he to tip me off as to the best way to approach and address the Minister of State in the Department of Transport, Mr Pádraig Flynn. He tells me that the people of this area are very fond of him as a result. *Go mbeirimid beo ar an am seo arís.*

"I take this opportunity of thanking my friend, Mr Sean Callery TD, on whom I have called very often for help in my difficulties. I owe him a deep debt of gratitude. While it is true that the government is giving us this airport, it is only fair to say when Dr Garrett Fitzgerald visited the site some months ago he told me that he was fully in favour of regional airports. It makes me very happy to know that the government have approved of it and that they have the full support of the main opposition party.

"The group of people who played the biggest part in making this airport possible were the people of Barnalyra, Barnacúige, Barcúil and Kilgarriff. Just as the word *Barr* before the names of their villages suggests, they are tops in my estimation, for being spunky, generous, public-spirited and delightful people. They made available this splendid, glorious and scenic site, which will become one of the most beautiful airports in Europe. The airport with its magnificent setting will become a great tourist attraction in its own right and I hope that it will bring them and their families great happiness and prosperity.

"I would like to pay a special tribute to Frank Harrington and his gallant men who have carried out the preliminary work on the site with enthusiasm and efficiency. They have done a superb job and they have done it in good time. They have certainly proved themselves fit to undertake any project no matter how demanding it may be. A friend of mine who called here, and who had seen Frank and his men in action, commented: 'I was happy to have seen, at last, a team of Irishmen doing the same efficient job in their own country as they have been doing in other countries for many years. I have no doubt that songs will be composed about Frank Harrington and his men like the one composed about McAlpine and his fusiliers.'

"The cynics for some time now have been trying to make up their minds as to whether this airport will be a white elephant or a monster to gobble up Shannon. However, they need not worry, for, nowadays, with modern technology, we can give the white elephant a lovely blue rinse. For, after all, who can say that Connaught is not entitled to its own airport and, I can assure you, Connaught will make good use of it. Certainly, we are not casting envious eyes at Shannon or posing any threat whatsoever. We are, on the other hand, convinced that with co-operation and good will we can be a great asset to Shannon's transatlantic traffic and Shannon will be a great boon to us. The young people of Mayo are in a majority and they want to live and work in their own country. If they have to go away, we want them to be able to come back as soon as possible to their own airport. Furthermore, a recent NESC survey has revealed that the average income for a family in the West of Ireland is 25% lower than for a family in any other part of the country. With that in mind, it is only reasonable that we need an airport as part of the necessary infrastructure to promote employment, industrial development and tourism. We are proud of Shannon, it is a great international airport, but who can expect us to starve for it?

"I would like to thank all the members of our committee who took such great interest in the airport and made it possible. Our gratitude goes to Dr Ken Holden of Transportation Analysis International. The success of this project is proof that he did his job well and he should be a proud man today. I would like to make a special mention of Jim Ryan who did a great job in public relations with the department and with the local people of the area. He may have spent much time over cups of tea in Barnalyra, but it was well worth it. At the end of the day the people of this area have the highest regard for him.

"I would like to thank Mr Sean Balfe, engineer, Claremorris, and Maloney & Millar, consultant engineers, Dublin, who have done a very efficient job in planning and layout. They had to work to a very tight schedule but they delivered in time. I thank Patrick McEllin and Son, solicitors, Claremorris, for the expert way they handled all legal matters. I thank Oliver Freaney & Company for keeping us on the straight and narrow in regard to fiscal matters.

"Last, but not least, I thank all the officials and engineers of the Department of Transport and Aer Rianta for their kindness and co-operation during the planning stages of the project. We may not have agreed on everything, but we all had a very pleasant and enjoyable time.

"I thank all the people who have helped me to organise this beautiful function, especially the people of Charlestown and Kilkelly. I thank all the people who organised bands for the occasion. I also thank the media and the press who have joined us in our celebrations. I owe them a great debt of gratitude because down through the years they never let people forget that I had a new project on hand and needed help.

"Last, but not least, I thank Most Rev. Dr Thomas Flynn, Bishop of Achonry and bishop of the airport, for performing the most important ceremony of all, the blessing of the site. Let's hope that the airport will bring countless blessings to the people of this province. *Moladh go deo le Dia.*"

Preparatory work on the airport was completed in late spring, 1981. In the January budget money had been made available for the airport and the committee was now informed that in order to qualify for grant aid it would have to form itself into a statutory body which would be known as the Connaught Regional Airport Company Ltd. About half of the committee now had to opt out as they could not be directors of the new company; they would not qualify as directors owing to positions or posts held by them in state agencies.

The contract for the construction of the airport was signed on June 1981. The contract had been awarded to Mr Patrick Harrington & Co Ltd, Kilkelly. The workers were all local people many of whom returned from England to work on the project. Work on the airport began in the first week of July 1981.

When the work was well advanced I had a visit from an Englishman who lived in Dublin. "Monsignor," he said, "I have just visited the airport and I could not pass without calling to tell you that I have seen a sight that delights my heart. I have seen Irishmen doing a job for their own country and its people that they have been doing for other countries for years. Who built the airports and roads throughout Great Britain? They were built by Irishmen, many of them from the West of Ireland. I'm proud of them!"

But many criticisms appeared in the news media about the airport being built on a bog. Yet the company prided itself on that decision. Why waste good arable land, which is at a premium in the West, when you can find disused land which is perfectly suitable? The site was a bog with a difference: when the peat was removed you have a gravel and rock base. It is well to remember that Kennedy Airport, New York, and our own Shannon Airport were built on swamps or boggy land.

The Gospel speaks of the wise man who built his house upon rock: "And the rain fell, and the floods came, and the winds blew, and they beat upon that house, and it fell not, for it was founded upon a rock." The truth was that an airport built upon such a foundation will not disintegrate or sink beneath the surface. But there was to be so much misrepresentation, lying propaganda and downright abuse unleashed on the airport site that it was impossible for the truth to catch up with it.

Airport Project Meets Hostility

When it came to dealing with Knock Airport and the role played by Charles J. Haughey, the media made all kinds of suggestions and insinuations about "deals", "strokes" and even "intrigue". I would like to know what part "intrigue" could play in making representations to politicians and to Taoiseachs; I have made representations to all kinds of politicians of every colour and of none, and consider it my right to do so.

In fact I never had, up to the time of writing, a private interview or any other kind of private meeting with Charles J. Haughey. I have known his mother and other members of his family, including his brother, Fr Eoghan, for many years. I first met Mr Haughey on the occasion of the funeral of two Gardaí from my parish who had been shot dead in the Ballaghaderreen bank-raid and whose funeral took place on 10 July 1980. He came to a lunch at the presbytery in Knock, to which all politicians had been invited, including Dr Garret Fitzgerald who though he did not attend the lunch called at the presbytery for some refreshments after the Requiem Mass. Mr Liam Cosgrave was also present. I made a little speech to welcome the Taoiseach and the other guests and I made reference in a light-hearted manner to the proposed airport. At that stage the Taoiseach had received a copy of the feasibility study carried out by TAI, and when he replied to my speech, in a similarly light-hearted way, he said that the airport would get sympathetic consideration, or words to that effect. Mr Jack Lynch, former Taoiseach, immediately warned: "That is not a commitment, Monsignor." I knew it was not a commitment, though it was encouraging.

The next meeting I had with Charles J. Haughey was at the opening ceremony for the Central Remedial Clinic on 23 September 1980 in Dublin. The Taoiseach was invited to perform the ceremony and I was invited for the occasion. There was lunch served but Mr Haughey did not attend the lunch. I had intended to discuss the airport with him and had even prepared my arguments, but, having thought about it on the journey to Dublin, I felt in the end that I should not take advantage of such an occasion to discuss the airport or any other business. After lunch Dr

Ken Holden invited the guests into a large drawing-room to meet the Taoiseach. I was standing in the midst of a large number of guests when he shook hands with me and jokingly said: "Will you have the red carpet out for me in Knock, when I attend Mass there on Sunday next?"

"Certainly," I said. "Knock will be honoured to receive the Taoiseach." He passed on and that was the end of the conversation. After the opening ceremony at the clinic I went on a tour of the building. In the corridor I met the Taoiseach and his entourage again. As he approached me he laid his hand on my shoulder and said: "I am hopeful that your airport will materialise."

"I hope so," I said. End of conversation.

On 28 September we had breakfast in my house after he had attended Mass in the basilica, together with Fianna Fáil politicians, on his tour of the western counties. I have no recollection of any references being made to the airport on this occasion, and neither had I any private meeting with the Taoiseach on the subject. More than 5,000 people were present at the Mass, when the Taoiseach occupied the place of honour at a special *prie-dieu*: on such an occasion the leader of our country gets a place of honour. After Mass he mingled with the huge crowd in the shrine grounds. He had that easy, natural and friendly touch that endeared him to the people. In a by-election in Donegal I had observed him on the streets of Letterkenny when he delighted the crowds with his winning manner.

The people of the West had decided to honour the new Fianna Fáil leader and Taoiseach by unveiling a plaque at the house where he was born in Castlebar. Mayo was proud of him as a native son. The guests assembled in Marsh House and walked in procession to the house of his birth in Mountain View Street. The streets along the way were thronged with people who clapped and cheered on his arrival. I had been asked to unveil the plaque and I opened the ceremony by making a speech as follows:

"Taoiseach, Archbishop, ladies and gentleman, I am most grateful for the privilege of unveiling this plaque at the birthplace of a very distinguished Irishman and Mayoman, Mr Charles J. Haughey.

"Taoiseach, I myself was born just down the road in the parish of Partry, and as a boy I attended the market at Staball at least once. Being an old neighbour and recipient of the Mayo *Meitheal*

Award with my Archbishop, Most Rev. Dr Joseph Cunnane, I was asked to perform this ceremony.

"Taoiseach, the measure of your popularity in Mayo can be gauged from the fact that you received the Mayoman of the Year Award in 1978, and your esteem and concern for the people of Mayo and Connaught has been proved by the recent announcement of a regional airport for our province. We are proud of the fact that you are the first Mayoman to reach the highest political office in this state, that of Taoiseach.

"As parish priest of Knock Shrine I am also happy to honour you as a member of a family that has been associated with the shrine for many years. Your family, and especially your mother and brother, Fr Eoghan OMI, have been personal friends of mine down the years, and I have always valued their friendship. I am glad that your wife, Mrs Maureen Haughey, your mother and Fr Eoghan are with us here today. Whenever your mother visited Knock she never failed to come along and greet me.

"Taoiseach, I know that you have just entered this very responsible office and I know that you have the business acumen, initiative and flair to make a great success of it. As Taoiseach you have the right to the support of every Irishman and woman in your efforts to guide our country through a period of worldwide recession. I hope and pray that your efforts will meet with great success and lead our beloved country to an era of peace and prosperity.

"*Go mairidh tú is go gcaithidh tú do nuaíocht!*"

At the mention of the airport he rose from his seat and shook my hand warmly. The cameras of the press clicked and flashed all around. The next day the pictures made the front page. This was Haughey's "honeymoon period" with the media, just after his election as Taoiseach. It was not to last long; soon he would be fighting for his political life with deadly opposition from the same media.

At no time did I meet Charles J. Haughey alone on this or any other occasion, or discuss Connaught Regional Airport with him. There was no opportunity for "strokes", "deals", or "intrigue". I did know that he had a sentimental attachment to the West of Ireland, the place of his birth. I am sure that Jack Lynch had the same attachment to Cork and Garret Fitzgerald to Dublin.

The next meeting, and the last to date, was when he visited the airport on 26 May 1981; he was on a General Election tour before polling day on 11 June. To preserve a political balance I had already met Garret Fitzgerald at the same site a few weeks previously, when I had been accompanied by Most Rev. Dr Joseph Cunnane. I have not met Charles J. Haughey since that day. I never met him in Dáil Éireann or in any other place. That will surprise many people who have liked to think otherwise.

I always admired Charles J. Haughey as a man of courage and determination, who kept his promises even at great personal or political cost. I regret the fact that a kind gesture by a Taoiseach to the people of his native province was used as a stick to beat him. In this game the ball was thrown in by a journalist who dubbed my action in unveiling the plaque as political and he labelled Charles J. Haughey's gift of an airport to his native Connaught as a political "stroke". In June Fianna Fáil failed to get an overall majority to form a government. Headed by Garret Fitzgerald, Fine Gael formed a coalition with Labour and a number of Independent TDs. It was a critical time for the airport and for the Connaught Regional Airport Company: would the coalition government honour the previous administration's commitment to the airport? The new Taoiseach, Garret Fitzgerald, had visited the site on his election tour and we felt sure that his government would not break the promise they had given before the election. Fine Gael had given a commitment not merely to an airport for Connaught but also to a £10m sports complex, and surely no government would turn down an airport project and build a sports complex. All the same, we were grateful when the new government confirmed that work would proceed on the airport. The contractor started work on the site in July 1981, the same week as the new government took office. The Coalition budget allocated £2.5m to the project.

Connaught Regional Airport was estimated to cost £8.5m at 1980 prices and, making due allowance for inflation, it remained on target. It is the only project in Ireland in recent years that has kept within its original budgets. If this happened in any other part of the country it would be acclaimed to the high heavens and set up as a model for others to follow, but this is not what happened to Connaught Airport. While no genuine argument was ever made against the airport, it was quickly assigned to the realm of the "Irish white elephants". I must say that that designation placed it in very select company. Among the original white elephants of Ireland are such prestigious projects as Shannon

Hydro-electric Scheme, Shannon Airport, Bórd na Móna and the Irish Sugar Company. Knock became a symbol of economic folly and this was most unfair and unjust. It was also used, on every possible occasion, to embarrass Charles J. Haughey, both as Taoiseach and as leader of the opposition. I remember that in two Herculean debates on television between Haughey and Garret Fitzgerald, Connaught Regional Airport was invariably pulled out of the hat. Elections were fought and won on an unfinished runway. I was often afraid to wake up in the morning and turn on the radio in case there would be another attack on the airport on the morning news, or in "What It Says in the Papers". At times the bashing of the airport and all concerned with it was so bad that my health was expected to crack. And enquiries about my health came from the most unexpected quarters. There was one particular journalist who concentrated so much on my age I am sure he was wondering how many years I had left.

There had been much speculation in the media and round the country as to what stance the new government would adopt towards the project. The Board of Directors of the Connaught Regional Airport Company were worried too, and I had asked a department official for his opinion as to the outcome. He replied that "it would only be a two-pence-halfpenny government that would renege on a decision of a previous government". The crucial decision had to be made when it came to the signing of the Grant-Aid Agreement, which was eventually signed on 20 August 1981.

So far, so good. Everything had gone well all through the summer; the board members, the contractor, the workers were all happy doing a great job for Connaught. But it was only the calm before the storm. On one of the last days of September I was driving in my car, listening to the news, when suddenly I heard a blistering attack being made on Charles J. Haughey, ex-Taoiseach. That was the flash-point, the signal for a protracted, concerted, relentless attack on what Barry Desmond insisted on calling "Knock Airport".

The basis of Barry Desmond's argument was an inter-departmental report which was leaked to the media. I quote from Barry Desmond's statement as reported in *The Irish Times*, 30 September 1981:

> The Minister of State at the Department of Finance, Mr Desmond, has asked the Taoiseach, Dr Fitzgerald, to suspend

all expenditure on the construction of Knock Airport pending a full review of the project.

Mr Desmond made his request in a letter to the Taoiseach and in a statement issued later to the press he repeated his criticism of the decision by the Fianna Fáil Government to build the airport in the first place, in view of the report by an inter-departmental working group which said that the airport could not be justified in purely economic/financial terms.

But a Government spokesman said later that some Ministers felt there was a commitment to support the project to the tune of £8m. The airport, he added, would go ahead but with a ceiling on expenditure set at £8m. The Minister for the Gaeltacht, Mr O'Toole, is understood to be one of those Ministers.

Mr Desmond commented that the original estimate of £8m for the airport was based on 1980 prices and was for a runway of 6,000 feet and basic installations. He added, however, that the promoters were now proceeding with an earthworks contract for a runway of 7,500 feet, 1,500 feet larger than Cork and capable of taking Jumbo Jet aircraft. A runway of that length would add massively to the cost of the project. Mr Desmond claimed that Aer Lingus and possibly Aer Rianta would have to be provided with additional State subsidies for losses on services there.

"My assessment," Mr Desmond said, "of a £20 million loss by 1985 is quite realistic. Thereafter, the annual operational loss will be £2 million and growing. As a former member of the Joint Committee on State-Sponsored Bodies which reported on Aer Lingus, Aer Rianta and other transport undertakings, I am aghast at this proposed waste of public monies," Mr Desmond said.

Mr Desmond said the decision in principle to go ahead – taken by the former Minister of State, Mr Pádraig Flynn – was taken on receipt of a feasibility study from the promoters which was later found to be based on false premises. The go-ahead for the airport was given, the Minister of State maintained, by Mr Haughey and the former Minister, Mr Reynolds, without having studied, costed and resolved such questions as: why an airport at Knock?

"Why were the serious and known deficiencies in the findings of the consultants, who prepared the feasibility study for the airport, ignored?" asked Mr Desmond. "Were the Taoiseach and the former Ministers, Gene Fitzgerald, Albert Reynolds and Pádraig Flynn, not fully aware that last February the report of the Inter-Departmental Working Group on the Knock Airport proposal stated that their assessment of the market potential did not suggest that there existed a solid foundation on which to mount a B737 style service? Did not this group of responsible public servants also report that 'There is no option which, in the view of the group, can be justified in purely financial/economic terms?'"

The study referred to was carried out by Aer Rianta, Aer Lingus, the Department of Transport, Department of the Taoiseach, Department of Finance and the Department of Industry, Commerce and Tourism, all of which had a vested interest in downgrading the idea of a Connaught Regional Airport. It was a packed jury but even so the report was not as bad as it was painted. All the so-called economic and government advisers took selective quotations from the report, but one can prove anything, even from the Bible, by taking quotations out of context. The critics only considered the project on financial/economic terms and not at all from the socio-economic point of view. The last paragraph of the report acknowledged:

> Overall, our work has shown that there is no option which, in the view of the group, can be justified in purely financial/economic terms. Decisions on the nature of the facilities and the scale of operations to be provided will, we suggest, have to take account, not only of the financial/economic aspects on which our study by its nature had to concentrate but also of wider issues of a socio-economic and political nature.

The socio-economic aspect is a vital part of a project like this. Airports are built as infrastructure, to boost industry, tourism etc. Yet the inter-departmental committee only considered the project from the point of view of whether it could make money or not; they considered it on a profit-and-loss basis. But an airport, like a road, is not built to make money: it is built to give service to a community. Connaught needed that service and was paying for it in taxes. The cost of the airport was estimated by Barry Desmond at £20 million by 1985; in January 1985 the almost completed airport had cost £10.3m, and the runway was 8,100 feet even at that cost. I claim, unless somebody is able to prove otherwise, that Connaught Regional Airport was the only project in the country in recent years that kept to its financial targets.

But though the Minister for the Gaeltacht went on television to assure the public that the project would be finished, once Barry Desmond had attacked the airport a concerted, planned and persistent campaign of denunciation, vilification, misrepresentation and downright lying began. The campaign to undermine the airport had many aspects. The political aspect was very much to the fore as it was combined with a campaign to vilify Charles J. Haughey, whose government had given approval to the project initially. There was also the East-West dimension which reflected the bias of those who think that any money – except dole – that may be spent in the West is "waste", "nonsense" and even "madness": these were some of the epithets used to describe the Connaught Regional Airport, which was soon better known as Knock Airport. And unfortunately, too, you had the traditional jealousies between different areas and counties in the West – the bickering of people foolish enough to fight amongst themselves for the crumbs that fell from the national table.

From Barry Desmond's outburst onward, the aim of the government was to scale down the operation. The mind of the government was revealed through deliberate leaks to the media. Most of it was kite-flying: they were probing to find out what the public reaction would be to any decision that they might take. It was clear at this stage that any decision they would make would be politically motivated.

As chairman of the Connaught Regional Airport Company I suspected that one of the options being considered by the Coalition government was to cut the airport down to a 4,000 feet runway. This proposal was suggested to us at two steering group meetings by an official from the Aeronautical Section of the Department of Transport, though I was of the opinion that the proposal came not from the department, as that particular aspect did not come within its ambit, but from the Minister for Transport, Mr Cooney. It got a cold reception from our board of directors: the proposal was rejected without discussion. Ken Holden, who had carried out the feasibility study, had made it quite clear that a 4,000-foot runway was useless for our purposes and it is quite easy to see why. The difference in fares between travelling on a small plane as compared to a large plane is the same as the difference between travelling in a motor-car or in a bus: the bus and the larger plane come much cheaper. The smaller the vehicle the higher the fare; this is real and undeniable logic, and quite clear even to people who are not transport experts. Connaught needed a runway capable of taking those larger planes.

On 1 December 1981 I called to the Department of Transport on my way to a press conference to promote a "Hymn for Knock" contest which was being held in the National Gallery. I had a discussion with two officials, who were also directors of the airport company, for more than two hours. They tried to persuade me to accept a runway of 4,000 feet, and suggested that the company should fight for the extra length later. They made it clear to me that if the company did not accept the shorter runway the airport might be axed, but I knew that if we compromised now we would never get anything more from the government. The government seemed to have become completely hostile to the project and had demonstrated such an attitude a number of times since taking office.

There was tension in the air, and a feeling of expectancy that a decision on the airport was imminent. Many journalists turned up for the press conference to interview me, not about the hymn for Knock but about the airport. In the circumstances I was not in the mood to be interviewed and, as talks at the Department of Transport had gone on much longer than expected, I was going to be late arriving at the press conference. I decided not to attend; after all, my archbishop Dr Joseph Cunnane and Fr Peter Waldron, director of the hymn contest, were present and they could give all the necessary information. It was only fair, too, that the reception would not be turned into a press conference on the fate of "Knock Airport".

The following day the press reported:

KNOCK AIRPORT PRIEST FAILS TO ATTEND BRIEFING

The Knock Airport promoter, Monsignor James Horan, failed to turn up at a news conference yesterday. It was understood that he had travelled to Dublin for the news conference which was called to announce details of a "Hymn for Knock" competition. But he, apparently, went to ground when he realised he was being sought after by the media.

An article by Denis Coughlan in one of the papers asked:

COONEY TO CLIP KNOCK'S WINGS?

The Government may not stand by contracts signed by Monsignor James Horan for work to be carried out at Knock International Airport if a report commissioned by the Minister for Transport and Communications, Mr Cooney, is acted upon.

A Government source indicated yesterday that the review of the Knock project carried out by officials of the Department of Transport had recommended that the work be scaled down to cost about £4 million. But it is understood that Monsignor Horan has already signed contracts for work on the site to the value of more than £5 million.

Traditionally, Governments recognise and underwrite contracts entered into by Departments and semi-state bodies, even if the projects involved are shelved or abandoned. But the Connaught Airport Development Company is a private concern and Government sanction has been given only for the spending of about £2 million on earthworks.

A Government source said that the decision to sign contracts, far in advance of works in progress, was not appreciated by the Minister concerned and that there was no guarantee that the Government would pick up the tab. If the work involved in the contracts had not been completed, he added, the work might have to be cancelled.

Last night Monsignor Horan was not available for comment at his home in Knock.

The day after I visited the Department of Transport I got a phone-call from the minister announcing the death of the airport. This phone-call was followed by a written statement the following day, 3 December 1981. It read:

The Government has decided, when the present earthworks contract has been completed, to cease its involvement in the Connaught Regional Airport project. Its involvement in the completion of the project will be renewed when financial conditions indicate.

In a way I was not surprised. I had refused to accept a watered-down version of an airport from the Department of Transport, and I knew then that the whole project might be axed, at least for the time being. Yet I could hardly believe that the Coalition government would abandon the project after such solemn election promises had been given by the Taoiseach, Dr Garret Fitzgerald, and Mr Paddy O'Toole, Minister for the Gaeltacht. Who could have expected that a project – especially an infrastructural project – would be abandoned after millions of pounds had already been spent on it? And not only had the government pledged to complete the airport but they had also promised to promote a sports complex near by. How wrong could I be?

Within days of the government's announcement meetings were set up in many of the western counties to seek support for the airport. As the weeks passed a growing and vociferous campaign got underway. The Connaught Airport Action Committee was set up in Charlestown under the chairmanship of Frank McCullough, Swinford. In a short time they had established an office and begun to raise funds to fight the case. The office was efficiently run by Mr Peter Walsh and devised many plans and schemes to save the airport, and it gave great moral support to the promoters of the project.

Fianna Fáil politicians rallied to the cause. The former Minister for Transport, Albert Reynolds, the former Minister of State at the Department of Transport, Pádraig Flynn, and the local Fianna Fáil TD, P.J. Morley, called on me to offer their support. They also visited the airport and met the workers. Their visits created a great atmosphere of hope and encouragement and were very much appreciated. I personally got hundreds of letters of support from all over the country. Most of the letters were from across the Shannon, many from supporters of Knock Shrine all over the world. I got messages from people who were disgusted by the short-sightedness of a government which would fund a project to the extent of £10m and then abandon it, a decision which must surely be the height of folly.

But on 3 December 1981 nobody could have foreseen what political development was going to take place within less than two months. When the news media had gloated sufficiently over the "knocking" of the airport, speculation began to grow about the contents of the budget due in January. Having disposed of "Knock Airport" without much fuss or political outrage, the government could now settle down to pursue its policy of fiscal rectitude. They turned to another of Charles J. Haughey's legacies, the subsidies on food and children's clothing, and gave these subsidies the chop in the forthcoming budget. There may have been other items in the budget which the public did not like, but the withdrawal of the subsidies was the straw that would break the camel's back.

On 27 January the budget was announced in the Dáil by the Minister for Finance, Mr John Bruton. The country was shocked at the withdrawal of all subsidies from food and clothing. The Independent TDs were particularly angry and their anger increased even more when they realised the reaction of their constituents. It would hit parents with families, and especially large families, very hard.

The most powerful politician in Ireland at that time, because he held the potential balance of power in the Dáil, was Mr Jim Kemmy of Limerick, who sat as an Independent. The Taoiseach could not sneeze without getting his approval. In every RTE programme which looked at the state of the country, he seemed to be there. His opinion on every national policy was sought by the newspapers who knew that his input on government policy could, on the day, be crucial. The fatal day of the budget was one of these days. He gave the government and the Taoiseach an ultimatum: if the subsidies on food and clothing were not restored he would vote against the government at the conclusion of the budget debate. Every artifice and attempt was made to persuade Kemmy to back the government in the vote but all in vain. He was adamant.

When the bell rang for the division in the Dáil the deputies in the various parties filed into the lobbies. Jim Kemmy was still seated. Garret Fitzgerald, on his way to the government lobby, stopped to speak to him and then proceeded on his way. Now the moment of truth had come; the fate of the whole country depended on the vote of this one man. Slowly he rose and entered the opposition lobby, a move which was greeted with an irreverent "whoopee" in the Dáil. The government had fallen and "Knock Airport" might live again! The Taoiseach, Dr Garret Fitzgerald, immediately went to the Phoenix Park and handed in his seal of office to the President, Dr Patrick Hillery. The President accepted his resignation and the date of the General Election was fixed for 18 February 1982, three weeks later.

Reprieve for Connaught Airport

It seemed inconceivable that Fine Gael could again have had the Connaught Regional Airport on its election manifesto, but they had. It was in the Fine Gael programme for East Mayo, Paddy O'Toole's constituency. As the only representative in the cabinet of people from Donegal to Shannon, he should, in all decency, have resigned when he found the people of the West being treated so shabbily. If he had done so he would have been a hero in the West for all time, his political future guaranteed.

With just one representative in the cabinet, the West fared very badly in the early eighties. The projects axed by a new Coalition government in 1984 were all in the West: Knock Airport, the chipboard factory in Clare and the briquette factory in Ballyforan, Co. Galway, and if the Minister of State, John Connaughton from Galway, had not laid his ministry on the line, the Tuam Beet Factory would also have been closed.* Fair play to him, he had the courage of his convictions and won the day. But it is quite clear that a Coalition government with Labour as one of the partners will never give anything to the West of Ireland. They have no support in the West and have no interest whatsoever in that part of the country. Indeed, there even seems to be a certain vindictiveness in their attitude to the people of the West.

Will the people, and especially our public representatives in the West ever wake up and fight for the rights of the region? There is downright discrimination against the people of the western seaboard. If "Knock" Airport were built in any other part of Ireland it would have been hailed as the achievement of the century. We built a complete airport for a third of the cost of building a runway in Dublin – it takes £32m at 1983 prices to build a runway in Dublin, while Connaught Regional Airport, its 8,000-foot runway and all amenities, was built for a mere £11m. More recently £2m was spent on resurfacing a runway in Dublin Airport which must now be scrapped. If that had happened in the West there would have been a hue-and-cry in all the daily newspapers.

The Tuam factory closed in 1991.

Once the election campaign got underway Knock Airport quickly became an issue. It became such a political football that even some Fianna Fáil TDs wanted to be in the fashion and criticise it. David Andrews TD, representing the same constituency as Barry Desmond, wanted the airport money to build a £50m ringroad in Dublin, another of the city's many expensive ventures. Just before polling day a very interesting feature appeared in the *Irish Press*. It gave an accurate picture of the views held by various political parties on the airport and evidence of dissension on the subject within Fianna Fáil. Perhaps it was the harbinger of more serious divisions within the party later in that year. The feature contained criticism by Mr P.J. Morley on the attitude of some of his colleagues in the Fianna Fáil party.

CURB PARTY CRITICS ON KNOCK – FF MAN

The controversial Knock Airport project led to the outgoing Fianna Fáil TD in Mayo East, Mr P.J. Morley, calling yesterday on his party leader to discipline Ms Síle de Valera and Mr Niall Andrews over their statements criticising the building of the airport.

Also yesterday, the *Irish Press* received an internal memo sent out by Fianna Fáil, dated January 30th, to brief candidates on what it termed "a highly sensitive issue, having regard to its potential support in Connacht and highly critical East Coast response".

The memo lists five "facts available to dispute any criticism of the Fianna Fáil pre- and post-election position" including the statement that a proposal to build a Connacht (the word "Western" crossed out) Regional Airport at Kilkelly had been in existence for several years, and was again raised by the Papal Visit.

It also stressed that the Fianna Fáil commitment was a once-off Grant-in-Aid of £8 million as costed in 1980.

A Fianna Fáil-established group to research traffic potential is quoted as saying: While it could not ascertain the hard facts about pilgrimage traffic, it concluded that a figure in the region of 40,000-50,000 would be generated annually, and in its view the project was viable. The memo also noted that Fine Gael supported the project publicly on two occasions, and the supplementary estimate of £2.2m prepared by the Coalition in mid-June was passed unanimously through the Dáil.

The Minister for the Gaeltacht, Mr O'Toole, meanwhile criticised critics of the airport issue yesterday, and alleged that the protest campaign about the Government postponement was politically motivated.

"Do they want me to build the damn thing myself?" demanded Mr O'Toole.

Though the election had been fiercely fought the outcome was inconclusive. Fianna Fáil held its lead but failed to gain an overall majority, and was dependent on the support of Independent TDs to form a government.

Now the real lobbying started. Jim Kemmy was no longer the key to power in the Dáil; this mantle fell on a Dublin TD, Tony Gregory, who threw in his lot with Charles J. Haughey. With Haughey as Taoiseach we now had a new government and hope for a reprieve from the death sentence of December 1981. John Wilson was appointed Minister for Transport and much to our surprise we discovered that the outgoing administration had left us a nice nest-egg in its last will and testament – £4.5m, the allocation for Connaught Regional Airport in the January budget. The change of regime was good news and lifted the gloom from the western world. We now had the money to complete the first phase of the work on the airport.

However, at steering group meetings and board meetings the atmosphere was not as bright as it should have been in the circumstances. We had three board members from two departments – two from Transport and one from Finance – and I found it hard as chairman to cope with members who wore two different hats. They were obliged to look after the ministers' interests as well as the interests of the board, and the two did not always coincide, especially when we faced a hostile government. They must have been caught at times on the horns of a dilemma; however, we always struck a balance and I think we never had to put any proposition to a vote. A very good record!

With a friendly government in power we had expected to achieve much in 1982, but that was not to be. Time and time again I tried to get permission to bring 3-phase electricity from Charlestown to the site and to proceed with the water scheme, but my plans were frowned upon by the departmental officials who insisted that they would not meet with ministerial approval. This was frustrating: how could we have an airport without these two essential commodities? Work at Barnalyra continued; the workers were intelligent, skilled and absolutely dedicated, and I was proud of their determination and enthusiasm, even though the media and politicians were trying to put them on the road. They did a mighty job and Knock Airport is a monument to their skill, courage and dedication. Surrounded by people of that calibre, an airport cannot fail and will not fail. At the same time the Connaught Airport Action Committee drew support from all over Connaught and beyond, though the need for such a group was not seen as urgent now that work on the airport was proceeding under the new government. Yet, though the Connaught Airport Action Group lost some if its impetus in promoting tourism and industrialisation in the province, it had done a good job for Connaught.

Despite the change of government, the onslaught on the airport continued; indeed, it became all the more vicious now that Charles J. Haughey was in power. A few weeks after the election an attack was made on the airport from a most unexpected quarter. The *Connaught Tribune* of 5 March 1982 carried a report of a meeting of the Galway Chamber of Commerce:

£16M "WASTED" ON KNOCK AIRPORT

Politicians are willing to sink £16 million in a boghole in County Mayo to build an airport which will probably never be used, rather than spend the money on improving infrastructure in the West of Ireland, a meeting of Galway Chamber of Commerce was told on Tuesday night.

In a stinging attack on the Connacht Regional Airport project at Knock, leading Galway businessman Mr Thomas McDonogh declared that Ireland was a misgoverned country where politicians were wasting money on such projects which would be better spent on improving roads in the West.

The Chamber was discussing the problem of growing unemployment in Galway when Mr McDonogh made his attack. He said that the two major problems in the West of Ireland were in the areas of infrastructure and communications.

"It's an absolute disgrace that public money should be used in this way. It's an absolute drain on the economy. This airport will never be used short of some fantastic miracle – this money should be used to make better roads," said Mr McDonogh.

"Our biggest problems in the West are infrastructure and communications. We're a misgoverned country when we are prepared to sink £16 million in a boghole in Mayo, which should be used to improve our roads. We are misdirecting the economy for short-term political gain and this is an absolute disgrace..."

As work progressed on the site, however, media coverage of the issue dwindled. There were many reasons for this strange new silence. Perhaps, with Fianna Fáil in power, the media took it for granted that the airport would go ahead on schedule and there was nothing to be gained by protest; after all, Charles J. Haughey and the Minister for Finance, Ray McSharry, had given a commitment in February, on assuming power, that the airport would be completed. As well as that, members of the airport board were reluctant to give interviews; they were very much aware that such interviews would only be used by the media to attack or embarrass the Fianna Fáil government. East-West cleavage on the issue was very much in evidence. The Dublin-based media had turned the project into a symbol of economic folly and placed it firmly at the door of the Taoiseach, Charles J. Haughey; Knock Airport became a slogan to rally the anti-Haughey brigades. The friends of the airport decided to "let the hare sit" for the time being.

Just six weeks after Barry Desmond had launched his attack on Knock Airport the members of the board panicked and passed a resolution on 12 November 1981 which agreed that "in future all statements relating to the airport should be cleared by the board and made by the chairman". The government representatives on the board had always pressed for this kind of action but I felt that it was literally tying the hands of the members in the important duty of answering criticism. The outcome of this decision was that the board issued no press statement of any kind from there on.

I am sure that the resolution of the board was a criticism of me personally, and I made it clear at that meeting that I had published some articles on the airport and that there were other features coming up in *Business & Finance* and on the *Today Tonight* television programme. I must have seemed unrepentant to the company members, but I felt that this resolution had been passed to silence me as chairman. I had given interviews to the media and had written articles to the press to counteract lying propaganda. I never revealed any information obtained at board meetings and never spoke on behalf of the board. I understood the reluctance of the government representatives in being party to any statement that would embarrass the minister or compromise their relations with him, and I always confined myself to the facts of the case and did not mete out criticism to any individual, political or otherwise. If that embarrassed people I felt sorry, but it was necessary and inevitable. My view was that I was entitled to make statements on my own behalf as long as I did not presume to speak for the board. Time proved that this policy was correct and the public admired my courage in taking up the challenge and speaking in defence of the airport.

Ever since work on the airport started I had been stalked by journalist, and when they caught up with me it was a question of either fobbing them off, as TDs do when entering the Dáil chambers, or standing one's ground and defending one's cause. If I fobbed them off they would write a story anyhow and perhaps not a true or complimentary one. I seemed to be very much in demand as chairman of the board and as the person believed to be responsible for the initiation of the scheme in the first place, and when I was cornered I always fought my way out. I am now convinced that I took the right decision and both journalists and the public seemed to have more respect for me as a result.

I was also swayed by the thought that journalists have a job to do and their livelihood depends on it. Generally speaking I got a lot of sympathy and backing for my point of view from journalists. One always found the odd case where a journalist went out to collect any little scrap of information that would back up his editor's point of view, or quite often one might find a screaming headline that had no bearing at all to the subject matter of the interview; such a headline is always the responsibility of the sub-editor and not the reporter. But if, on the other hand, I refused to give an interview to journalists they could easily assume that I was trying to hide something. An interview is always a challenge and my general policy had always been to meet the challenge.

Nevertheless, the members of the board and I as chairman kept a low profile. We moved cautiously and kept our heads down to avoid the flak. The situation was very well summarised by Frank Byrne in the *Sunday Independent* of 22 August 1982:

> At present, the directors of the airport development scheme, of which the Monsignor is one, would appear to have taken a vow of silence with regard to the media; they have admittedly been deluged with criticism from that particular quarter.
>
> All publicity, almost, has been bad publicity as far as the airport has been concerned. Even if it is completed, the experts have given it no chance of operating on an economically viable

basis. No wonder the directors are anxious to keep their heads down while C.J. and his high-flying crew decide about that extra £5 million. ...

The site, on a high plateau, resembled a lunar landscape; it was alive with heavy earth-moving equipment excavating, dumping, levelling. A miracle being made in mud. Up to one hundred men have been employed on the project for over a year. Most of them are locals, some with experience of working on airport sites in England. They returned to build an airport for their own country.

Blasting was in progress as the flying of red flags and the presence of armed soldiers indicated. Such operations are carried out three times a week and at present are being used to smooth out difficult terrain. As yet there is no sign of the terminal buildings or the aviation fuel stores – but the assurance is that it will be ready by the completion date set for 1984. George Orwell couldn't have planned it better.

Against all the odds and the outrage, the "miracle" they said should never happen has transformed a bleak mountainside in Co. Mayo into an airport runway almost fit for the jet age. Light planes are capable already of landing and taking off on barren Barr na Cúige where the first phase of Connaught's much-debated regional airport is nearing completion. However, all that is needed now to make it usable for the big jets is another £5 million, which depends on the continuing good-will of the Fianna Fáil Government. Word on site is that the money will be forthcoming, but this is not gospel.

A new pilgrim road to Knock, six miles away, is being built by the Mayo County Council; it will by-pass Kilkelly, a village with no claim to fame except that it is the nearest to the airport and at the heart of what is known locally as the "Black Triangle" – an area blighted by lack of development over the decades.

Regardless of our progress, Barry Desmond still continued to blaze away at the airport. The *Sunday Independent* reported that

Barry Desmond, TD, the *bête noire* of the airport plan, is totally unrepentant about his trenchant opposition to it as former Junior Minister for State at the Department of Finance. "It is wholly unwarranted, even more so today because of our economic situation that it was in 1980," he said. "Even at this late stage it should be stopped."

His reasoning may sound logical to the objective taxpayer but it is unlikely to deter the dedicated people behind the Connaught Regional Airport plan. It seems that nothing short of national bankruptcy will stop them now.

The *Independent* had a word for me, too:
But still nobody quite believes that it can all come true – except perhaps Monsignor Horan of Knock whose faith, after all, has already moved a mountain. But he is keeping a distinct and uncharacteristic low profile at the moment.

He was unavailable for comment although he was at home on Wednesday in his presbytery at Knock where hundreds of August pilgrims were making a Novena for the most elusive gift – peace in the world.

Should the Monsignor's prayers be answered, then by the second half of the eighties the hundreds will have swollen to thousands of Marian worshippers jetting in from all over Europe to plead the cause of humanity. By then, the xenophobia which seems to sprout among local officialdom as soon as Knock Airport is mentioned will hopefully have disappeared.

While public criticism of the project had waned, we did run into trouble with the trade unions in September. The press reported that:
The building trades' group in the region has written to the Minister for Transport, Mr John Wilson, asking him not to allocate the £5m funds for the second stage of the project until the unions, the Brick and Stonelayers Trade Union, the ITGWU and UCATT are allowed on site.

The organisation has pointed out to the Minister that unless the contractor and the airport development company co-operate in bringing about the situation they will be requesting the Irish Congress of Trade Unions to "black" the development...

Michael Kilcoyne, the local ITGWU official, had visited the site on at least two occasions and had spoken to the workers. The majority of workers there were self-employed men who owned their own lorries and they were not interested in unions. As chairman of the board I knew that no member had any objection to men joining a union, but neither the contractor nor the company had any authority to force men to join. The matter was raised at a company meeting when a letter to me from Mr Kilcoyne was discussed. In the letter Mr Kilcoyne explained that the site was not unionised, and somehow or other he seemed to feel that this was the responsibility of the company. In a short reply to Mr Kilcoyne it was explained that the company had no responsibility in this regard and that he should contact the contractor, Mr Frank Harrington. Mr Ward McEllin, the company's solicitor, pointed out, too, that Mr Harrington had written to Mr Kilcoyne to say that he had no objection to the union official calling to the site; our solicitor added that in his opinion Mr Harrington's letter to Mr Kilcoyne fulfilled the company's obligation in the matter. As chairman I also wrote to Michael Kilcoyne telling him that I had no objection to the men joining a union. The issue remained unresolved. In the spring of 1983 the *Evening Press* of 16 March reported:

Mr Michael Kilcoyne, a spokesman for the Federation [of Trade Unions] said: "We are not for or against Knock Airport, but we are angry that the scheme has been allowed to continue in a non-union situation.

"We find it hard to accept that public money can continue to be pumped into a project which is blatantly anti-union. We are seeking a clause from the government to have it inserted into the contracts that union officials be permitted to enter the site.

"If this fails then we are asking Congress to support our motion to have the site declared black. This is the last thing, however, we want to happen," he said.

He brought his complaint to the Western Federation of Trade Unions and through them to the Irish Congress of Trade Unions. A motion was finally introduced at the ICTU Congress to "black" the site. It was defeated. It did not, however, help the cause of the Connaught Regional Airport; it left strained relations and misunderstanding which was most unfortunate. The *Irish Independent* of 17 March 1983:

The Irish Congress of Trade Unions yesterday attacked the use of non-union labour on the construction of the Government-financed Knock Airport development scheme.

The ICTU condemned the use of non-union labour as outrageous and disgraceful. But the Congress executive, at a meeting in Dublin, decided not to sanction any move to have the site of the £12 million-plus development blacked by West of Ireland trade unions as this would be illegal.

Instead, the ICTU will issue a statement, within days, condemning the use of non-union labour and detailing plans to pressure and embarrass the Government and airport developers into accepting union representation on the site.

The Congress move followed complaints from the Western Federation of Trade Unions that efforts since October 1981 to have discussions with the airport Board of Directors, under the chairmanship of Knock Parish Priest, Monsignor James Horan, regarding union representation for the workforce of over 170, have failed.

Some of the unions have alleged that they were prevented from entering the site four miles from Charlestown where the main contractor is Mr Frank Harrington, from nearby Kilkelly, who has a number of sub-contractors working for him.

Up to 170 men have been employed on the site since July 1981, building a foundation for a 7,500 foot long runway. This phase of the scheme is now almost completed and the laying of 6,000 feet of asphalt surface will begin about May. This operation will bring the workforce to nearly 200.

According to the Western Federation of Trades Councils, Monsignor Horan insists he has no responsibility regarding the workforce on the site. Mr Harrington has told the unions he has had no approach from any of the workers requesting union representation.

But in a letter to the Federation a year ago he stated: "We are not, however, prepared to allow you interfere with the normal progress of work that is taking place."

Mr Harrington said that if any of the workforce wanted to join a union he would contact the Federation.

The ICTU Executive yesterday decided to refer the problem to its Industrial Relations Committee to prepare a formula that may be acceptable to the developers. The Western Federation spokesman, Castlebar ITGWU official, Mr Michael Kilcoyne, said that they were seeking to have a clause inserted by the Government into the contract that union officials should be allowed free access on to the site.

To be fair to Michael Kilcoyne, he had the courage to change his mind about the airport later and to say so publicly. He stated that, irrespective of unions, workers are workers and work should be provided for them. On behalf of Castlebar No. 1 Branch he put down a motion for the ITGWU annual conference calling on the government to allocate funds to finish Knock Airport. He stated that that part of Mayo had an unemployment rate of 49%, and that the only hope of attracting suitable industry and investment to the region was to provide the necessary infrastructure.

Mr Kilcoyne want on to say (*Irish Press,* 21 May 1984):

"We are very critical of the use of non-union labour on the airport site, but that does not take away from the fact that we feel an airport is necessary to provide the infrastructure for the additional jobs we need in the West," he said.

Neither could his Branch accept that the airport should be run by a private company when the State had already invested close to £10 million in the project.

His motion calling for the allocation of funds to finish Knock Airport was defeated.

"When Mr Kilcoyne suggested his motion should be referred back to the Union Executive Council, Union President John Carroll commented: 'It will be referred back to the waste-paper basket.'"

This remark by the president of the ITGWU was scandalous. The president of the most prestigious union in our country should have the interests of all workers at heart, irrespective of unions. The unions exist only for the protection of the workers' rights and conditions and if, by any irresponsible word or action, they deny these rights, then they undermine the whole basis of their existence as trade unions. Moreover, I had called on John Carroll, together with an officer of the Co. Mayo Planning Authority, in the spring of 1980, before any approach had been made to the government or the Department of Transport on the Connaught Regional Airport. We explained fully what we had in mind and our hopes and expectations for the future. He did not express any strong views nor any opposition on that occasion. The meeting in relation to the airport took place in his office, as General Secretary of the ITGWU. I met him on two other occasions with the directors of Bord Fáilte. I remarked to him that he appeared to be more severe on television than in the flesh; I found him a most charming person and not at all as he appears when defending the rights of members of his union on TV. I would like to think that he was not serious when he suggested that the proposal calling on the government to allocate funds to Knock Airport should be thrown into the waste-paper basket.

Despite our problems with the ITGWU work continued on the runway, but we found ourselves saddled with immense difficulties when it came to providing the other basic facilities. The board was frustrated all through the Fianna Fáil term of office from February to November 1982. Mr John Wilson, Minister for

Transport, curbed our activities considerably. The board sought permission to go to tender for such things as the airport terminal building: he refused us permission even though it did not require funding in that particular year. He forbade us to bring water or 3-phase electricity to the site. This was very serious as the absence of these services was likely to delay the eventual opening of the airport considerably. It would also have been quite in order for the minister to allow the company to borrow an allocation in the budget for 1983. I do not know what influence the upheaval within Fianna Fáil which surfaced in August had on our situation, although I have my views on the matter.

Trouble on the Horizon

The Fianna Fail government was voted out of office once more on 24 November 1982. It had, however, prepared its capital expenditure programme for 1983 which contained £2.7m for contract no. 2, which had been signed between the contractor and the company on 27 August 1982 and provided for the laying of asphalt on 6,000 feet of runway. The incoming Coalition government honoured that contract before finally axing the project on 14 December 1983. December seems to have been an unlucky month for the company.

At a meeting of the board on 15 February 1983 we decided to invite Jim Mitchell, the new Minister for Communications, to visit the site. A proposal was also made to place before the minister a report of the expected traffic, running costs and total cost of the completed airport. A sub-committee was appointed to draw up a draft report for the minister which was later forwarded to him with an invitation to visit the site. He accepted.

In July the minister was entertained to lunch in Knock presbytery with all the members of the board present. The minister's demeanour and personality impressed me very much. He was tight-lipped in regard to any future plans he may have had for the airport, but I got the idea that he was favourably disposed towards the project. It was not his first visit to Knock Shrine as he had come on a number of occasions as a pilgrim. Taking all things into account, I was very impressed with him.

It was a beautiful day and an ideal day on which to view the airport; it is a most scenic area and looks beautiful on a fine sunny day. The minister was taken on a tour of the airport and given a resumé of our hopes and expectations for the project. He seemed very happy and relaxed during his visit and I was convinced that he was well disposed towards the airport.

A very interesting comment on Jim Mitchell's visit to Knock had appeared in *The Irish Times* of 9 July 1983:

> Jim is going West early next week. He is making a political pilgrimage to Knock. The Monsignor is calling for a meeting of minds. The Monsignor likes a politician who gets things done. He is not much given to orthodoxy when it comes to getting

the show on the road.

The Monsignor and friends have a problem with the Connaught Regional Airport. The job is practically finished bar the terminal building. And what's that but a couple of truckloads of building blocks – all made of Irish material – and the job is out and finished! Any political snags and Jim'll fix it.

Yes.

The word is out locally that Mitchell is down to arrange for the funeral and will do the undertaking bit now that the Dáil is up and there will be no platform for the Fianna Fáil chaps.

I wouldn't like to take bets on that. Mitchell is his own man and in his own bulldozing way he exercises his clout.

While I won't say he could give the Fianna Fáil crowd lessons, I'll reassure you he has precious little to learn from that party. I have the utmost confidence that if the ride gets a bit rough, with a bit of political turbulence showing, a discreet repairing by the pair of them to the sitting-room, where the safety belts can be fastened, will save the day. That is, if there's a saving to be done. Mitchell isn't such a political clunch that, once he sees the tarmac down, the runway laid, and the whole project gone past the point of no return, he is going to be the one to bury, still further, the forlorn hope of a second Fine Gael seat in East Mayo.

There were some surprises in store for us though. Towards the end of the year there was a little turbulence in the Coalition camp when Minister Frank Cluskey resigned in protest at a grant of £65m given to the Dublin Gas Company to help it make the conversion from commercial to natural gas. He objected in principle to the government giving such grants to private companies; nevertheless the Coalition government granted the money to the Gas Company. I do not know what bargaining took place in the cabinet or whether the Connaught Regional Airport was part of the deal in keeping the Coalition intact after Frank Cluskey's resignation, but I was worried that the airport might be used as a sacrificial lamb to hold the Coalition together.

Throughout 1983 there had been leaks of information from some sources close to the new Coalition government in regard to the ever-imminent abandonment of Knock Airport. These leaks could well have been meant to act as feelers on public opinion in the matter; the government would have liked to find out how popular or otherwise the axing of the airport would be. An extract from an unsigned news item in the *Irish Independent* of 21 September 1983 read:

KNOCK CRUNCH COMING

The Government is likely to decide within weeks whether to make a huge cash handout to complete the controversial Knock Airport. The next Book of Estimates is now being drawn up. Already more than £7 million of taxpayers' money has been poured into the project on a hillside 10 miles from Knock Shrine, visited by Pope John Paul II four years ago.

It was the Papal trip that convinced Monsignor Horan that an airport was needed to cater for the anticipated two million pilgrims he expected to visit Knock each year.

Construction began in 1980 after Monsignor Horan won approval from the then Haughey administration. Under the Coalition Government of 1981 work was suspended. But Dr Fitzgerald's Government stayed in office just seven months and Mr Haughey, back as Taoiseach, permitted the Knock Scheme's reactivation.

Now Knock Airport needs £4 million more to emerge in its fully planned glory. Already, the often mist-shrouded site has a 6,000 feet long runway capable of taking Boeing 737 size airlines. An extra £400,000 would permit Jumbo jets to land.

Local T.D. Pádraig Flynn said yesterday: "People who don't believe it's possible will find it very difficult to stop it now. It would be political and economic lunacy. What we want, now, is a clear indication from the Government about its intentions."

But it could be that the Government will ask the Connacht Regional Airport Development Company and its chairman, Monsignor Horan, to find a private investor to put up the rest of the money.

There were some fair-minded men amongst the economists and "public advisers" who commented on the airport. Earlier in the year Mr Colm Rapple had had the courage and conviction to stand out on a limb and write, in the *Sunday Independent* of 16 January:

Hopefully, however, the Government will be careful about where the axe falls on capital projects. Capital spending creates a lot of employment – even sometimes when it appears wasteful. By all means cut back on imports of expensive machinery whether it be for hospitals or ESB power stations. But do not cut back on employment-creating construction work.

There might even be a conversion to the view that laying the runway at Knock Airport was not simply throwing money into a boghole. Those employed would otherwise be on the dole. Instead of drawing state funds, they are contributing to the coffers. Most of the materials are domestic so the firms supplying them are paying extra tax. There is less leakage of money from the Irish economy from that spent at Knock than from many other supposedly wise investment decisions...

However, such counsels did not prevail. My worst fears were realised when the letter arrived on 14 December 1983 with the bad news. Knock Airport was axed and this time for good. The letter bore the minister's signature.

It was total withdrawal; it not merely withdrew any further exchequer funds for the project itself but also any further exchequer support to subsidise the running costs of the airport. That was indeed surprising as any losses sustained by Shannon, Dublin or Cork airports are made good from exchequer funds.

The minister's letter referred back to a submission made by the company to his department earlier in the year, seeking clarification of the government's commitment to the airport, though it had been always my view that such a submission should never have been made as the government had a legal and moral commitment under the Grant-Aid Agreement to provide funds to complete the airport:

> Earlier this year you sent me a submission on behalf of the Board of the Connaught Airport Development Company Ltd seeking what was, in effect, a commitment that the airport project will continue to be financed by the Exchequer and the work will proceed at a sufficient pace to enable the airport to be completed by April, 1985. Your request has been considered by the Government in the context of the 1984 Estimates.
>
> In view of the magnitude of the budgetary problems facing it, the Government decided that the most that it could do is to allocate a sum not exceeding £650,000 to the Company in 1984 to meet the existing contractual commitments of the Company on the project.
>
> The Government has also decided that when this allocation has been expended, thus bringing the total Exchequer expenditure on the project to almost £10m, no further Exchequer contribution will be forthcoming.
>
> Your Board's submission also referred to the possibility, when

the airport is open for traffic, of annual losses on its operations, losses which your Company would hope to meet from its own resources derived mainly from local contributions. In this connection I should mention that no Exchequer support would be forthcoming to subsidise the running costs of the airport.

I am sorry that I am not able to give you better news but, in view of the difficult position of the public finances, the Government feels that it has gone as far as possible in its contribution to the construction of the airport.

Very early in 1984 the work on the airport ground to a standstill; a site that had been a hive of activity lay silent and deserted. I felt sad but not disheartened, and that was true of every member of the Connaught Regional Airport Company Board. I also felt that truth and justice must surely prevail in the end.

I had great respect for Mr Mitchell's decision to make £650,000 available for the completion of the apron at the airport, but during the six months from January to June 1984 the business of the board mostly concerned the scaling down of operations and laying off the technical staff employed by the company. The technical staff were put on a week-to-week notice and the secretary of the company, the former liaison officer, was given three months notice. It was so sad to put workers on the dole.

The board looked at the possibility of reactivating our application to the EEC for a grant based on the document *Development Strategy to 2004* commissioned jointly by the Galway/Mayo Regional Development Organisation and the Commission of the European Communities. The government representatives on the board had not informed us that the board's application to the EEC for funds had already been officially withdrawn by a Fianna Fáil minister, John Wilson, late in 1982. Most extraordinary! I have heard that Mr Wilson did so on the advice of department officials, who said that it was a foolish venture and not a worthy project for EEC aid. Who were the wise officials? During this period the Minister for Finance withdrew his representative from the board. His resignation was accepted.

Many people have asked me about my state of mind while the airport was the subject of such controversy and particularly when it was postponed and then finally axed. I must admit that at no time did the whole affair worry me; I certainly never lost a night's sleep over it. I was not even embarrassed by the apparent failure; I simply felt sorry for an administration that could have shown such vindictiveness as to postpone or abandon the project. I suppose I really felt like the old man at Knock Shrine who said: "Monsignor, don't worry about the airport. If God and Our Lady herself wants it, it will be there, notwithstanding all opposition."

I felt sure that he was right.

I never had any doubts about the airport being finished. I probably had no cogent reason for my confidence; it was just a hunch. Perhaps, too, I was living in hope that the government might change its mind and honour its legal commitment.

The foreign media, press, television and radio took an obsessive interest in what was now known as "Knock Airport". News items were constantly fed to the foreign press by Irish journalists who poured scorn and ridicule on the project. It got such headlines as: "Airport leading to nowhere", "Airport for a village of 400 people". The net result was world-wide publicity for "Knock Airport" and Knock Shrine. Journalists, television and radio crews visited Knock from all parts of the world. They came in scores from the USA, Canada, Great Britain, Australia, Germany, France and the Netherlands, to mention but a few. It got extensive coverage in *Time, Newsweek,* the *New York Times, The Times* and newspapers and magazines all over the world.

The press of our country did a great disservice to Ireland in the way it presented the story of Knock Airport, holding our politicians and Irishmen in general up to ridicule. It is hard to say whether it was the foreign press resident in this country or Irish journalists themselves that were responsible for this "stage-Irishman" performance in the world press. It is most extraordinary how Irish journalists seem to have absolutely no discretion in the kind of story they feed to the foreign press; we Irish seem to have a death wish as far as our image abroad is concerned.

But the more ridicule that was heaped on the airport, the more my stature grew in the home and foreign press. It was obviously so vicious that people did not believe it. It also made Knock Shrine known all over the world. Maybe there is no such thing as a bad press. As a result of my appearance on the prestigious *Sixty Minutes* on CBS I received an invitation to the official opening of an airport in Cairns, North Queensland, a town situated in the Tropics and very close to the Barrier Reef. Having seen the programme on which I was interviewed, they had decided to invite me to address tour operators from all over the world who were gathered there for the opening. I and a companion got free tickets to Australia and back. We stayed in the Catholic bishop's residence and had cars and couriers at our disposal during our sojourn. We arrived in late March and left in early April – autumn in Australia. It was an opportune time to be away as it was during that period when work had stopped at the airport and the scene there was sad and lonely; it was good to be away from all that and to have the opportunity to visit a brand-new airport and speak with its promoters. They seemed to be in a similar situation to the people of the West of Ireland. They lived far from the seat of power in Canberra and, like the people of the West, were often forgotten and neglected. We brought them a gift which showed the solidarity of the people in the West of Ireland with their brothers and sisters in North Queensland. Brothers and sisters they certainly were as many of them were from Ireland. Many were descendants of the original settlers in Australia, and they told me that 40% of Australians claim Irish heritage.

I was so proud of the Irish that I met in Australia. The sister in charge of the local Mercy Convent in Cairns was a native of the parish of Aghamore where I had worked for some years. The Catholic faith was very strong there and the Catholic community was held in great respect by all. The pioneers of the faith in that part of Australia, or at least in the Catholic Diocese of Cairns, were members of the Augustinian Order from Ireland. The bishops of the diocese were Augustinians. The present bishop, Most Rev. Dr Torpie, is of Irish descent.

The Queenslanders had their own dialect and distinct pronunciation of English words and phrases. Cairns itself is off the beaten path. The birds sport gay colours in the sunshine and there are exotic animals, birds and fish – I even saw live crocodiles and kangaroos in the wild. The weather was beautiful in autumn, which is the rainy season. When it rains in Australia it literally pours. For some strange reason the rain falls mostly at night; at least, that was my experience. During our first night in Australia the heavens opened and there was a downpour – some five inches of rain. A strange phenomenon in Queensland is that in a glorious climate of sunshine they still get up to 80-90 inches of rain each year, twice what we get in parts of Ireland.

I was asked by my Australian friends to do some publicity work for them with the media on my journey through the various cities in Australia. I gave many press, television and radio interviews and found the journalists very gentlemanly, courteous and helpful. I met the heads of government in Queensland, who joined in the celebrations at Cairns. I met Bjelke-Petersen the Premier and had my picture taken with him. I also met the Governor of Queensland, Sir James Ramsay. I hope that my efforts to help this Australian airport were of some help to my friends in Cairns.

The Problem with the Media

Whenever I think of the media I think of the day which Tom Neary, Chief Steward of Knock Shrine, and myself spent in Dublin visiting the various newspaper offices. Up until that time, around 1977, Knock Shrine had received very little publicity in the press; the local correspondent for the daily papers usually sent a report on the Sundays during the pilgrimage season, but this was normally very short and scrappy and merely mentioned the bare essentials of the pilgrimage – the shrine where it took place and the numbers which attended. I had often been told that there were people in Dublin who had never heard of Knock Shrine, and it was suggested that I should do something about it. So I found myself in Dublin trying to peddle articles on the shrine from one newspaper office to another, only to be told that it was not "newsy" or controversial and they were not interested. The day in Dublin was not my first encounter with the media and, as time would prove, it would not be my last. I myself became the focus of a great deal of media attention, as did at least one of the projects I was involved in. The encounter taught me a lot about myself, and of course a lot about the media.

Reporters occasionally came then to Knock to ask me for an interview, but this usually became a long enquiry on "commercialism" at the shrine. When asked about this side of Knock I always explained that pilgrims wanted this kind of service, as they liked to bring home some pious objects and present them to their families and relatives. The people in the stalls gave this service and made a modest living from it. I explained that I could not see anything wrong with this and that "commercialism" was too strong a word for it.

Another hobby-horse of journalists, especially non-Catholic journalists, was holy water! They regarded this as one of the superstitions of the Catholic Church. I explained that water was very common in the liturgy of the Church, for example in baptism; holy water is a sacramental and gets its efficacy from the prayer of the Church used in the blessing ceremony. After this was explained to them non-Catholic journalists then went on to ask of statues and their place in Catholic worship, and this I usually explained by drawing a comparison with the visual-aids used in schools. There was no question of giving worship to a statue made of stone or plaster of Paris as that would be idolatry. The statues of Our Lord, Our Lady and the saints simply help us keep our minds on the persons whom the statues represent, and any aid that helps us to keep our minds on the spiritual must be very useful. We have the example of the crib which reminds us of the birth of Christ in the stable at Bethlehem. The crib stirs our imagination; it helps to make the scene at Bethlehem vivid and real and speaks to us of the love of God down through the centuries.

The next aspect of Knock that journalists never failed to investigate was the question of our methods of getting the necessary finance. Catholic or non-Catholic, Christian or unbeliever, they always attended Mass. The first shock they got was on entering the church, when they saw that there was no question or sign of a collection at the door. When they had recovered from this they made up their minds that there must be some snag, and perhaps the collection would come later at the offertory. Again they drew a blank, and then they came to me hot-foot, asking for an explanation. I explained to them that we had no collections whatsoever at Knock Shrine but that we did have donation boxes placed at strategic positions. I would add that perhaps they were not strategic enough, as the journalist had missed them. But as the old people used to say, "God looks after his own," and thank God we always got sufficient funds to keep going.

Journalists were always interested in watching people touch the stones of the gable where the apparition took place; they felt that this smacked of superstition. They had also heard that many cures were wrought through the application of the mortar or clay from the gable to the sick person. I must say that this aspect bothered me until I realised that Jesus himself had used such simple things as dust, spittle and water to cure the man born blind. It occurs in St John's Gospel, Chapter 9: "Jesus spat on the ground and made clay of the spittle and anointed the man's eyes with the clay saying to him, 'Go, wash in the pool of Siloam.' So he went and washed and came back seeing." This is an example of how God used ordinary things to produce extraordinary results, both spiritual and temporal. Praised be Jesus Christ. For journalists the question was always: "Have there been any miracles lately?" I would reply that we had many cures but I was not always sure whether they were miracles or not. I would then explain that God can cure sick people in two ways. Firstly, he can cure people by using the ordinary healing powers inherent in their own bodies. And God can of course cure people in an extraordinary way, beyond the power of any human healing. If this happens and if there is proof, then there may be a question of a miracle. Up to the present we have had no medical bureau at Knock, so the word "miracle" cannot be used in the case of the numerous people that have been cured down through the years. That does not mean that some cures may not have been miraculous, but I personally did not think it served any useful purpose to set up a medical bureau to analyse individual cures. The hand of God must be in every cure whether wrought by a natural or supernatural means. Our Lord Jesus Christ did not have a medical bureau with him as he did the rounds in Palestine.

I have often entertained journalists at Knock Shrine and have always found them very interesting and stimulating. An interview with a journalist always seemed to me like a cat-and-mouse encounter. They usually came with false notions of my character and personality gleaned from various reports in the newspapers, reports which were often written with prejudice, not to me personally but to various projects in which I was involved. I am a fairly good judge of character and often I knew that the gentleman or lady interviewing me was not interested in the true facts, but wanted some isolated statements that might back up the slant that the editor wished to project. This situation very often arose because I was involved in projects, genuine projects but nevertheless controversial, which sometimes aroused envy, jealousy and fear. If vested interests were powerful enough they could sometimes influence the media against such schemes. This might have lead to discouragement and frustration in many people, but I always took it as a challenge to ride the waves of opposition. You must depend on the Holy Spirit to "give you [the words] to speak". So the journalists who came to me were frequently very cautious and almost antagonistic at first, but when they found that I was very human, with a good sense of humour, they thawed out and became friendly and informal. They could even begin to see shrines and airports in a totally different light from what they had expected; you might almost say that the journalist who came to criticise went home to praise. In general I have a very good relationship with journalists and I can claim many good friends among them. I always try to believe in the integrity, honesty and truthfulness of newspapers reports and editors but, unfortunately, my experiences do not always make it easy for me to do so.

When news of the Papal visit to Knock and Ireland was flashed across the world I was besieged by journalists seeking interviews. For weeks my whole time was taken up talking to the press, radio and television. Fortunately, some years previously I had attended two courses given by Bunny Carr, Tom Savage and Barry Barker on dealing with media interviews. They taught me how to woo the camera and how to relax. I also learned some techniques that were useful in answering, or not answering, awkward and hypothetical questions. There is one politician that comes to mind who is expert at not answering difficult questions but holds tightly to his own hobby-horse: I admire him very much.

When I get an invitation to take part in a television or radio programme, I consider it very carefully and cautiously. There is always a considerable risk involved; it might help your cause, or it might do it a lot of damage. In a way that is true of every venture, but in the case of the media your cause may be irretrievably damaged by one bad presentation. It is not your arguments that count so much as the image of your character and personality that comes across to the listener or viewer: if they get the impression that you are a warm, honest, sincere and likable character, then you have won the day. When people spoke to me about my performances they used words like "sincere", "honest", "good humoured", and above all that "you are yourself". It would be fatal to try to impress or put on any kind of an act; the motto is to be yourself, warts and all.

Having made my decision to go on a programme, I work hard to gather all the information possible on the topics likely to be discussed and then I feel confident that I know as much about the particular subject as the interviewer. I usually have a special friend who discusses the matter with me and we finish by having a question-and-answer session.

During my preparation I school myself on what I call "a humility exercise". The object of the exercise is to help me to disregard any idea that I may have of winning popularity or of image-making. My aim always is to get my message across, clearly and accurately. I am convinced that the best way to do that is to "be myself", to be natural, completely at ease and unmindful of my image. I convince myself that mistakes do not really matter as long as people see me as I really am. I go on the assumption that anybody who never made a mistake never made anything. My friends have tapes of some of the most important programmes on which I featured but I have never viewed them because I would be worried that they might influence my performance on future programmes. It is better to be my true self. Media interviews deal with projects that mean a lot to me, projects about which I pray and think a lot.

When I pray about a project I usually finish with an old Irish prayer: "Welcome be God's Holy Will." I was going on a programme one morning and, waiting for the call outside the studio, I was very silent. I never feel nervous. I would describe my condition as an unease or alertness, the same kind of feeling that an athlete has before running a race; all my faculties are geared for the performance. A friend who was with me that day remarked on my quietness.

"Yes!" I said, "I am praying."

As well as being a prayer of petition, it is an offering of myself to God. I place myself on the altar of sacrifice convinced that I am doing it for a good cause, and having offered myself, I leave everything to God and Our Lady. And having made all my preparations and having geared myself mentally to the performance, I sit in the hot seat. Hey Presto! I forget completely where I am and enjoy the programme. I feel that I have always performed better on live programmes than on edited ones. On an edited programme you have no audience and the only reaction you get is from a tough, severe-looking interviewer. Their routine has made them tough and arrogant, though of course there are many notable exceptions. In an edited programme, your interview goes in at one end of the machine but God only knows what may come out at the other, whereas, live, the story comes out just as you have told it.

The most daunting of all shows on Irish television is the *Late Late Show*. When I got my first invitation to go on the *Late Late* I lost my appetite for several days. I tried to make a decision. My archbishop would not advise me to accept, but neither did he discourage me. I studied Gay Byrne's tactics on Saturday nights trying to sum up his character and above all his style, and after some weeks I decided that he was human after all and might treat me sympathetically. The subject of the interview was to be Knock

Shrine and I felt confident that supernatural help would be forthcoming.

To prepare myself for the programme I got a friend who resembled Gay Byrne and had him ask me the most awkward questions. I studied my subject for weeks until I felt sure that I knew as much about it as any interviewer could and perhaps a little more. My greatest fear was that I would make a fool of myself and that I would be the laughing-stock of the whole country, but in the end I decided that I was lacking in humility and that, if I had the proper attitude, I would not mind whether I made a fool of myself or not. In the event the interview worked out very well, and of all the shows I appeared on I got the greatest reaction from my appearances on the *Late Late Show*.

As a result of the worldwide publicity regarding Knock Airport we came under the notice of the producer of one of the most prestigious programmes in the world, CBS's *Sixty Minutes*. On my first meeting with Morley Safer I expressed some doubt as to whether I should become involved in this programme or not, but he assured me that he would do a good programme and that I would be very pleased with it. *Sixty Minutes*, he went on to say, was syndicated to the whole English-speaking world, including Australia, Canada, South Africa, South Korea and New Zealand, and it has some ninety-four million viewers across the globe. "Do you know what a thirty-second advertisement would cost on this programme?" he asked me.

"I do not."

"$340,000."

The value of the programme to Knock and the airport, at that rate, would be $13m.

Very few people have been fortunate enough to have the vast experience I have had on radio and television and with the world press. I had always feared television and radio but admired the courage of all the valiant people who took part. Being involved in a marriage introductions bureau many years ago I was inundated with calls for interviews from media people intent on turning a very important service to the community into material for buffoonery. I did a few programmes and was inclined to "freeze" when standing before a camera – the thought of all those people out there listening to me scared me out of my wits. My mind would go blank unless I had what I wanted to say well and truly rehearsed. All that has changed nowadays through sheer practice and experience. It is interesting also to look back and evaluate the differences in my experiences as between one country and another. Being a priest I always felt a special responsibility in talking to the media, and I feared misrepresentation or being misunderstood. I always felt safer in giving an interview to the foreign media than to our Irish boys. This may have been because I was not as well known in foreign parts as on my home ground, but I also found that the foreign media was more conscious of the status and respect due to a minister of religion.

In Ireland it seems to be the "in-thing" to criticise religion, religious attitudes and even the moral fibre of our society. If a priest or bishop fails to respond to the needs of a community he is severely criticised, but if on the other hand he does respond he can be told that the matter is none of his business or that he is acting politically. As a priest, what am I to do? Unfortunately, we are very close to Great Britain and we have a slavish habit of copying the style and attitudes of the British media. I do not know why this should be the case, but a large number of the liberal element in our society finds its way into the media and press. Perhaps it is because they are usually more vocal and articulate when good people who should speak out in defence of our institutions and traditions choose to remain silent. It reminds me of Edmund Burke's oft-quoted words: "All that is necessary for evil to triumph is that good men remain silent."

I have always suspected that Irish journalists export copy to the foreign press which is very often derogatory to the Irish people and to Church and state institutions. This to my mind is offensive and unworthy of journalism; it makes a laughing-stock of our country, its culture and traditions. Connaught Airport is a good example of this abuse: it was blazoned in the foreign press as an example of irresponsible and foolish expenditure. After these fabricated stories appeared in newspapers such as *The Times* and the *New York Times*, they were then reprinted in Ireland as examples of what the foreign press was saying about us, when it was really the work of Irish journalists that had been exported and re-imported. A foreign saboteur could not do more damage to our country than this irresponsible journalism.

Coming from the West of Ireland and being steeped in Irish culture and the Irish language, I am of the opinion that our traditional Irish values have been neglected ever since we became an independent state. When I was young, in the twenties, there was great euphoria in the air as to the future of Ireland, its language and its culture. Everybody was enthusiastic and there was a rush to the Irish colleges for the learning of Irish. Down the years this enthusiasm has waned, even though Herculean efforts were made by many governments to revive the Irish language.

I am a person who was born near the Gaeltacht, if not in the Gaeltacht. I am a person who always appreciated and studied the Irish language, Irish culture and Irish music. Nothing inspires me more than the music and traditions of my country, and the older I get the more inspiration I take from it. The Irish language, music and culture should get time and space in the media, where it will help to dilute the flood of foreign cultural influence that is invading our country.

But the media have prejudices and they have their favourites. I have never subscribed to the theory that journalists, unlike other people, are infallible. Everybody knows that certain newspapers take up certain stances in politics, as in religion, and print what best backs up their point of view. If you want to prove any pet theory nowadays, all you have to do is commission an opinion poll and ask the right questions. I have known journalists who would deny infallibility to the Pope in matters of faith and morals, and at the same time speak "ex-cathedra" from the privileged position of their news desks. It makes me sad when I read between the lines in newspapers and find journalists allowing themselves to be used to promote the interests of pressure groups and sectional or political lobbies. This abuse of the news media can be quite apparent to the more critical reader – the bias on the part of some journalists can be unashamedly obvious – but it can be grossly misleading to the general public. I am sure that some projects in the West of Ireland have suffered because of a bias shown towards a part of our country that has always been neglected.

The media thrives on controversy: sometimes I think that it is obsessed by the need for controversy to promote sales. By the same token I have often found the result of interviews unsatisfactory and frustrating. At times I did a lot of research into a particular subject and marshalled my arguments with care, only to be bitterly disappointed with the superficial manner in which the interviewer dealt with the matter.

Still and all, as chairman of the Connaught Regional Airport and as a prominent victim of "media bashing" in the home and foreign press, I should be most grateful to the media. Every new airport needs publicity. To get a good airing in the world press would cost millions of pounds, but the Connaught Airport got it free, gratis and for nothing. We should be very grateful to the politicians who kindled the torch in this worldwide publicity marathon: the result is that there is no airport as well known as the "Knock Airport", and there is no shrine better known than Knock Shrine.

I was very often asked about my attitude towards the media when Connaught Regional Airport was being so bitterly and unfairly attacked. I always felt that media personnel had nothing against me personally, rather they used the airport to launch an attack on the economic policy of Charles J. Haughey and Fianna Fáil. Unjustly, unfairly and unscrupulously, they turned a genuine infrastructural project into a symbol of wastefulness and irresponsibility. If it had been built in Dublin then it would have been lauded to the high heavens and paraded as an economic miracle but, alas, nothing good could come out of the West!

Personally I feel that I have a wonderful relationship with the media and I always try to facilitate journalists in every possible way. I realise that journalists have to meet a tight schedule for their features and articles and they are entitled to co-operation and understanding in all circumstances. However, the scripture says there is a time to be silent and a time to speak. Unfortunately, journalists may have approached me when it was a time to be silent and I hope that, at that moment, they realised that I had such a duty.

As administrator of Knock Shrine and as chairman of "Knock" Airport Committee I am most grateful to journalists: their help was invaluable through the years. I remember, particularly, their kindness and co-operation before, during and after the Papal visit to Knock. During that period I got to know journalists better than I had ever known them before and I learned to appreciate the tedious and exacting job they have to do. Thank God, ever since, I have had a wonderful relationship with the media people. I hope that the sentiments are reciprocated, for then I will have a happy and peaceful life.

I have a kind of love-hate relationship with the media. They may not like what I am doing or even what I stand for, but they still like to interview me. I have always treated journalists with great courtesy and rarely refused to give an interview and in turn

The Problem with the Media

I have found journalists very professional, gentlemanly and honourable, again with a few exceptions. I have been interviewed by journalists from all over the world and have entertained and shown many journalists over the Connaught Regional Airport, and that includes journalists who had written about it but had never seen it. I found it difficult to understand how journalists could pour abuse and invective on a project they had never seen; it seemed so callous and even dishonest. John Healy of *The Irish Times* referred to such practices as the work of "hired mouths". But I loved to watch their reaction when they saw the sheer size and beauty of the airport. They had, of course, heard about the "foggy-boggy" airport or the "bog-hole on top of a mountain", yet to see "Knock Airport" was to be absolutely impressed and amazed at the marvellous spirit which built it.

Taking the good with the bad, I have fared well with the media and the publicity received was beneficial to my work in many ways. The image of me that was portrayed was generally good, perhaps that of a sincere person engaged – unfortunately – in silly projects!

Back on the Agenda

SHORTLY AFTER I arrived back from Australia I wrote to Jim Mitchell, on 7 May 1984, pointing out clearly the government's legal commitment to complete the airport. In the same letter I asked the minister to receive a deputation from the board to discuss the government's decision of 14 December 1983. The minister replied to my letter on 14 May. He refused to receive our deputation and reiterated his decision that no further funds would be made available to complete the airport:

In view of the fact that the decision notified to you in December last was taken by the government, you will appreciate that I would be unable to add to or take from the decision myself. Pressure of business has dictated that I must curtail the number of deputations that I can receive. I cannot therefore accede to your request for a meeting. However, I will arrange that officials of my department will be available to meet you, Mr M. O'Malley and Mr J. Ryan, should you require any clarification to the government decision.

With regard to the question whether the statement that "no further Exchequer contribution will be forthcoming" refers to this year only, I have to advise you that it is not the intention to provide any further State finances for the project after this year.

On behalf of the board, on 18 June I again requested the minister to meet a deputation. At the minister's request – in a letter to me of 13 June – I submitted proposals for the completion and operation of the airport.

My dear Minister,

I thank you for your letter dated 13th June, 1984. You are aware that the airport runway, the taxi-way and the apron are completed, all to ICAO standards.

 1. Is there any point in the Airport Development Company expecting further aid from the Exchequer for the completion and operation of the airport?

 2. Can the company expect the government to seek financial aid from the EEC in order to complete the project?

 3. What future role does the government propose to take in relation to the completion and operation of the airport?

4. In certain circumstances, would the government hand over, free of charge and without conditions, full ownership of the project, as completed to date, to the company?
5. Would the government consider favourably, in principle, the establishment of a Duty-Free Zone in the vicinity of the airport?
6. If the airport is completed in accordance with acceptable standards for international air transport operation, will:
 (a) an airport licence, consistent with these standards, be issued?
 (b) will authorisation be given for scheduled international air transport movements?

In view of the holiday period and impending meetings of the company it is highly desirable that the meeting takes place before July 1st, when we would be willing to travel to Dublin at your convenience.

Within a day or two the minister went to Galway to speak at the launching of a project to develop the airport at Carnmore. On a night when I thought that the Connaught Regional Airport was dead, or was at least in moth-balls, I got an unexpected phone-call from a reporter from an evening newspaper. He told me that the Minister for Communications was to make a speech in Galway the very next day and that the script had been handed to the newspapers. I asked was it for or against the project.

"Against," he said, and he read the few punch lines over the telephone. I could hardly believe my ears. I said that I would not make any statement until I got the full text of the speech.

In the speeh delivered at Carnmore Airport, Galway, prior to the European elections, the Minister for Communications must have thought that there was jealousy in Connaught over the siting of the regional airport. "Knock Airport" was already dead and the minister, Mr Mitchell, went to Galway to bury the corpse. The Americans have a saying that "they never flay a dead dog" but here was Jim Mitchell flogging away for all he was worth:

"The Knock project was ill-advised in the extreme, far-distant from any sizeable town, high on a foggy and boggy hill, and the cost equalling the cost of ten airports similar to the one now proposed for Galway. Moreover, by absorbing so much state money, Knock Airport has severely depleted the resources available to the government for other airport projects."

I felt that it could not have been the same Jim Mitchell who had visited the airport site some months previously and who had been so impressed. What was extraordinary about the story was that he had visited the site under clear blue skies and had seen a most scenically situated airport; he certainly offered no criticism of it, though I had heard earlier that a brother of his had made a statement saying that "not one more penny would be given to Knock Airport".

What a pity that the minister's speech seemed to have the effect of sowing the seed of enmity between the different counties in the West. Surely he could have honoured Galway, and rightly so, without insulting the rest of Connaught?

I had great respect for Jim Mitchell as a minister and a person but I was disappointed, very disappointed, by his Galway performance. If the minister had consulted his files he would have found that Mr Williams, meteorologist at Dublin Airport, had reported that the meteorological conditions at the site of the Connaught Airport are much better than Cork and in some aspects better than Dublin. In his speech the minister criticised the cost of Connaught Regional Airport, but the cost would have been as low as £9 million if the government had allocated sufficient funds each year and allowed the work to continue on schedule. They did not, and it cost the project dearly. The state's total contribution to the project was £9.8 million and for that sum the runway, taxi-way, apron and approach roads had all been completed. That figure can be contrasted with the estimate for a new runway in Dublin Airport, costing £32 million at 1983 prices.

Mr Mitchell also said that the company built the airport against the advice of experts. The fact is that the airport was built on the advice of consultants recommended by officials of his department! They recommended Transportation Analysis International, a company based in Shannon and Dublin which had previously carried out a survey on airports in Ireland, and the conclusion they came to was that if another airport were to be built in Ireland it should be built in the area in which the present Connaught Regional Airport has now been built.

Some months after this controversy we finally got to meet the minister, on 12 October 1984. I submitted the following memorandum:

> The Board of the Connaught Regional Airport Development Company Ltd wish to thank the Minister for granting us this interview.

The Board of Directors would like to ask the Minister if any further funds will be made available from the Exchequer for the completion of the Connaught Regional Airport. If the government has decided not to grant any further funds for the airport then the company regrets that the government has failed to honour a legal commitment which arises from a grant-aid agreement signed between the Government and the company on 20th August 1981.

As well as the grant-aid agreement, all the circumstances of the case, and statements by various Ministers, prove the original intention of the administration to grant-aid the airport 100%. This is not merely the opinion of the majority of the Board, it is also the legal advice that we have received from a very distinguished Senior Counsel. It is quite clear that the company have a legal case against the government for breach of contract. This option, however, will only be taken as a last resort. It is extraordinary that up to £10 million has already been spent by the government on a project which they now seem to have abandoned. For instance, no provision has been made for the appointment of a caretaker to protect the site.

We therefore ask the Minister if he has considered the legal commitment of the government to finish the airport, and if so, is it still his intention to deny further financial aid to the project?

The company is also surprised that no effort has been made by the government to procure EEC funds for the completion of the airport. The Minister must be aware that we have made application through his department and through the Department of Finance for an EEC grant. Our information is that this application was not pursued actively in Brussels. We would now like to ask the government and the Minister to press the case in Brussels and to allocate any funds forthcoming directly to the company. If the government decides not to support the company's case, the company seeks permission to make a direct approach to the EEC for funds.

If no further funds can be expected from the Exchequer then the government is in breach of the grant-aid agreement. Therefore, the Minister should release the company from any obligation or restrictions arising from the said agreement. We thus make the following proposals to the Minister:

1. To treat the £10 million as a non-repayable grant.

2. The removal by the Minister for Finance and Communications, as per Articles of Association and Grant-Aid Agreement, of all restrictions binding on the company.

3. Permission to invite equity from outside interests for the completion and running of the airport.

4. To establish at the airport duty/tax-free facilities including duty-free sales for passengers and a "free port" type industrial area designed to accommodate potential demand (three or four acres). The company understands that the officials of Mayo County Council would have no objection in principle to these proposals.

The company would, therefore, propose to complete the airport on certain conditions:

1. If the Minister hands over, free-of-charge and without conditions, full ownership of the project as completed to date.

2. If the Minister gives an assurance to the company that when the airport is completed in accordance with accepted international standards:

    (a) An airport licence, consistent with these standards will be issued.

    (b) Authorisation be given for scheduled international air-transport movements as follows:

        (i) Internal

        (ii) Scheduled Flights to the U.K. and Europe, and Charter Flights as at (i), (ii) above and North America.

The meeting with the minister was decisive in that the outcome was taken to mean that the Connaught Regional Airport Company was authorised to proceed with the completion of the airport subject to compliance with international standards and recommended practices, though without any further state funding.

Epilogue

THE MONSIGNOR'S MEMOIRS end with his report on the meeting of the Airport Management Board in October 1984. Three months later, in January 1985, James Horan was given one of the greatest honours that can be awarded to people associated with Co. Mayo when he was declared Mayo Man of the Year. The occasion was celebrated in the Burlington Hotel in Dublin in the presence of almost one thousand paying guests. Accompanying the monsignor were his mother, Catherine, members of his family, and Mayo friends from far and near.

The following summer, on 21 June, Monsignor Horan's mother passed away at the age of ninety-seven years. The monsignor was in the United States with Archbishop Cunnane and Fr Tom Shannon at the time. News of her death affected him badly; he wept at her funeral and in the months that followed felt very lonely for his late mother.

Among the many messages of sympathy he received was a letter from the Minister for Transport and Tourism, Jim Mitchell. The monsignor appreciated this act of kindness and often referred to it later. Despite the difficulties between them over the financing of the airport, the monsignor had great regard for Jim Mitchell as a person.

After the collapse of state support for the airport Monsignor Horan and his friends more than doubled their efforts to raise funds for the basic services essential to an international airport. Their appeal for funds, which were raised through voluntary subscriptions and the proceeds of a major raffle, brought in over £3m. At the end of the day it was the modest contributions of ordinary people which filled the financial vacuum created by the government's withdrawal from the project. The bulk of the money came from contributions of relatively small amounts paid by people throughout Ireland, Britain and the USA.

The monsignor proceeded to extend the runway despite pressure from the government, via the Department of Communications and Transport, to limit its length to a maximum of 6,000 feet. He pressed on and built a runway of 8,000 feet to which were later added two turning circles of 100 feet diameter each. This gave the airport the second longest runway in the State – Shannon had a 10,000-foot runway – capable of allowing a fully loaded Jumbo jet to take off at Connaught Regional Airport in most weather conditions.

Three Aer Lingus aircrafts, a Boeing 707 and two 737s, took off from the airport on 25 October on the inaugural flights to Rome. A special effort had been made to have everything ready on the day. The minister, Jim Mitchell, promised every help – short of finance – to get the flights off the ground. The stewards of Knock Shrine, under the direction of Tom Neary, policed the perimeter of the airfield, while a retired pilot, Captain Aidan Quigley, was appointed honorary Airport Director for the duration of the inaugural flights. The County Mayo Chief Fire Officer, Civil Defence units, members of the Red Cross and the Knights of Malta offered their services. Aer Rianta loaned firemen and fire-engines for the occasion and other services were given by Department of Transport staff stationed at Shannon.

After celebrating a special Mass asking for God's blessing on the historic flights, Monsignor Horan proudly led the pilgrim passengers from the new airport to the Eternal City. It was a moment of great joy for him and for all who had worked with such determination to give Connaught a regional and international airport. The Barnacúige plateau was now alive to the world of aviation. The flights returned to Connaught on 1 November 1985 and those who had accompanied Monsignor Horan were delighted with their journey, and at having participated in the making of history in the West of Ireland.

The official opening of the airport did not take place until seven months later. Charles J. Haughey, former Taoiseach, was chosen to perform the official opening ceremoney. The decision touched political sensitivities, especially in Mayo. The *Western People* reported: "A political storm is raging ... over the decision of the Knock Airport Committee to invite the Leader of the Opposition to open the £13m airport. ... The decision ... was slammed by Deputy O'Toole, Minister for Defence, and by Senator Jim Higgins (Fine Gael). Last evening Monsignor Horan made no comment, saying he had no authority to make statements without the Board's approval."

The formal ceremony was carefully planned and a large crowd of well-wishers and media was expected. As the day grew closer

Epilogue

Monsignor Horan was in buoyant form. "Let us rejoice and be glad," he told the *Western People*. "This airport is a monument to the skill, intelligence and dedication of the people of the West. It has kindled a fire of enthusiasm that will not be extinguished..."

On 30 May 1986, a day which turned out unusually wet and stormy, thousands of people made their way to Barnacúige to celebrate the formal opening of Connaught Regional Airport. The rain and gale-force winds symbolised the achievement of "triumph over adversity". With some £400,000 still needed for lighting and navigational aids, the tape was cut by Charles J. Haughey TD, whose faith in the project had contributed much to its completion. Mr Haughey was met by most of his shadow cabinet; the government was not represented at the formal opening of the airport. The airport was blessed ecumenically by Most Rev. Drs Thomas Flynn, Catholic Bishop of Achony, and John Neill, Church of Ireland Bishop of the united diocese of Tuam, Killala and Achonry. Most Rev. Dr Joseph Cunnane, Archbishop of Tuam, and member of the airport board, was also present.

In his address to the assembled gathering, many of whose toil and support had helped build the airport, Mr Haughey said:

"From Barnacúige today we send forth a message which is of significance to the entire nation. It is a message of triumph over adversity, of difficulties overcome, of critics confounded... This airport will have a profound impact on this region of our country and may well be the turning point of historic significance for the whole Province of Connaught."

Monsignor Horan, chairperson of the board, replied to Mr Haughey and thanked him for his support. Were it not for him, "There would be no opening today. ... In all the controversy, in all the name-calling, Charles J. Haughey's faith in the project never wavered." In the end, however, the monsignor pointed out that the airport was completed by the generous support of the people. "There's 'Live Aid' and 'Sport Aid' and 'Self Aid'," he said, but, "the people of Mayo have been practicing self aid for generations. Otherwise they would have disappeared."

There were still many problems to be solved and further construction to take place at the airport. The board had been informed by Aer Rianta and Aer Lingus respectively that they did not wish to undertake the management of the airport or provide a regular air service from it – the latter was not considered to be commercially viable by Aer Lingus. In the absence of such arrangements Monsignor Horan negotiated an agreement for the management and development of the airport with British Airports International and with Celtic Air for flying and handling operations. These agreements got the airport off the ground, though they did not work out satisfactorily later. In all his efforts to develop the airport Monsignor Horan was loyally supported by a hard-working team of friends.

Sadly, Monsignor James Horan had only two more months to live. During those final months he carried many burdens relating to financing and organising the airport's completion, and he continued his pastoral role as parish priest and administrator of Knock. It had been agreed that he would retire as parish priest in September 1986 and would continue as administrator of the shrine. His successor was to be his close friend and colleague Fr Dominic Grealy, who was administrator of Tuam at the time.

On 23 June the monsignor went to Dublin on the national school's annual tour, as he had done in previous years. While there he visited a consultant for a check-up and on his advice agreed to undergo an operation for a hernia, which took place on 1 July. Everything went well. He was released from hospital in mid-July and spent two weeks convalescing at his sister Nancy's home. He was in good spirits and felt he had recovered sufficiently to feel capable of going on a pilgrimage to the Shrine of Our Lady of Lourdes in the company of his sisters Mary, Margaret, Bridie and Nancy. He also pushed himself to go so as not to dissapoint his friends.

He was the last passenger to board the flight for Lourdes as he was busy making the final arrangements for the lighting of the runway, and signed the contract just before he left. On arrival at Lourdes the pilgrims from Knock booked into their hotel, had an evening meal and went to the shrine to take part in the rosary procession. The next day Monsignor Horan was relaxed and in good humour, preparing to entertain the pilgrims later that evening. He said Mass in the local church and went to the grotto for the group photograph. In the afternoon he returned to the Shrine of Our Lady on his own and read the Office of the day.

Later that evening he went to his room to rest for an hour so that he would be in good form for the party which took place after the rosary procession. When everyone had assembled in the hotel lounge the monsignor entertained them with some of his favourite ballads, among them "Moonlight in Mayo", "Red is the

Rose" and "Galway Bay". The party ended shortly after half-past twelve with his spirited rendition of "If I Can Help Somebody". Shortly after retiring to his room his sister, Nancy, knocked on his door to bid him goodnight.

"How did I do?" he asked her.

"You did very well," she said. "Everyone enjoyed the party."

The monsignor asked her to call him at half-seven as they were going on a tour.

Next morning Nancy knocked on his door and called "Jimmy" several times. There was no reply. She alerted her sister, Bridie. They thought that he may have got up earlier as was his custom and would be back, but no one had seen him. Nancy went and knocked at his door again but still there was no reply. She went down to the hotel reception and got a key. When she opened the door she saw that her brother Jimmy had passed away in his sleep. His hands were crossed on his chest with the watch hand on top. His expression was very peaceful.

The hotel management summoned a priest and a doctor and the monsignor's remains were taken to the local hospital. The doctor certified that the cause of death was pulmonary embolism – a clot – which was probably a delayed reaction to his operation one month earlier. The family in Mayo were notified immediately and the late monsignor's brothers, Pat and Bartley, accompanied by Fr Porter of Knock, flew to Lourdes to join the mourning sisters. Knock parish made the arrangements for the funeral. Fr Colm Kilcoyne rang Nancy to enquire if the monsignor had indicated to the family where at Knock he would like to be buried. "No, he hadn't," she replied. He had, however, told the chief steward, Tom Neary, the actual spot he had chosen for his grave.

Monsignor Horan's death was headline news in Ireland and abroad. His stature as a public figure was now manifested. A sense of genuine sadness descended upon many, many people in the West of Ireland and throughout the country.

On Saturday, 2 August, Requiem Mass was offered in the Church of the Poor Clares in Lourdes and on the following day the Bishop of Dumbarton, Dr Logan, offered Mass at the shrine. On Monday, 4 August, a special Requiem Mass was offered in Lourdes' parish church by Fr Pat Munroe of Cong, a second-cousin of the monsignor's, and the monsignor's remains were then taken to the airport and flown directly to Connaught, accompanied by the pilgrimage group. The plane was greeted by tens of thousands of mourners from all over Ireland, but especially from Mayo. After a brief service led by the monsignor's great friend, Archbishop Cunnane, the cortège moved to Knock Shrine which was crowded with pilgrims waiting to mourn this "giant among men", as the *Western People* described him.

The monsignor's successor, Fr Dominic Grealy, received the monsignor's remains into the Basilica of Our Lady. He told the congregation that it was appropriate to welcome home a great pastor on the feast of the patron of pastors – the Curé of Ars, St John Vianney. The remains of the late monsignor lay in state in the basilica until Requiem Mass was celebrated on the following day by Dr Joseph Cunnane, accompanied by the Papal Nuncio, Archbishop Alibrandi. Most of the Irish hierarchy and a large and representative number of priests, brothers and sisters from all over the country were present at the ceremony, at which Cardinal Tomás Ó Fiaich presided. Dr Joseph Cunnane paid tribute to his lifelong friend:

"He was a very human and good person, gentle and nice until he was crossed. Then he could be a tough man, and he needed all his toughness when tackling a project like the Connaught Regional Airport and seeing it through. He needed all his optimism and all his realism to face up to the opposition he got with the airport project. ... He was a very powerful influence in the diocese and an outstanding example to other priests and myself, and it is not going to be easy to find someone to take his place."

Charles Haughey paid him tribute in the following terms:

"He had a deep committment to the people of the West of Ireland and knew what they wanted. He had a vision of what was needed there and what the people needed in terms of religious, economic and social development. He was a power-house, a man of great vision and tremendous business capacity. But the man was also deeply religious and it was his deep committment to his religion which spurred on everything else. He was a brilliant and able man who liked a challenge."

The words of Senator Martin J. O'Toole sum up the effect which Monsignor Horan had on those who worked with him. The monsignor, he said, had done more than any man in modern times to encourage the people of the West to have faith in themselves. "He will certainly be missed by the people of Connaught, but I believe he has inspired and motivated us all to continue his good work."

Epilogue

The laying to rest of the remains of Monsignor James Horan was the biggest coming together of the people of the West of Ireland since the visit of Pope John Paul II in 1979. They came to bid farewell to one of their own, a man whom they had come to know and love and who knew and loved them in return. Shortly after his death Connaught Regional Airport was renamed Horan International Airport in his honour.

Ar dheis Dé go raibh a anam uasal.